To dea

With

GW00792469

2

180
SELECTED POEMS OF
BYRON

Oxford University Press, Ely House, London W. 1

GLASGOW NEW YORK TORONTO MELBOURNE WELLINGTON
CAPE TOWN SALISBURY IBADAN NAIROBI DAR ES SALAAM LUSAKA ADDIS ABABA
BOMBAY CALCUTTA MADRAS KARACHI LAHORE DACCA
KUALA LUMPUR SINGAPORE HONG KONG TOKYO

Selected Poems of
BYRON

London
OXFORD UNIVERSITY PRESS

GEORGE GORDON, LORD BYRON

Born, London . . . 22 January 1788
Died, Missolonghi, Greece . . 19 April 1824

The present selection of Byron's poems was first published in The World's Classics *in 1913 and reprinted in* 1923, 1924, 1928, 1931, 1936, 1942, 1947, 1950, 1960, 1966, *and* 1970

SBN 19 250180 1

CONTENTS

POEMS

LACHIN Y GAIR

Away, ye gay landscapes, ye gardens of roses !
   In you let the minions of luxury rove ;
Restore me the rocks, where the snow-flake reposes,
   Though still they are sacred to freedom and love :
Yet, Caledonia, beloved are thy mountains,
   Round their white summits though elements war ;
Though cataracts foam 'stead of smooth-flowing fountains,
   I sigh for the valley of dark Loch na Garr.

Ah ! there my young footsteps in infancy wander'd ;
   My cap was the bonnet, my cloak was the plaid ;
On chieftains long perish'd my memory ponder'd,   11
   As daily I strode through the pine-cover'd glade ;
I sought not my home till the day's dying glory
   Gave place to the rays of the bright polar star ;
For fancy was cheer'd by traditional story,
   Disclosed by the natives of dark Loch na Garr.

" Shades of the dead ! have I not heard your voices
   Rise on the night-rolling breath of the gale ? "
Surely the soul of the hero rejoices,   19
   And rides on the wind, o'er his own Highland vale.
Round Loch na Garr while the stormy mist gathers,
   Winter presides in his cold icy car :
Clouds there encircle the forms of my fathers ;
   They dwell in the tempests of dark Loch na Garr.

" Ill-starr'd, though brave, did no visions foreboding
   Tell you that fate had forsaken your cause ? "
Ah ! were you destined to die at Culloden,
   Victory crown'd not your fall with applause :

Still were you happy in death's earthly slumber,
    You rest with your clan in the caves of Braemar;
The pibroch resounds, to the piper's loud number,   31
    Your deeds on the echoes of dark Loch na Garr.

Years have roll'd on, Loch na Garr, since I left you,
    Years must elapse ere I tread you again:
Nature of verdure and flow'rs has bereft you,
    Yet still are you dearer than Albion's plain.
England! thy beauties are tame and domestic
    To one who has roved o'er the mountains afar:
Oh for the crags that are wild and majestic!
    The steep frowning glories of dark Loch na Garr.   40

WHEN WE TWO PARTED

WHEN we two parted
    In silence and tears,
Half broken-hearted
    To sever for years,
Pale grew thy cheek and cold,
    Colder thy kiss;
Truly that hour foretold
    Sorrow to this.

The dew of the morning
    Sunk chill on my brow—   10
It felt like the warning
    Of what I feel now.
Thy vows are all broken,
    And light is thy fame:
I hear thy name spoken,
    And share in its shame.

They name thee before me,
    A knell to mine ear;
A shudder comes o'er me—
    Why wert thou so dear?   20

They know not I knew thee,
  Who knew thee too well :—
Long, long shall I rue thee,
  Too deeply to tell.

In secret we met—
  In silence I grieve,
That thy heart could forget,
  Thy spirit deceive.
If I should meet thee
  After long years,   30
How should I greet thee ?—
  With silence and tears.

                                    1808.

WELL! THOU ART HAPPY

WELL ! thou art happy, and I feel
  That I should thus be happy too ;
For still my heart regards thy weal
  Warmly, as it was wont to do.

Thy husband 's blest—and 'twill impart
  Some pangs to view his happier lot :
But let them pass—Oh ! how my heart
  Would hate him if he loved thee not !

When late I saw thy favourite child,
  I thought my jealous heart would break ;   10
But when the unconscious infant smiled,
  I kiss'd it for its mother's sake.

I kiss'd it,—and repress'd my sighs
  Its father in its face to see ;
But then it had its mother's eyes,
  And they were all to love and me.

Mary, adieu ! I must away :
  While thou art blest I'll not repine ;
But near thee I can never stay ;
  My heart would soon again be thine   20

I deem'd that time, I deem'd that pride,
    Had quench'd at length my boyish flame;
Nor knew, till seated by thy side,
    My heart in all,—save hope,—the same.

Yet was I calm: I knew the time
    My breast would thrill before thy look;
But now to tremble were a crime—
    We met,—and not a nerve was shook.

I saw thee gaze upon my face,
    Yet meet with no confusion there: 30
One only feeling could'st thou trace;
    The sullen calmness of despair.

Away! away! my early dream
    Remembrance never must awake:
Oh! where is Lethe's fabled stream?
    My foolish heart, be still, or break.
                November 2, 1808.

FILL THE GOBLET AGAIN

A SONG

FILL the goblet again! for I never before
Felt the glow which now gladdens my heart to its core;
Let us drink!—who would not?—since, through life's
    varied round,
In the goblet alone no deception is found.

I have tried in its turn all that life can supply;
I have bask'd in the beam of a dark rolling eye;
I have loved!—who has not?—but what heart can
    declare
That pleasure existed while passion was there?

In the days of my youth, when the heart's in its spring,
And dreams that affection can never take wing,   10
I had friends!—who has not?—but what tongue will
    avow,
That friends, rosy wine! are so faithful as thou?

The heart of a mistress some boy may estrange,
Friendship shifts with the sunbeam—thou never canst
    change ;
Thou grow'st old—who does not ?—but on earth what
    appears,
Whose virtues, like thine, still increase with its years ?

Yet if blest to the utmost that love can bestow,
Should a rival bow down to our idol below,
We are jealous !—who 's not ?—thou hast no such alloy ;
For the more that enjoy thee, the more we enjoy. 20

Then the season of youth and its vanities past,
For refuge we fly to the goblet at last ;
There we find—do we not ?—in the flow of the soul,
That truth, as of yore, is confined to the bowl.

When the box of Pandora was opened on earth,
And Misery's triumph commenced over Mirth,
Hope was left,—was she not ?—but the goblet we kiss,
And care not for Hope, who are certain of bliss.

Long life to the grape ! for when summer is flown,
The age of our nectar shall gladden our own : 30
We must die—who shall not ?—May our sins be for-
    given,
And Hebe shall never be idle in heaven.

LINES TO MR. HODGSON

WRITTEN ON BOARD THE LISBON PACKET

Huzza ! Hodgson, we are going,
    Our embargo 's off at last ;
Favourable breezes blowing
    Bend the canvas o'er the mast.
From aloft the signal 's streaming,
    Hark ! the farewell gun is fired ;
Women screeching, tars blaspheming,
    Tell us that our time 's expired.

Here 's a rascal
       Come to task all,   10
   Prying from the custom-house;
       Trunks unpacking,
       Cases cracking,
Not a corner for a mouse
'Scapes unsearch'd amid the racket,
Ere we sail on board the Packet.

Now our boatmen quit their mooring,
   And all hands must ply the oar;
Baggage from the quay is lowering,
   We're impatient, push from shore.   20
" Have a care ! that case holds liquor—
   Stop the boat—I'm sick—oh Lord ! "
" Sick, ma'am, damme, you'll be sicker
   Ere you've been an hour on board."
       Thus are screaming
       Men and women,
   Gemmen, ladies, servants, Jacks;
       Here entangling,
       All are wrangling,
Stuck together close as wax.—   30
Such the general noise and racket,
Ere we reach the Lisbon Packet.

Now we've reach'd her, lo ! the captain,
   Gallant Kidd, commands the crew;
Passengers their berths are clapt in,
   Some to grumble, some to spew.
" Heyday ! call you that a cabin ?
   Why 'tis hardly three feet square :
Not enough to stow Queen Mab in—
Who the deuce can harbour there ? "   40
       " Who, sir ? plenty—
       Nobles twenty
Did at once my vessel fill."—
       " Did they ? Jesus,
       How you squeeze us !
Would to God they did so still:

Then I'd scape the heat and racket
Of the good ship, Lisbon Packet."

Fletcher! Murray! Bob! where are you?
  Stretch'd along the deck like logs—   50
Bear a hand, you jolly tar, you!
  Here's a rope's end for the dogs.
Hobhouse muttering fearful curses,
  As the hatchway down he rolls,
Now his breakfast, now his verses,
  Vomits forth—and damns our souls.
      " Here's a stanza
        On Braganza—
  Help!"—" A couplet?"—" No, a cup
    Of warm water—"   60
      " What's the matter?"
  " Zounds! my liver's coming up;
I shall not survive the racket
Of this brutal Lisbon Packet."

Now at length we're off for Turkey,
  Lord knows when we shall come back!
Breezes foul and tempests murky
  May unship us in a crack.
But, since life at most a jest is,
  As philosophers allow,   70
Still to laugh by far the best is,
  Then laugh on—as I do now.
      Laugh at all things,
      Great and small things,
  Sick or well, at sea or shore;
      While we're quaffing,
      Let's have laughing—
Who the devil cares for more?—
Some good wine! and who would lack it,
Ev'n on board the Lisbon Packet?   80

          Falmouth Roads, *June* 30, 1809.

STANZAS WRITTEN IN PASSING THE AMBRACIAN GULF

THROUGH cloudless skies, in silvery sheen,
    Full beams the moon on Actium's coast:
And on these waves, for Egypt's queen,
    The ancient world was won and lost.

And now upon the scene I look,
    The azure grave of many a Roman;
Where stern Ambition once forsook
    His wavering crown to follow woman.

Florence! whom I will love as well
    As ever yet was said or sung   10
(Since Orpheus sang his spouse from hell),
    Whilst thou art fair and I am young;

Sweet Florence! those were pleasant times,
    When worlds were staked for ladies' eyes:
Had bards as many realms as rhymes,
    Thy charms might raise new Antonies.

Though Fate forbids such things to be,
    Yet, by thine eyes and ringlets curl'd!
I cannot lose a world for thee,
    But would not lose thee for a world.   20

November 14, 1809.

WRITTEN AFTER SWIMMING FROM SESTOS TO ABYDOS

IF, in the month of dark December,
    Leander, who was nightly wont
(What maid will not the tale remember?)
    To cross thy stream, broad Hellespont!

If, when the wintry tempest roar'd,
    He sped to Hero, nothing loth,
And thus of old thy current pour'd,
    Fair Venus! how I pity both!

For *me*, degenerate modern wretch,
  Though in the genial month of May,   10
My dripping limbs I faintly stretch,
  And think I've done a feat to-day.

But since he cross'd the rapid tide,
  According to the doubtful story,
To woo,—and—Lord knows what beside,
  And swam for Love, as I for Glory;

'Twere hard to say who fared the best:
  Sad mortals! thus the gods still plague **you**!
He lost his labour, I my jest;
  For he was drown'd, and I've the ague.   20

May 9, 1810.

MAID OF ATHENS, ERE WE PART

Ζώη μοῦ, σᾶς ἀγαπῶ.

MAID of Athens, ere we part,
Give, oh give me back my heart!
Or, since that has left my breast,
Keep it now, and take the rest!
Hear my vow before I go,
Ζώη μοῦ, σᾶς ἀγαπῶ.

By those tresses unconfined,
Woo'd by each Ægean wind;
By those lids whose jetty fringe
Kiss thy soft cheeks' blooming tinge;   10
By those wild eyes like the roe,
Ζώη μοῦ, σᾶς ἀγαπῶ.

By that lip I long to taste;
By that zone-encircled waist;
By all the token-flowers that tell
What words can never speak so well;
By love's alternate joy and woe,
Ζώη μοῦ, σᾶς ἀγαπῶ.

Maid of Athens! I am gone:
Think of me, sweet! when alone.   20
Though I fly to Istambol,
Athens holds my heart and soul:
Can I cease to love thee? No!
Ζώη μοῦ, σᾶς ἀγαπῶ.

Athens, 1810.

ONE STRUGGLE MORE, AND I AM FREE

ONE struggle more, and I am free
    From pangs that rend my heart in twain;
One last long sigh to love and thee,
    Then back to busy life again.
It suits me well to mingle now
    With things that never pleased before:
Though every joy is fled below,
    What future grief can touch me more?

Then bring me wine, the banquet bring;
    Man was not form'd to live alone: 10
I'll be that light, unmeaning thing
    That smiles with all, and weeps with none.
It was not thus in days more dear,
    It never would have been, but thou
Hast fled, and left me lonely here;
    Thou'rt nothing—all are nothing now.

In vain my lyre would lightly breathe!
    The smile that sorrow fain would wear
But mocks the woe that lurks beneath,
    Like roses o'er a sepulchre.   20
Though gay companions o'er the bowl
    Dispel awhile the sense of ill:
Though pleasure fires the maddening soul,
    The heart,—the heart is lonely still!

On many a lone and lovely night
    It sooth'd to gaze upon the sky;
For then I deem'd the heavenly light
    Shone sweetly on thy pensive eye:

And oft I thought at Cynthia's noon,
  When sailing o'er the Ægean wave,   30
" Now Thyrza gazes on that moon "—
  Alas, it gleam'd upon her grave !

When stretch'd on fever's sleepless bed,
  And sickness shrunk my throbbing veins,
" 'Tis comfort still," I faintly said,
  " That Thyrza cannot know my pains : "
Like freedom to the time-worn slave,
  A boon 'tis idle then to give,
Relenting Nature vainly gave
  My life, when Thyrza ceased to live !   40

My Thyrza's pledge in better days,
  When love and life alike were new !
How different now thou meet'st my gaze !
  How tinged by time with sorrow's hue !
The heart that gave itself with thee
  Is silent—ah, were mine as still !
Though cold as e'en the dead can be,
  It feels, it sickens with the chill.

Thou bitter pledge ! thou mournful token !
  Though painful, welcome to my breast !   50
Still, still preserve that love unbroken,
  Or break the heart to which thou'rt press'd.
Time tempers love, but not removes,
  More hallow'd when its hope is fled :
Oh ! what are thousand living loves
  To that which cannot quit the dead ?

EUTHANASIA

When Time, or soon or late, shall bring
  The dreamless sleep that lulls the dead,
Oblivion ! may thy languid wing
  Wave gently o'er my dying bed !

No band of friends or heirs be there,
  To weep, or wish, the coming blow :
No maiden, with dishevelled hair,
  To feel, or feign, decorous woe.

But silent let me sink to earth,
  With no officious mourners near :   10
I would not mar one hour of mirth,
  Nor startle friendship with a tear.

Yet Love, if such an hour
  Could nobly check its useless sighs,
Might then exert its latest power
  In her who lives, and him who dies.

'Twere sweet, my Psyche ! to the last
  Thy features still serene to see :
Forgetful of its struggles past,
  E'en Pain itself should smile on thee.   20

But vain the wish—for Beauty still
  Will shrink, as shrinks the ebbing breath ;
And Woman's tears, produced at will,
  Deceive in life, unman in death.

Then lonely be my latest hour,
  Without regret, without a groan ;
For thousands Death hath ceas'd to lower,
  And pain been transient or unknown.

" Ay, but to die, and go," alas !
  Where all have gone, and all must go !   30
To be the nothing that I was
  Ere born to life and living woe !

Count o'er the joys thine hours have seen,
  Count o'er thy days from anguish free,
And know, whatever thou hast been,
  'Tis something better not to be.

AND THOU ART DEAD, AS YOUNG AND FAIR

" Heu, quanto minus est cum reliquis versari quam tui
meminisse ! "

AND thou art dead, as young and fair
    As aught of mortal birth ;
And form so soft, and charms so rare,
    Too soon return'd to Earth !
Though Earth received them in her bed
And o'er the spot the crowd may tread
    In carelessness or mirth,
There is an eye which could not brook
A moment on that grave to look.

I will not ask where thou liest low,   10
    Nor gaze upon the spot ;
There flowers or weeds at will may grow,
    So I behold them not :
It is enough for me to prove
That what I loved, and long must love,
    Like common earth can rot ;
To me there needs no stone to tell,
'Tis Nothing that I loved so well.

Yet did I love thee to the last
    As fervently as thou,   20
Who didst not change through all the past,
    And canst not alter now.
The love where Death has set his seal,
Nor age can chill, nor rival steal,
    Nor falsehood disavow :
And, what were worse, thou canst not see
Or wrong, or change, or fault in me.

The better days of life were ours ;
    The worst can be but mine :
The sun that cheers, the storm that lowers,   30
    Shall never more be thine.

The silence of that dreamless sleep
I envy now too much to weep;
    Nor need I to repine,
That all those charms have pass'd away;
I might have watch'd through long decay.

The flower in ripen'd bloom unmatch'd
    Must fall the earliest prey;
Though by no hand untimely snatch'd,
    The leaves must drop away: 40
And yet it were a greater grief
To watch it withering, leaf by leaf,
    Than see it pluck'd to-day;
Since earthly eye but ill can bear
To trace the change to foul from fair.

I know not if I could have borne
    To see thy beauties fade;
The night that follow'd such a morn
    Had worn a deeper shade:
Thy day without a cloud hath pass'd,   50
And thou wert lovely to the last;
    Extinguish'd, not decay'd;
As stars that shoot along the sky
Shine brightest as they fall from high.

As once I wept, if I could weep,
    My tears might well be shed,
To think I was not near to keep
    One vigil o'er thy bed;
To gaze, how fondly! on thy face,
To fold thee in a faint embrace,   60
    Uphold thy drooping head;
And show that love, however vain,
Nor thou nor I can feel again.

Yet how much less it were to gain,
    Though thou hast left me free,
The loveliest things that still remain,
    Than thus remember thee!

The all of thine that cannot die
Through dark and dread Eternity
  Returns again to me,   70
And more thy buried love endears
  Than aught except its living years.
                              February, 1812.

IF SOMETIMES IN THE HAUNTS OF MEN

IF sometimes in the haunts of men
  Thine image from my breast may fade,
The lonely hour presents again
  The semblance of thy gentle shade :
And now that sad and silent hour
  Thus much of thee can still restore,
And sorrow unobserved may pour
  The plaint she dare not speak before.

Oh, pardon that in crowds awhile
  I waste one thought I owe to thee,   10
And self-condemn'd, appear to smile,
  Unfaithful to thy memory :
Nor deem that memory less dear,
  That then I seem not to repine ;
I would not fools should overhear
  One sigh that should be wholly *thine*.

If not the goblet pass unquaff'd,
  It is not drain'd to banish care ;
The cup must hold a deadlier draught,
  That brings a Lethe for despair.   20
And could Oblivion set my soul
  From all her troubled visions free,
I'd dash to earth the sweetest bowl
  That drown'd a single thought of thee.

For wert thou vanish'd from my mind,
  Where could my vacant bosom turn ?
And who would then remain behind
  To honour thine abandon'd Urn ?

No, no—it is my sorrow's pride
 That last dear duty to fulfil: 30
Though all the world forget beside,
 'Tis meet that I remember still.

For well I know, that such had been
 Thy gentle care for him, who now
Unmourn'd shall quit this mortal scene,
 Where none regarded him, but thou:
And, oh! I feel in *that* was given
 A blessing never meant for me;
Thou wert too like a dream of Heaven
 For earthly Love to merit thee. 40
        March 14, 1812.

LINES TO A LADY WEEPING

WEEP, daughter of a royal line,
 A Sire's disgrace, a realm's decay;
Ah! happy if each tear of thine
 Could wash a father's fault away!

Weep—for thy tears are Virtue's tears—
 Auspicious to these suffering isles;
And be each drop in future years
 Repaid thee by thy people's smiles!
        March, 1812.

REMEMBER HIM WHOM PASSION'S POWER

REMEMBER him whom passion's power
 Severely, deeply, vainly proved:
Remember thou that dangerous hour,
 When neither fell, though both were loved.

That yielding breast, that melting eye,
 Too much invited to be bless'd:
That gentle prayer, that pleading sigh,
 The wilder wish reproved, repress'd.

Oh! let me feel that all I lost
 But saved thee all that conscience fears; 10
And blush for every pang it cost
 To spare the vain remorse of years.

Yet think of this when many a tongue,
　　Whose busy accents whisper blame,
Would do the heart that loved thee wrong,
　　And brand a nearly blighted name.

Think that, whate'er to others, thou
　　Hast seen each selfish thought subdued:
I bless thy purer soul even now,
　　Even now, in midnight solitude. 　　　20

Oh, God! that we had met in time,
　　Our hearts as fond, thy hand more free;
When thou hadst loved without a crime,
　　And I been less unworthy thee!

Far may thy days, as heretofore,
　　From this our gaudy world be past!
And that too bitter moment o'er,
　　Oh! may such trial be thy last.

This heart, alas! perverted long,
　　Itself destroy'd might there destroy; 　　30
To meet thee in the glittering throng,
　　Would wake Presumption's hope of joy.

Then to the things whose bliss or woe,
　　Like mine, is wild and worthless all,
That world resign—such scenes forego,
　　Where those who feel must surely fall.

Thy youth, thy charms, thy tenderness,
　　Thy soul from long seclusion pure;
From what even here hath pass'd, may guess
　　What there thy bosom must endure. 　　　40

Oh! pardon that imploring tear,
　　Since not by Virtue shed in vain,
My frenzy drew from eyes so dear;
　　For me they shall not weep again.

Though long and mournful must it be,
　　The thought that we no more may meet;
Yet I deserve the stern decree,
　　And almost deem the sentence sweet.

> Still, had I loved thee less, my heart
> Had then less sacrificed to thine; 50
> It felt not half so much to part
> As if its guilt had made thee mine.

1813.

SONNET, TO GENEVRA

THINE eyes' blue tenderness, thy long fair hair,
And the wan lustre of thy features—caught
From contemplation—where serenely wrought,
Seems Sorrow's softness charm'd from its despair—
Have thrown such speaking sadness in thine air,
That—but I know thy blessed bosom fraught
With mines of unalloy'd and stainless thought—
I should have deem'd thee doom'd to earthly care.
With such an aspect by his colours blent,
When from his beauty-breathing pencil born
(Except that *thou* hast nothing to repent),
The Magdalen of Guido saw the morn—
Such seem'st thou—but how much more excellent!
With nought Remorse can claim—nor Virtue scorn.

December 17, 1813.

SONNET, TO THE SAME

THY cheek is pale with thought, but not from woe,
And yet so lovely, that if Mirth could flush
Its rose of whiteness with the brightest blush,
My heart would wish away that ruder glow:
And dazzle not thy deep-blue eyes—but, oh!
While gazing on them sterner eyes will gush,
And into mine my mother's weakness rush,
Soft as the last drops round heaven's airy bow.
For, through thy long dark lashes low depending,
The soul of melancholy Gentleness
Gleams like a seraph from the sky descending,
Above all pain, yet pitying all distress;
At once such majesty with sweetness blending,
I worship more, but cannot love thee less.

December 17, 1813.

ODE TO NAPOLEON BUONAPARTE

"Expende Annibalem :—quot libras in duce summo
   Invenies ? "—Juvenal, *Sat.* x.

"The Emperor Nepos was acknowledged by the Senate,
by the Italians, and by the Provincials of Gaul ; his moral
virtues, and military talents, were loudly celebrated ; and
those who derived any private benefit from his government
announced in prophetic strains the restoration of public
felicity. . . . By this shameful abdication, he protracted
his life a few years, in a very ambiguous state, between
an Emperor and an Exile, till ——."—Gibbon's *Decline
and Fall*, vol. vi., p. 220.

I

'Tis done—but yesterday a King !
   And arm'd with Kings to strive—
And now thou art a nameless thing :
   So abject—yet alive !
Is this the man of thousand thrones,
Who strew'd our earth with hostile bones,
   And can he thus survive ?
Since he, miscall'd the Morning Star,
Nor man nor fiend hath fallen so far.

II

Ill-minded man ! why scourge thy kind   10
   Who bow'd so low the knee ?
By gazing on thyself grown blind,
   Thou taught'st the rest to see.
With might unquestion'd,—power to save,—
Thine only gift hath been the grave,
   To those that worshipp'd thee ;
Nor till thy fall could mortals guess
Ambition's less than littleness !

III

Thanks for that lesson—It will teach
   To after-warriors more   20
Than high Philosophy can preach,
   And vainly preach'd before.

That spell upon the minds of men
Breaks never to unite again,
 That led them to adore
Those Pagod things of sabre sway,
With fronts of brass, and feet of clay.

IV

The triumph and the vanity,
 The rapture of the strife—
The earthquake voice of Victory,   30
 To thee the breath of life;
The sword, the sceptre, and that sway
Which man seem'd made but to obey,
 Wherewith renown was rife—
All quell'd !—Dark Spirit ! what must be
The madness of thy memory !

V

The Desolator desolate !
 The Victor overthrown !
The Arbiter of others' fate
 A Suppliant for his own !   40
Is it some yet imperial hope
That with such change can calmly cope
 Or dread of death alone ?
To die a prince—or live a slave—
Thy choice is most ignobly brave.

VI

He who of old would rend the oak,
 Dream'd not of the rebound :
Chain'd by the trunk he vainly broke—
 Alone—how look'd he round ?
Thou, in the sternness of thy strength, 50
An equal deed hast done at length,
 And darker fate hast found :
He fell, the forest prowlers' prey ;
But thou must eat thy heart away !

VII

The Roman, when his burning heart
    Was slaked with blood of Rome,
Threw down the dagger—dared depart,
    In savage grandeur, home—
He dared depart in utter scorn
Of men that such a yoke had borne,   60
    Yet left him such a doom!
His only glory was that hour
Of self-upheld abandon'd power.

VIII

The Spaniard, when the lust of sway
    Had lost its quickening spell,
Cast crowns for rosaries away,
    An empire for a cell;
A strict accountant of his beads,
A subtle disputant on creeds,
    His dotage trifled well: 70
Yet better had he neither known
A bigot's shrine, nor despot's throne.

IX

But thou—from thy reluctant hand
    The thunderbolt is wrung—
Too late thou leav'st the high command
    To which thy weakness clung;
All Evil Spirit as thou art,
It is enough to grieve the heart
    To see thine own unstrung;
To think that God's fair world hath been   80
The footstool of a thing so mean;

X

And Earth hath spilt her blood for him,
    Who thus can hoard his own!
And Monarchs bow'd the trembling limb,
    And thank'd him for a throne!

Fair Freedom ! we may hold thee dear,
When thus thy mightiest foes their fear
    In humblest guise have shown.
Oh ! ne'er may tyrant leave behind
A brighter name to lure mankind !   90

XI

Thine evil deeds are writ in gore,
    Nor written thus in vain—
Thy triumphs tell of fame no more,
    Or deepen every stain :
If thou hadst died as honour dies,
Some new Napoleon might arise,
    To shame the world again—
But who would soar the solar height,
To set in such a starless night ?

XII

Weigh'd in the balance, hero dust   100
    Is vile as vulgar clay ;
Thy scales, Mortality ! are just
    To all that pass away ;
But yet methought the living great
Some higher sparks should animate,
    To dazzle and dismay :
Nor deem'd Contempt could thus make mirth
Of these, the Conquerors of the earth.

XIII

And she, proud Austria's mournful flower,
    Thy still imperial bride ;   110
How bears her breast the torturing hour ?
    Still clings she to thy side ?
Must she too bend, must she too share
Thy late repentance, long despair,
    Thou throneless Homicide ?
If still she loves thee, hoard that gem,—
'Tis worth thy vanish'd diadem !

XIV

Then haste thee to thy sullen Isle,
   And gaze upon the sea;
That element may meet thy smile—   120
   It ne'er was ruled by thee!
Or trace with thine all idle hand
In loitering mood upon the sand
   That Earth is now as free!
That Corinth's pedagogue hath now
Transferr'd his by-word to thy brow.

XV

Thou Timour! in his captive's cage
   What thoughts will there be thine,
While brooding in thy prison'd rage?
   But one—" The world *was* mine!"   130
Unless, like he of Babylon,
All sense is with thy sceptre gone,
   Life will not long confine
That spirit pour'd so widely forth—
So long obey'd—so little worth!

XVI

Or, like the thief of fire from heaven,
   Wilt thou withstand the shock?
And share with him, the unforgiven,
   His vulture and his rock!
Foredoom'd by God—by man accurst,   140
And that last act, though not thy worst,
   The very Fiend's arch mock;
He in his fall preserved his pride,
And, if a mortal, had as proudly died!

XVII

There was a day—there was an hour,
   While earth was Gaul's—Gaul thine—
When that immeasurable power
   Unsated to resign

Had been an act of purer fame
Than gathers round Marengo's name,   150
    And gilded thy decline,
Through the long twilight of all time,
Despite some passing clouds of crime.

XVIII

But thou forsooth must be a king,
    And don the purple vest,
As if that foolish robe could wring
    Remembrance from thy breast.
Where is that faded garment ? where
The gewgaws thou wert fond to wear,
    The star, the string, the crest ?   160
Vain froward child of empire ! say,
Are all thy playthings snatched away ?

XIX

Where may the wearied eye repose
    When gazing on the Great ;
Where neither guilty glory glows,
    Nor despicable state ?
Yes—one—the first—the last—the best—
The Cincinnatus of the West,
    Whom envy dared not hate,
Bequeath'd the name of Washington,   170
To make man blush there was but one !

STANZAS FOR MUSIC

I SPEAK not, I trace not, I breathe not thy name,
There is grief in the sound, there is guilt in the fame :
But the tear which now burns on my cheek may impart
The deep thoughts that dwell in that silence of heart.

Too brief for our passion, too long for our peace,
Were those hours—can their joy or their bitterness cease?
We repent, we abjure, we will break from our chain,—
We will part, we will fly to—unite it again !

Oh ! thine be the gladness, and mine be the guilt !
Forgive me, adored one !—forsake, if thou wilt ;— 10
But the heart which is thine shall expire undebased,
And *man* shall not break it—whatever *thou* mayst.

And stern to the haughty, but humble to thee,
This soul, in its bitterest blackness, shall be ;
And our days seem as swift, and our moments more
    sweet,
With thee by my side, than with worlds at our feet.

One sigh of thy sorrow, one look of thy love,
Shall turn me or fix, shall reward or reprove ;
And the heartless may wonder at all I resign—
Thy lip shall reply, not to them, but to *mine*. 20

May, 1814.

TO BELSHAZZAR

BELSHAZZAR ! from the banquet turn,
   Nor in thy sensual fulness fall ;
Behold ! while yet before thee burn
   The graven words, the glowing wall,
Many a despot men miscall
   Crown'd and anointed from on high ;
But thou, the weakest, worst of all—
   Is it not written, thou must die ?

Go ! dash the roses from thy brow—
   Grey hairs but poorly wreathe with them ; 10
Youth's garlands misbecome thee now,
   More than thy very diadem,
Where thou hast tarnish'd every gem :—
   Then throw the worthless bauble by,
Which, worn by thee, ev'n slaves contemn ;
   And learn like better men to die !

Oh ! early in the balance weigh'd,
   And ever light of word and worth,
Whose soul expired ere youth decay'd,
   And left thee but a mass of earth. 20
To see thee moves the scorner's mirth :
   But tears in Hope's averted eye
Lament that even thou hadst birth—
   Unfit to govern, live, or die.

HEBREW MELODIES

ADVERTISEMENT

The subsequent poems were written at the request of my friend, the Hon. Douglas Kinnaird, for a Selection of Hebrew Melodies, and have been published, with the music, arranged by Mr. Braham and Mr. Nathan.

January, 1815.

SHE WALKS IN BEAUTY

I

She walks in beauty, like the night
  Of cloudless climes and starry skies;
And all that 's best of dark and bright
  Meet in her aspect and her eyes:
Thus mellow'd to that tender light
  Which heaven to gaudy day denies.

II

One shade the more, one ray the less,
  Had half impair'd the nameless grace
Which waves in every raven tress,
  Or softly lightens o'er her face;   10
Where thoughts serenely sweet express
  How pure, how dear their dwelling-place.

III

And on that cheek, and o'er that brow,
  So soft, so calm, yet eloquent,
The smiles that win, the tints that glow,
  But tell of days in goodness spent,
A mind at peace with all below,
  A heart whose love is innocent!

THE HARP THE MONARCH MINSTREL SWEPT

I

THE harp the monarch minstrel swept,
  The King of men, the loved of Heaven,
Which Music hallow'd while she wept
  O'er tones her heart of hearts had given,
  Redoubled be her tears, its chords are riven !
It soften'd men of iron mould,
  It gave them virtues not their own ;
No ear so dull, no soul so cold,
  That felt not, fired not to the tone,   9
  Till David's lyre grew mightier than his throne !

II

It told the triumphs of our King,
  It wafted glory to our God ;
It made our gladden'd valleys ring,
  The cedars bow, the mountains nod ;
  Its sound aspired to heaven and there abode !
Since then, though heard on earth no more,
  Devotion and her daughter Love
Still bid the bursting spirit soar
  To sounds that seem as from above,   19
  In dreams that day's broad light can not remove.

IF THAT HIGH WORLD

I

IF that high world, which lies beyond
  Our own, surviving Love endears ;
If there the cherish'd heart be fond,
  The eye the same, except in tears—
How welcome those untrodden spheres !
  How sweet this very hour to die !
To soar from earth and find all fears
  Lost in thy light—Eternity !

II

It must be so : 'tis not for self
  That we so tremble on the brink ;   10
And striving to o'erleap the gulf,
  Yet cling to Being's severing link.

Oh ! in that future let us think
    To hold each heart the heart that shares ;
With them the immortal waters drink,
    And soul in soul grow deathless theirs !

THE WILD GAZELLE

I

THE wild gazelle on Judah's hills
    Exulting yet may bound,
And drink from all the living rills
    That gush on holy ground :
Its airy step and glorious eye
May glance in tameless transport by :—

II

A step as fleet, an eye more bright,
    Hath Judah witness'd there ;
And o'er her scenes of lost delight
    Inhabitants more fair.
The cedars wave on Lebanon,   10
But Judah's statelier maids are gone !

III

More blest each palm that shades those plains
    Than Israel's scatter'd race ;
For, taking root, it there remains
    In solitary grace :
It cannot quit its place of birth,
It will not live in other earth.

IV

But we must wander witheringly,
    In other lands to die ;   20
And where our fathers' ashes be,
    Our own may never lie :
Our temple hath not left a stone,
And Mockery sits on Salem's throne.

OH! WEEP FOR THOSE

I

OH ! weep for those that wept by Babel's stream,
Whose shrines are desolate, whose land a dream ;
Weep for the harp of Judah's broken shell ;
Mourn—where their God hath dwelt the godless dwell !

II

And where shall Israel lave her bleeding feet ?
And when shall Zion's songs again seem sweet ?
And Judah's melody once more rejoice
The hearts that leap'd before its heavenly voice ?

III

Tribes of the wandering foot and weary breast,
How shall ye flee away and be at rest !
The wild-dove hath her nest, the fox his cave,
Mankind their country—Israel but the grave !

10

ON JORDAN'S BANKS

I

ON Jordan's banks the Arab's camels stray,
On Sion's hill the False One's votaries pray,
The Baal-adorer bows on Sinai's steep—
Yet there—even there—Oh God ! thy thunders sleep:

II

There—where thy finger scorch'd the tablet stone !
There—where thy shadow to thy people shone !
Thy glory shrouded in its garb of fire :
Thyself—none living see and not expire !

III

Oh ! in the lightning let thy glance appear ;
Sweep from his shiver'd hand the oppressor's spear !
How long by tyrants shall thy land be trod ?
How long thy temple worshipless, Oh God ?

9

JEPHTHA'S DAUGHTER

I

SINCE our Country, our God—Oh, my Sire !
Demand that thy Daughter expire ;
Since thy triumph was bought by thy vow—
Strike the bosom that 's bared for thee now !

II

And the voice of my mourning is o'er,
And the mountains behold me no more:
If the hand that I love lay me low !
There cannot be pain in the blow!

III

And of this, oh, my Father ! be sure—
That the blood of thy child is as pure   10
As the blessing I beg ere it flow,
And the last thought that soothes me below.

IV

Though the virgins of Salem lament,
Be the judge and the hero unbent !
I have won the great battle for thee,
And my Father and Country are free !

V

When this blood of thy giving hath gush'd,
When the voice that thou lovest is hush'd,
Let my memory still be thy pride,
And forget not I smiled as I died !   20

OH ! SNATCH'D AWAY IN BEAUTY'S BLOOM

I

OH ! snatch'd away in beauty's bloom,
On thee shall press no ponderous tomb ;
  But on thy turf shall roses rear
  Their leaves, the earliest of the year ;
And the wild cypress wave in tender gloom :

II

And oft by yon blue gushing stream
    Shall Sorrow lean her drooping head,
And feed deep thought with many a dream,
    And lingering pause and lightly tread ;   **9**
    Fond wretch ! as if her step disturb'd the dead !

III

Away ! we know that tears are vain,
    That death nor heeds nor hears distress :
Will this unteach us to complain ?
    Or make one mourner weep the less ?
And thou—who tell'st me to forget,
Thy looks are wan, thine eyes are wet.

MY SOUL IS DARK

I

My soul is dark—Oh ! quickly string
    The harp I yet can brook to hear ;
And let thy gentle fingers fling
    Its melting murmurs o'er mine ear.
If in this heart a hope be dear,
    That sound shall charm it forth again :
If in these eyes there lurk a tear,
    'Twill flow, and cease to burn my brain.

II

But bid the strain be wild and deep,
    Nor let thy notes of joy be first :   **10**
I tell thee, minstrel, I must weep,
    Or else this heavy heart will burst ;
For it hath been by sorrow nursed,
    And ach'd in sleepless silence long ;
And now 'tis doom'd to know the worst,
    And break at once—or yield to song.

I SAW THEE WEEP

I

I SAW thee weep—the big bright tear
   Came o'er that eye of blue ;
And then methought it did appear
   A violet dropping dew ;
I saw thee smile—the sapphire's blaze
   Beside thee ceased to shine ;
It could not match the living rays
   That fill'd that glance of thine.

II

As clouds from yonder sun receive
   A deep and mellow dye,
Which scarce the shade of coming eve   10
   Can banish from the sky,
Those smiles unto the moodiest mind
   Their own pure joy impart ;
Their sunshine leaves a glow behind
   That lightens o'er the heart.

THY DAYS ARE DONE

I

THY days are done, thy fame begun ;
   Thy country's strains record
The triumphs of her chosen Son,
   The slaughters of his sword !
The deeds he did, the fields he won,
   The freedom he restored !

II

Though thou art fall'n, while we are free
   Thou shalt not taste of death !
The generous blood that flow'd from thee
   Disdain'd to sink beneath :   10
Within our veins its currents be,
   Thy spirit on our breath !

III

Thy name, our charging hosts along,
　Shall be the battle-word !
Thy fall, the theme of choral song
　From virgin voices pour'd !
To weep would do thy glory wrong :
　Thou shalt not be deplored.

SAUL

I

THOU whose spell can raise the dead,
　Bid the prophet's form appear.
"Samuel, raise thy buried head !
　King, behold the phantom seer ! "
Earth yawn'd ; he stood the centre of a cloud :
Light changed its hue, retiring from his shroud.
Death stood all glassy in his fixed eye ;
His hand was wither'd, and his veins were dry ;
His foot, in bony whiteness, glitter'd there,
Shrunken and sinewless, and ghastly bare ;　　10
From lips that moved not and unbreathing frame,
Like cavern'd winds, the hollow accents came.
Saul saw, and fell to earth, as falls the oak,
At once, and blasted by the thunder-stroke.

II

"Why is my sleep disquieted ?
Who is he that calls the dead ?
Is it thou, O King ? Behold,
Bloodless are these limbs, and cold :
Such are mine ; and such shall be
Thine to-morrow, when with me :　　20
Ere the coming day is done,
Such shalt thou be, such thy son.
Fare thee well, but for a day,
Then we mix our mouldering clay.
Thou, thy race, lie pale and low,
Pierced by shafts of many a bow :

And the falchion by thy side
To thy heart thy hand shall guide :
Crownless, breathless, headless fall,
Son and sire, the house of Saul ! "   30

SONG OF SAUL BEFORE HIS LAST BATTLE

I

WARRIORS and chiefs ! should the shaft or the sword
Pierce me in leading the host of the Lord,
Heed not the corse, though a king's, in your path :
Bury your steel in the bosoms of Gath !

II

Thou who art bearing my buckler and bow,
Should the soldiers of Saul look away from the foe,
Stretch me that moment in blood at thy feet !
Mine be the doom which they dared not to meet.

III

Farewell to others, but never we part,
Heir to my royalty, son of my heart !   10
Bright is the diadem, boundless the sway,
Or kingly the death, which awaits us to-day !

"ALL IS VANITY, SAITH THE PREACHER'

I

FAME, wisdom, love, and power were mine,
    And health and youth possess'd me ;
My goblets blush'd from every vine,
    And lovely forms caress'd me ;
I sunn'd my heart in beauty's eyes,
    And felt my soul grow tender ;
All earth can give, or mortal prize,
    Was mine of regal splendour.

II

I strive to number o'er what days
　Remembrance can discover,　　　　　　10
Which all that life or earth displays
　Would lure me to live over.
There rose no day, there roll'd no hour
　Of pleasure unembitter'd ;
And not a trapping deck'd my power
　That gall'd not while it glitter'd.

III

The serpent of the field, by art
　And spells, is won from harming ;
But that which coils around the heart,
　Oh ! who hath power of charming ?　　20
It will not list to wisdom's lore,
　Nor music's voice can lure it ;
But there it stings for evermore
　The soul that must endure it.

WHEN COLDNESS WRAPS THIS SUFFERING CLAY

I

WHEN coldness wraps this suffering clay,
　Ah ! whither strays the immortal mind ?
It cannot die, it cannot stay,
　But leaves its darken'd dust behind.
Then, unembodied, doth it trace
　By steps each planet's heavenly way ?
Or fill at once the realms of space,
　A thing of eyes, that all survey ?

II

Eternal, boundless, undecay'd,
　A thought unseen, but seeing all,　　10
All, all in earth or skies display'd,
　Shall it survey, shall it recall :

Each fainter trace that memory holds
  So darkly of departed years,
In one broad glance the soul beholds,
  And all, that was, at once appears.

III

Before Creation peopled earth,
  Its eye shall roll through chaos back;
And where the furthest heaven had birth,
  The spirit trace its rising track.   20
And where the future mars or makes,
  Its glance dilate o'er all to be,
While sun is quench'd or system breaks,
  Fix'd in its own eternity.

IV

Above or Love, Hope, Hate, or Fear,
  It lives all passionless and pure:
An age shall fleet like earthly year;
  Its years as moments shall endure.
Away, away, without a wing,
  O'er all, through all, its thought shall fly,   30
A nameless and eternal thing,
  Forgetting what it was to die.

VISION OF BELSHAZZAR

I

THE King was on his throne,
  The Satraps throng'd the hall:
A thousand bright lamps shone
  O'er that high festival.
A thousand cups of gold,
  In Judah deem'd divine—
Jehovah's vessels hold
  The godless Heathen's wine!

II

In that same hour and hall,
  The fingers of a hand   10
Came forth against the wall,
  And wrote as if on sand:
The fingers of a man ;—
  A solitary hand
Along the letters ran,
  And traced them like a wand.

III

The monarch saw, and shook,
  And bade no more rejoice ;
All bloodless wax'd his look,
  And tremulous his voice.   20
" Let the men of lore appear,
  The wisest of the earth,
And expound the words of fear,
  Which mar our royal mirth."

IV

Chaldea's seers are good,
  But here they have no skill ;
And the unknown letters stood
  Untold and awful still.
And Babel's men of age
  Are wise and deep in lore ;   30
But now they were not sage,
  They saw—but knew no more.

V

A captive in the land,
  A stranger and a youth,
He heard the king's command,
  He saw that writing's truth.
The lamps around were bright,
  The prophecy in view ;
He read it on that night,—
  The morrow proved it true.   40

VI

" Belshazzar's grave is made,
His kingdom pass'd away,
He, in the balance weigh'd,
Is light and worthless clay;
The shroud his robe of state,
His canopy the stone;
The Mede is at his gate!
The Persian on his throne!"

SUN OF THE SLEEPLESS!

Sun of the sleepless! melancholy star!
Whose tearful beam glows tremulously far,
That show'st the darkness thou canst not dispel,
How like art thou to joy remember'd well!
So gleams the past, the light of other days,
Which shines, but warms not with its powerless rays;
A night-beam Sorrow watcheth to behold,
Distinct, but distant—clear—but, oh how cold!

WERE MY BOSOM AS FALSE AS THOU DEEM'ST IT TO BE

I

Were my bosom as false as thou deem'st it to be,
I need not have wander'd from far Galilee;
It was but abjuring my creed to efface
The curse which, thou say'st, is the crime of my race.

II

If the bad never triumph, then God is with thee!
If the slave only sin, thou art spotless and free!
If the Exile on earth is an Outcast on high,
Live on in thy faith, but in mine I will die.   8

III

I have lost for that faith more than thou canst bestow,
As the God who permits thee to prosper doth know;
In his hand is my heart and my hope—and in thine
The land and the life which for him I resign.

HEROD'S LAMENT FOR MARIAMNE

I

Oh, Mariamne! now for thee
  The heart for which thou bled'st is bleeding;
Revenge is lost in agony,
  And wild remorse to rage succeeding.
Oh, Mariamne! where art thou?
  Thou canst not hear my bitter pleading:
Ah! could'st thou—thou would'st pardon now,
  Though Heaven were to my prayer unheeding.

II

And is she dead?—and did they dare
  Obey my frenzy's jealous raving?   10
My wrath but doom'd my own despair:
  The sword that smote her 's o'er me waving.—
But thou art cold, my murder'd love!
  And this dark heart is vainly craving
For her who soars alone above,
  And leaves my soul unworthy saving.

III

She 's gone, who shared my diadem;
  She sunk, with her my joys entombing;
I swept that flower from Judah's stem,
  Whose leaves for me alone were blooming;   20
And mine 's the guilt, and mine the hell,
  This bosom's desolation dooming;
And I have earn'd those tortures well,
  Which unconsumed are still consuming!

ON THE DAY OF THE DESTRUCTION OF
JERUSALEM BY TITUS

I

From the last hill that looks on thy once holy dome,
I beheld thee, oh Sion! when render'd to Rome:
'Twas thy last sun went down, and the flames of thy fall
Flash'd back on the last glance I gave to thy wall.

II

I look'd for thy temple, I look'd for my home,
And forgot for a moment my bondage to come ;
I beheld but the death-fire that fed on thy fane,
And the fast-fetter'd hands that made vengeance in vain.

III

On many an eve, the high spot whence I gazed
Had reflected the last beam of day as it blazed ;   10
While I stood on the height, and beheld the decline
Of the rays from the mountain that shone on thy shrine.

IV

And now on that mountain I stood on that day,
But I mark'd not the twilight beam melting away ;
Oh ! would that the lightning had glared in its stead,
And the thunderbolt burst on the conqueror's head !

V

But the gods of the Pagan shall never profane
The shrine where Jehovah disdain'd not to reign ;
And scatter'd and scorn'd as thy people may be,
Our worship, oh Father ! is only for thee.   20

BY THE RIVERS OF BABYLON WE SAT DOWN AND WEPT

I

We sat down and wept by the waters
    Of Babel, and thought of the day
When our foe, in the hue of his slaughters,
    Made Salem's high places his prey ;
And ye, oh her desolate daughters !
    Were scatter'd all weeping away.

II

While sadly we gazed on the river
    Which roll'd on in freedom below,
They demanded the song ; but, oh never
    That triumph the stranger shall know !   10
May this right hand be wither'd for ever,
    Ere it string our high harp for the foe !

III

On the willow that harp is suspended,
  Oh Salem ! its sound should be free ;
And the hour when thy glories were ended
  But left me that token of thee :
And ne'er shall its soft tones be blended
  With the voice of the spoiler by me !

THE DESTRUCTION OF SENNACHERIB

I

THE Assyrian came down like the wolf on the fold,
And his cohorts were gleaming in purple and gold ;
And the sheen of their spears was like stars on the sea,
When the blue wave rolls nightly on deep Galilee.

II

Like the leaves of the forest when Summer is green,
That host with their banners at sunset were seen :
Like the leaves of the forest when Autumn hath blown,
That host on the morrow lay wither'd and strown.

III

For the Angel of Death spread his wings on the blast,
And breath'd in the face of the foe as he pass'd ;   10
And the eyes of the sleepers wax'd deadly and chill,
And their hearts but once heaved, and for ever grew
    still !

IV

And there lay the steed with his nostril all wide,
But through it there roll'd not the breath of his pride ;
And the foam of his gasping lay white on the turf,
And cold as the spray of the rock-beating surf.

V

And there lay the rider distorted and pale,
With the dew on his brow, and the rust on his mail :
And the tents were all silent, the banners alone,
The lances unlifted, the trumpet unblown.   20

VI

And the widows of Asshur are loud in their wail,
And the idols are broke in the temple of Baal;
And the might of the Gentile, unsmote by the sword,
Hath melted like snow in the glance of the Lord!

A SPIRIT PASS'D BEFORE ME

FROM JOB

I

A SPIRIT pass'd before me: I beheld
The face of immortality unveil'd—
Deep sleep came down on every eye save mine—
And there it stood,—all formless—but divine:
Along my bones the creeping flesh did quake;
And as my damp hair stiffen'd, thus it spake:

II

" Is man more just than God? Is man more pure
Than he who deems even Seraphs insecure?
Creatures of clay—vain dwellers in the dust!
The moth survives you, and are ye more just?   10
Things of a day! you wither ere the night,
Heedless and blind to Wisdom's wasted light!"

STANZAS FOR MUSIC

THERE be none of Beauty's daughters
     With a magic like thee;
And like music on the waters
     Is thy sweet voice to me:
When, as if its sound were causing
The charmed ocean's pausing,
The waves lie still and gleaming,
And the lull'd winds seem dreaming:

And the midnight moon is weaving
    Her bright chain o'er the deep;   10
Whose breast is gently heaving,
    As an infant's asleep:
So the spirit bows before thee,
To listen and adore thee;
With a full but soft emotion,
Like the swell of Summer's ocean.

STANZAS FOR MUSIC

    " O Lachrymarum fons, tenero sacros
        Ducentium ortus ex animo: quater
        Felix! in imo qui scatentem
        Pectore te, pia Nympha, sensit."
                             GRAY'S *Poemata.*

THERE's not a joy the world can give like that it takes
    away,
When the glow of early thought declines in feeling's dull
    decay;
'Tis not on youth's smooth cheek the blush alone, which
    fades so fast,
But the tender bloom of heart is gone, ere youth itself
    be past.

Then the few whose spirits float above the wreck of
    happiness
Are driven o'er the shoals of guilt or ocean of excess:
The magnet of their course is gone, or only points in vain
The shore to which their shiver'd sail shall never stretch
    again.

Then the mortal coldness of the soul like death itself
    comes down;
It cannot feel for others' woes, it dare not dream its
    own;   10
That heavy chill has frozen o'er the fountain of our
    tears,
And though the eye may sparkle still, 'tis where the ice
    appears.

Though wit may flash from fluent lips, and mirth dis-
    tract the breast,
Through midnight hours that yield no more their former
    hope of rest ;
'Tis but as ivy-leaves around the ruin'd turret wreath,
All green and wildly fresh without, but worn and grey
    beneath.

Oh could I feel as I have felt,—or be what I have been,
Or weep as I could once have wept o'er many a vanish'd
    scene ;
As springs in deserts found seem sweet, all brackish
    though they be,
So, midst the wither'd waste of life, those tears would
    flow to me.   20

                                        March, 1815.

ODE FROM THE FRENCH

I

We do not curse thee, Waterloo !
Though Freedom's blood thy plain bedew ;
There 'twas shed, but is not sunk—
Rising from each gory trunk,
Like the water-spout from ocean,
With a strong and growing motion—
It soars, and mingles in the air,
With that of lost Labedoyère—
With that of him whose honour'd grave
Contains the " bravest of the brave."   10
A crimson cloud it spreads and glows,
But shall return to whence it rose ;
When 'tis full 'twill burst asunder—
Never yet was heard such thunder
As then shall shake the world with wonder—
Never yet was seen such lightning
As o'er heaven shall then be bright'ning !
Like the Wormwood Star foretold
By the sainted Seer of old,
Show'ring down a fiery flood,   20
Turning rivers into blood.

II

The Chief has fallen, but not by you,
Vanquishers of Waterloo!
When the soldier citizen
Sway'd not o'er his fellow-men—
Save in deeds that led them on
Where Glory smiled on Freedom's son—
Who, of all the despots banded,
  With that youthful chief competed?
  Who could boast o'er France defeated,   30
Till lone Tyranny commanded?
Till, goaded by ambition's sting,
The Hero sunk into the King?
Then he fell:—so perish all,
Who would men by man enthral!

III

And thou, too, of the snow-white plume!
Whose realm refused thee ev'n a tomb;
Better hadst thou still been leading
France o'er hosts of hirelings bleeding,
Than sold thyself to death and shame   40
For a meanly royal name;
Such as he of Naples wears,
Who thy blood-bought title bears.
Little didst thou deem, when dashing
  On thy war-horse through the ranks,
  Like a stream which burst its banks,
While helmets cleft, and sabres clashing,
Shone and shiver'd fast around thee—
Of the fate at last which found thee:
Was that haughty plume laid low   50
By a slave's dishonest blow?
Once—as the moon sways o'er the tide,
It roll'd in air, the warrior's guide;
Through the smoke-created night
Of the black and sulphurous fight,
The soldier raised his seeking eye
To catch that crest's ascendancy,—

And, as it onward rolling rose,
So moved his heart upon our foes.
There, where death's brief pang was quickest,   60
And the battle's wreck lay thickest,
Strew'd beneath the advancing banner
    Of the eagle's burning crest—
(There with thunder-clouds to fan her,
    Who could then her wing arrest—
    Victory beaming from her breast ?)
While the broken line enlarging
    Fell, or fled along the plain ;
There be sure was Murat charging !
    There he ne'er shall charge again !   70

IV

O'er glories gone the invaders march,
Weeps Triumph o'er each levell'd arch—
But let Freedom rejoice,
With her heart in her voice ;
But, her hand on her sword,
Doubly shall she be adored ;
France hath twice too well been taught
The " moral lesson " dearly bought—
Her safety sits not on a throne,
With Capet or Napoleon !   80
But in equal rights and laws,
Hearts and hands in one great cause—
Freedom, such as God hath given
Unto all beneath his heaven,
With their breath, and from their birth,
Though guilt would sweep it from the earth ;
With a fierce and lavish hand
Scattering nations' wealth like sand ;
Pouring nations' blood like water,
In imperial seas of slaughter !   90

V

But the heart and the mind,
And the voice of mankind,
Shall arise in communion—
And who shall resist that proud union ?

The time is past when swords subdued—
Man may die—the soul's renew'd:
Even in this low world of care
Freedom ne'er shall want an heir;
Millions breathe but to inherit
Her for ever bounding spirit—   100
When once more her hosts assemble,
Tyrants shall believe and tremble—
Smile they at this idle threat?
Crimson tears will follow yet.

NAPOLEON'S FAREWELL

[FROM THE FRENCH]

I

FAREWELL to the Land where the gloom of my Glory
Arose and o'ershadow'd the earth with her name—
She abandons me now—but the page of her story,
The brightest or blackest, is fill'd with my fame.
I have warr'd with a world which vanquish'd me only
When the meteor of conquest allured me too far;
I have coped with the nations which dread me thus
        lonely,
The last single Captive to millions in war.

II

Farewell to thee, France! when thy diadem crown'd
        me,
I made thee the gem and the wonder of earth,   10
But thy weakness decrees I should leave as I found
        thee,
Decay'd in thy glory, and sunk in thy worth.
Oh! for the veteran hearts that were wasted
In strife with the storm, when their battles were won—
Then the Eagle, whose gaze in that moment was
        blasted,
Had still soar'd with eyes fix'd on victory's sun!

III

Farewell to thee, France!—but when Liberty rallies
Once more in thy regions, remember me then,—
The violet still grows in the depth of thy valleys;
Though wither'd, thy tear will unfold it again—   20
Yet, yet, I may baffle the hosts that surround us,
And yet may thy heart leap awake to my voice—
There are links which must break in the chain that has
  bound us,
Then turn thee and call on the Chief of thy choice!

FARE THEE WELL

FARE thee well! and if for ever,
  Still for ever, fare thee well:
Even though unforgiving, never
  'Gainst thee shall my heart rebel.

Would that breast were bared before thee
  Where thy head so oft hath lain,
While that placid sleep came o'er thee
  Which thou ne'er canst know again:

Would that breast, by thee glanced over,
  Every inmost thought could show!   10
Then thou wouldst at last discover
  'Twas not well to spurn it so.

Though the world for this commend thee—
  Though it smile upon the blow,
Even its praises must offend thee,
  Founded on another's woe:

Though my many faults defaced me,
  Could no other arm be found,
Than the one which once embraced me,
  To inflict a cureless wound?   20

Yet, oh yet, thyself deceive not;
  Love may sink by slow decay,
But by sudden wrench, believe not
  Hearts can thus be torn away:

Still thine own its life retaineth,
  Still must mine, though bleeding, beat;
And the undying thought which paineth
  Is—that we no more may meet.

These are words of deeper sorrow
  Than the wail above the dead;   30
Both shall live, but every morrow
  Wake us from a widow'd bed.

And when thou wouldst solace gather,
  When our child's first accents flow,
Wilt thou teach her to say "Father!"
  Though his care she must forego?

When her little hands shall press thee,
  When her lip to thine is press'd,
Think of him whose prayer shall bless thee,
  Think of him thy love had bless'd!   40

Should her lineaments resemble
  Those thou never more may'st see,
Then thy heart will softly tremble
  With a pulse yet true to me.

All my faults perchance thou knowest,
  All my madness none can know;
All my hopes, where'er thou goest,
  Wither, yet with *thee* they go.

Every feeling hath been shaken;
  Pride, which not a world could bow,   50
Bows to thee—by thee forsaken,
  Even my soul forsakes me now:

But 'tis done—all words are idle—
  Words from me are vainer still;
But the thoughts we cannot bridle
  Force their way without the will.

Fare thee well! thus disunited,
  Torn from every nearer tie,
Sear'd in heart, and lone, and blighted,
  More than this I scarce can die.   60

March 17, 1816.

ENDORSEMENT TO THE DEED OF SEPARATION

IN THE APRIL OF 1816

A YEAR ago, you swore, fond she!
  "To love, to honour," and so forth:
Such was the vow you pledged to me,
  And here's exactly what 'tis worth.

STANZAS TO AUGUSTA

I

WHEN all around grew drear and dark,
  And reason half withheld her ray—
And hope but shed a dying spark
  Which more misled my lonely way;

II

In that deep midnight of the mind,
  And that internal strife of heart,
When dreading to be deem'd too kind,
  The weak despair—the cold depart;

III

When fortune changed—and love fled far,
  And hatred's shafts flew thick and fast,   10
Thou wert the solitary star
  Which rose and set not to the last.

IV

Oh! blest be thine unbroken light!
  That watch'd me as a seraph's eye,
And stood between me and the night,
  For ever shining sweetly nigh.

V

And when the cloud upon us came,
  Which strove to blacken o'er thy ray—
Then purer spread its gentle flame,
  And dash'd the darkness all away.   20

VI

Still may thy spirit dwell on mine,
  And teach it what to brave or brook—
There 's more in one soft word of thine
  Than in the world's defied rebuke.

VII

Thou stood'st, as stands a lovely tree,
  That still unbroke, though gently bent,
Still waves with fond fidelity
  Its boughs above a monument.

VIII

The winds might rend—the skies might pour,
  But there thou wert—and still wouldst be   30
Devoted in the stormiest hour
  To shed thy weeping leaves o'er me.

IX

But thou and thine shall know no blight,
  Whatever fate on me may fall ;
For Heaven in sunshine will requite
  The kind—and thee the most of all.

X

Then let the ties of baffled love
  Be broken—thine will never break ;
Thy heart can feel—but will not move ;
  Thy soul, though soft, will never shake.   40

XI

And these, when all was lost beside,
  Were found and still are fix'd in thee ;—
And bearing still a breast so tried,
  Earth is no desert—ev'n to me.

STANZAS TO AUGUSTA

I

THOUGH the day of my destiny's over,
 And the star of my fate hath declined,
Thy soft heart refused to discover
 The faults which so many could find;
Though thy soul with my grief was acquainted,
 It shrunk not to share it with me,
And the love which my spirit hath painted
 It never hath found but in *thee*.

II

Then when nature around me is smiling,
 The last smile which answers to mine,   10
I do not believe it beguiling,
 Because it reminds me of thine;
And when winds are at war with the ocean,
 As the breasts I believed in with me,
If their billows excite an emotion,
 It is that they bear me from *thee*.

III

Though the rock of my last hope is shiver'd,
 And its fragments are sunk in the wave,
Though I feel that my soul is deliver'd
 To pain—it shall not be its slave.   20
There is many a pang to pursue me:
 They may crush, but they shall not contemn;
They may torture, but shall not subdue me;
 'Tis of *thee* that I think—not of them.

IV

Though human, thou didst not deceive me,
 Though woman, thou didst not forsake,
Though loved, thou forborest to grieve me,
 Though slander'd, thou never couldst shake;
Though trusted, thou didst not disclaim me,
 Though parted, it was not to fly,   30
Though watchful, 'twas not to defame me,
 Nor, mute, that the world might belie.

V

Yet I blame not the world, nor despise it,
  Nor the war of the many with one ;
If my soul was not fitted to prize it,
  'Twas folly not sooner to shun :
And if dearly that error hath cost me,
  And more than I once could foresee,
I have found that, whatever it lost me,
  It could not deprive me of *thee*.   40

VI

From the wreck of the past, which hath perish'd,
  Thus much I at least may recall,
It hath taught me that what I most cherish'd
  Deserved to be dearest of all :
In the desert a fountain is springing,
  In the wide waste there still is a tree,
And a bird in the solitude singing,
  Which speaks to my spirit of *thee*.

July 24, 1816.

EPISTLE TO AUGUSTA

I

My sister ! my sweet sister ! if a name
Dearer and purer were, it should be thine ;
Mountains and seas divide us, but I claim
No tears, but tenderness to answer mine :
Go where I will, to me thou art the same—
A loved regret which I would not resign.
There yet are two things in my destiny,—
A world to roam through, and a home with thee.

II

The first were nothing—had I still the last,
It were the haven of my happiness ;   10
But other claims and other ties thou hast,
And mine is not the wish to make them less.
A strange doom is thy father's son's, and past
Recalling, as it lies beyond redress ;
Reversed for him our grandsire's fate of yore,—
He had no rest at sea, nor I on shore.

III

If my inheritance of storms hath been
In other elements, and on the rocks
Of perils, overlook'd or unforeseen,
I have sustain'd my share of worldly shocks,   20
The fault was mine ; nor do I seek to screen
My errors with defensive paradox ;
    I have been cunning in mine overthrow,
The careful pilot of my proper woe.

IV

Mine were my faults, and mine be their reward.
My whole life was a contest, since the day
That gave me being, gave me that which marr'd
The gift,—a fate, or will, that walk'd astray ;
And I at times have found the struggle hard,
And thought of shaking off my bonds of clay :   30
    But now I fain would for a time survive,
If but to see what next can well arrive.

V

Kingdoms and empires in my little day
I have outlived, and yet I am not old ;
And when I look on this, the petty spray
Of my own years of trouble, which have roll'd
Like a wild bay of breakers, melts away :
Something—I know not what—does still uphold
    A spirit of slight patience ;—not in vain,
Even for its own sake, do we purchase pain.   40

VI

Perhaps the workings of defiance stir
Within me—or perhaps a cold despair,
Brought on when ills habitually recur,—
Perhaps a kinder clime, or purer air,
(For even to this may change of soul refer,
And with light armour we may learn to bear,)
    Have taught me a strange quiet, which was not
The chief companion of a calmer lot.

VII

I feel almost at times as I have felt
In happy childhood; trees, and flowers, and brooks,
Which do remember me of where I dwelt   51
Ere my young mind was sacrificed to books,
Come as of yore upon me, and can melt
My heart with recognition of their looks;
And even at moments I could think I see
Some living thing to love—but none like thee.

VIII

Here are the Alpine landscapes which create
A fund for contemplation;—to admire
Is a brief feeling of a trivial date;
But something worthier do such scenes inspire: 60
Here to be lonely is not desolate,
For much I view which I could most desire,
And, above all, a lake I can behold
Lovelier, not dearer, than our own of old.

IX

Oh that thou wert but with me!—but I grow
The fool of my own wishes, and forget
The solitude which I have vaunted so
Has lost its praise in this but one regret;
There may be others which I less may show;—
I am not of the plaintive mood, and yet   70
I feel an ebb in my philosophy,
And the tide rising in my alter'd eye.

X

I did remind thee of our own dear Lake,
By the old Hall which may be mine no more.
Leman's is fair; but think not I forsake
The sweet remembrance of a dearer shore:
Sad havoc Time must with my memory make,
Ere *that* or *thou* can fade these eyes before;
Though, like all things which I have loved, they are
Resign'd for ever, or divided far.   80

XI

The world is all before me ; I but ask
Of Nature that with which she will comply—
It is but in her summer's sun to bask,
To mingle with the quiet of her sky,
To see her gentle face without a mask,
And never gaze on it with apathy.
She was my early friend, and now shall be
My sister—till I look again on thee.

XII

I can reduce all feelings but this one ;
And that I would not ;—for at length I see   90
Such scenes as those wherein my life begun.
The earliest—even the only paths for me—
Had I but sooner learnt the crowd to shun,
I had been better than I now can be ;
The passions which have torn me would have slept ;
I had not suffer'd, and *thou* hadst not wept.

XIII

With false Ambition what had I to do ?
Little with Love, and least of all with Fame ;
And yet they came unsought, and with me grew,
And made me all which they can make—a name.
Yet this was not the end I did pursue ;   101
Surely I once beheld a nobler aim.
But all is over—I am one the more
To baffled millions which have gone before.

XIV

And for the future, this world's future may
From me demand but little of my care ;
I have outlived myself by many a day ;
Having survived so many things that were ;
My years have been no slumber, but the prey
Of ceaseless vigils ; for I had the share   110
Of life which might have fill'd a century,
Before its fourth in time had pass'd me by.

XV

And for the remnant which may be to come
I am content ; and for the past I feel
Not thankless,—for within the crowded sum
Of struggles, happiness at times would steal,
And for the present, I would not benumb
My feelings further.—Nor shall I conceal
That with all this I still can look around,
And worship Nature with a thought profound.   120

XVI

For thee, my own sweet sister, in thy heart
I know myself secure, as thou in mine ;
We were and are—I am, even as thou art—
Beings who ne'er each other can resign ;
It is the same, together or apart,
From life's commencement to its slow decline
We are entwined—let death come slow or fast,
The tie which bound the first endures the last !

THE DREAM

I

OUR life is two-fold : Sleep hath its own world,
A boundary between the things misnamed
Death and existence : Sleep hath its own world,
And a wide realm of wild reality.
And dreams in their development have breath,
And tears, and tortures, and the touch of joy ;
They leave a weight upon our waking thoughts,
They take a weight from off our waking toils,
They do divide our being ; they become
A portion of ourselves as of our time,   10
And look like heralds of eternity ;
They pass like spirits of the past,—they speak
Like Sibyls of the future : they have power—
The tyranny of pleasure and of pain ;
They make us what we were not—what they will,
And shake us with the vision that's gone by,
The dread of vanish'd shadows—Are they so ?

Is not the past all shadow ?—What are they ?
Creations of the mind ?—The mind can make
Substance, and people planets of its own   20
With beings brighter than have been, and give
A breath to forms which can outlive all flesh.
I would recall a vision which I dream'd
Perchance in sleep—for in itself a thought,
A slumbering thought, is capable of years,
And curdles a long life into one hour.

II

I saw two beings in the hues of youth
Standing upon a hill, a gentle hill,
Green and of mild declivity, the last
As 'twere the cape of a long ridge of such,   30
Save that there was no sea to lave its base,
But a most living landscape, and the wave
Of woods and corn-fields, and the abodes of men
Scatter'd at intervals, and wreathing smoke
Arising from such rustic roofs ;—the hill
Was crown'd with a peculiar diadem
Of trees, in circular array, so fix'd,
Not by the sport of nature, but of man :
These two, a maiden and a youth, were there
Gazing—the one on all that was beneath   40
Fair as herself—but the boy gazed on her ;
And both were young, and one was beautiful :
And both were young—yet not alike in youth.
As the sweet moon on the horizon's verge,
The maid was on the eve of womanhood ;
The boy had fewer summers, but his heart
Had far outgrown his years, and to his eye
There was but one beloved face on earth,
And that was shining on him : he had look'd
Upon it till it could not pass away ;   50
He had no breath, no being, but in hers ;
She was his voice ; he did not speak to her,
But trembled on her words ; she was his sight,
For his eye follow'd hers, and saw with hers,
Which colour'd all his objects :—he had ceased

To live within himself ; she was his life,
The ocean to the river of his thoughts,
Which terminated all : upon a tone,
A touch of hers, his blood would ebb and flow,
And his cheek change tempestuously—his heart   60
Unknowing of its cause of agony.
But she in these fond feelings had no share :
Her sighs were not for him ; to her he was
Even as a brother—but no more ; 'twas much,
For brotherless she was, save in the name
Her infant friendship had bestow'd on him ;
Herself the solitary scion left
Of a time-honour'd race.—It was a name
Which pleased him, and yet pleased him not—and
       why ?
Time taught him a deep answer—when she loved   70
Another ; even *now* she loved another,
And on the summit of that hill she stood
Looking afar if yet her lover's steed
Kept pace with her expectancy, and flew.

III

A change came o'er the spirit of my dream.
There was an ancient mansion, and before
Its walls there was a steed caparison'd :
Within an antique Oratory stood
The Boy of whom I spake ;—he was alone,
And pale, and pacing to and fro : anon   80
He sate him down, and seized a pen, and traced
Words which I could not guess of ; then he lean'd
His bow'd head on his hands, and shook as 'twere
With a convulsion—then arose again,
And with his teeth and quivering hands did tear
What he had written, but he shed no tears,
And he did calm himself, and fix his brow
Into a kind of quiet : as he paused,
The Lady of his love re-entered there ;
She was serene and smiling then, and yet   90
She knew she was by him beloved,—she knew,
For quickly comes such knowledge, that his heart

Was darken'd with her shadow, and she saw
That he was wretched, but she saw not all.
He rose, and with a cold and gentle grasp
He took her hand; a moment o'er his face
A tablet of unutterable thoughts
Was traced, and then it faded, as it came;
He dropp'd the hand he held, and with slow steps
Retired, but not as bidding her adieu,   100
For they did part with mutual smiles; he pass'd
From out the massy gate of that old Hall,
And mounting on his steed he went his way;
And ne'er repass'd that hoary threshold more.

IV

A change came o'er the spirit of my dream.
The Boy was sprung to manhood: in the wilds
Of fiery climes he made himself a home,
And his soul drank their sunbeams: he was girt
With strange and dusky aspects; he was not
Himself like what he had been; on the sea   110
And on the shore he was a wanderer:
There was a mass of many images
Crowded like waves upon me, but he was
A part of all; and in the last he lay
Reposing from the noontide sultriness,
Couch'd among fallen columns, in the shade
Of ruin'd walls that had survived the names
Of those who rear'd them; by his sleeping side
Stood camels grazing, and some goodly steeds
Were fasten'd near a fountain; and a man   120
Clad in a flowing garb did watch the while,
While many of his tribe slumber'd around:
And they were canopied by the blue sky,
So cloudless, clear, and purely beautiful,
That God alone was to be seen in heaven.

V

A change came o'er the spirit of my dream.
The Lady of his love was wed with One
Who did not love her better:—in her home,

A thousand leagues from his,—her native home,
She dwelt, begirt with growing Infancy,   130
Daughters and sons of Beauty,—but behold!
Upon her face there was the tint of grief,
The settled shadow of an inward strife,
And an unquiet drooping of the eye,
As if its lid were charged with unshed tears.
What could her grief be?—she had all she loved,
And he who had so loved her was not there
To trouble with bad hopes, or evil wish,
Or ill-repress'd affliction, her pure thoughts.
What could her grief be?—she had loved him not,   141
Nor given him cause to deem himself beloved,
Nor could he be a part of that which prey'd
Upon her mind—a spectre of the past.

VI

A change came o'er the spirit of my dream.
The Wanderer was return'd.—I saw him stand
Before an Altar—with a gentle bride;
Her face was fair, but was not that which made
The Starlight of his Boyhood;—as he stood
Even at the altar, o'er his brow there came
The self-same aspect, and the quivering shock   150
That in the antique Oratory shook
His bosom in its solitude; and then—
As in that hour—a moment o'er his face
The tablet of unutterable thoughts
Was traced,—and then it faded as it came,
And he stood calm and quiet, and he spoke
The fitting vows, but heard not his own words,
And all things reel'd around him; he could see
Not that which was, nor that which should have been—
But the old mansion, and the accustom'd hall,   160
And the remember'd chambers, and the place,
The day, the hour, the sunshine, and the shade,
All things pertaining to that place and hour,
And her who was his destiny,—came back
And thrust themselves between him and the light:
What business had they there at such a time?

VII

A change came o'er the spirit of my dream.
The Lady of his love :—Oh ! she was changed
As by the sickness of the soul ; her mind
Had wander'd from its dwelling, and her eyes   170
They had not their own lustre, but the look
Which is not of the earth ; she was become
The queen of a fantastic realm ; her thoughts
Were combinations of disjointed things ;
And forms impalpable and unperceived
Of others' sight familiar were to hers.
And this the world calls frenzy ; but the wise
Have a far deeper madness, and the glance
Of melancholy is a fearful gift ;
What is it but the telescope of truth ?   180
Which strips the distance of its fantasies,
And brings life near in utter nakedness,
Making the cold reality too real !

VIII

A change came o'er the spirit of my dream.
The Wanderer was alone as heretofore,
The beings which surrounded him were gone,
Or were at war with him ; he was a mark
For blight and desolation, compass'd round
With Hatred and Contention ; Pain was mix'd
In all which was served up to him, until,   190
Like to the Pontic monarch of old days,
He fed on poisons, and they had no power,
But were a kind of nutriment ; he lived
Through that which had been death to many men,
And made him friends of mountains : with the stars
And the quick Spirit of the Universe
He held his dialogues ; and they did teach
To him the magic of their mysteries ;
To him the book of Night was open'd wide,
And voices from the deep abyss reveal'd   200
A marvel and a secret—Be it so.

IX

My dream was past ; it had no further change.
It was of a strange order, that the doom
Of these two creatures should be thus traced out
Almost like a reality—the one
To end in madness—both in misery.

July, 1816.

LINES ON HEARING THAT LADY BYRON WAS ILL

AND thou wert sad—yet I was not with thee ;
   And thou wert sick, and yet I was not near ;
Methought that joy and health alone could be
   Where I was *not*—and pain and sorrow here !
And is it thus ?—it is as I foretold,
   And shall be more so ; for the mind recoils
Upon itself, and the wreck'd heart lies cold,
   While heaviness collects the shatter'd spoils.
It is not in the storm nor in the strife
   We feel benumb'd, and wish to be no more,   10
   But in the after-silence on the shore,
When all is lost, except a little life.

I am too well avenged !—but 'twas my right ;
   Whate'er my sins might be, *thou* wert not sent
To be the Nemesis who should requite—
   Nor did Heaven choose so near an instrument.
Mercy is for the merciful !—if thou
   Hast been of such, 'twill be accorded now.
Thy nights are banish'd from the realms of sleep !—
   Yes ! they may flatter thee, but thou shalt feel   20
   A hollow agony which will not heal,
For thou art pillow'd on a curse too deep ;
Thou hast sown in my sorrow, and must reap
   The bitter harvest in a woe as real !
I have had many foes, but none like thee ;
   For 'gainst the rest myself I could defend,
   And be avenged, or turn them into friend ;
But thou in safe implacability

Hadst nought to dread—in thy own weakness shielded,
And in my love, which hath but too much yielded,   30
  And spared, for thy sake, some I should not spare ;
And thus upon the world—trust in thy truth,
And the wild fame of my ungovern'd youth—
  On things that were not, and on things that are—
Even upon such a basis hast thou built
A monument, whose cement hath been guilt!
  The moral Clytemnestra of thy lord,
And hew'd down, with an unsuspected sword,
Fame, peace, and hope—and all the better life,
  Which, but for this cold treason of thy heart,   40
Might still have risen from out the grave of strife,
  And found a nobler duty than to part.
But of thy virtues didst thou make a vice,
  Trafficking with them in a purpose cold,
  For present anger, and for future gold—
And buying other's grief at any price.
And thus once enter'd into crooked ways,
The early truth, which was thy proper praise,
Did not still walk beside thee—but at times,
And with a breast unknowing its own crimes,   50
Deceit, averments incompatible,
Equivocations, and the thoughts which dwell
  In Janus-spirits—the significant eye
Which learns to lie with silence—the pretext
Of prudence, with advantages annex'd—
The acquiescence in all things which tend,
No matter how, to the desired end—
  All found a place in thy philosophy.
The means were worthy, and the end is won—
I would not do by thee as thou hast done !   60

September, 1816.

DARKNESS

I HAD a dream, which was not all a dream.
The bright sun was extinguish'd, and the stars
Did wander darkling in the eternal space,
Rayless, and pathless, and the icy earth

Swung blind and blackening in the moonless air;
Morn came and went—and came, and brought no day,
And men forgot their passions in the dread
Of this their desolation; and all hearts
Were chill'd into a selfish prayer for light:
And they did live by watchfires—and the thrones,   10
The palaces of crowned kings—the huts,
The habitations of all things which dwell,
Were burnt for beacons; cities were consumed,
And men were gather'd round their blazing homes
To look once more into each other's face;
Happy were those who dwelt within the eye
Of the volcanos, and their mountain-torch:
A fearful hope was all the world contain'd;
Forests were set on fire—but hour by hour
They fell and faded—and the crackling trunks   20
Extinguish'd with a crash—and all was black.
The brows of men by the despairing light
Wore an unearthly aspect, as by fits
The flashes fell upon them; some lay down
And hid their eyes and wept; and some did rest
Their chins upon their clenched hands, and smiled;
And others hurried to and fro, and fed
Their funeral piles with fuel, and look'd up
With mad disquietude on the dull sky,
The pall of a past world; and then again   30
With curses cast them down upon the dust,
And gnash'd their teeth and howl'd: the wild birds
    shriek'd,
And, terrified, did flutter on the ground,
And flap their useless wings; the wildest brutes
Came tame and tremulous; and vipers crawl'd
And twined themselves among the multitude,
Hissing, but stingless—they were slain for food!
And War, which for a moment was no more,
Did glut himself again:—a meal was bought   40
With blood, and each sate sullenly apart
Gorging himself in gloom: no love was left;
All earth was but one thought—and that was death
Immediate and inglorious; and the pang

Of famine fed upon all entrails—men
Died, and their bones were tombless as their flesh;
The meagre by the meagre were devour'd,
Even dogs assail'd their masters, all save one,
And he was faithful to a corse, and kept
The birds and beasts and famish'd men at bay,
Till hunger clung them, or the dropping dead   50
Lured their lank jaws; himself sought out no food,
But with a piteous and perpetual moan,
And a quick desolate cry, licking the hand
Which answer'd not with a caress—he died.
The crowd was famish'd by degrees; but two
Of an enormous city did survive,
And they were enemies: they met beside
The dying embers of an altar-place
Where had been heap'd a mass of holy things
For an unholy usage; they raked up,   60
And shivering scraped with their cold skeleton hands
The feeble ashes, and their feeble breath
Blew for a little life, and made a flame
Which was a mockery; then they lifted up
Their eyes as it grew lighter, and beheld
Each other's aspects—saw, and shriek'd, and died—
Even of their mutual hideousness they died,
Unknowing who he was upon whose brow
Famine had written Fiend.   The world was void,
The populous and the powerful was a lump,   70
Seasonless, herbless, treeless, manless, lifeless,
A lump of death—a chaos of hard clay.
The rivers, lakes, and ocean all stood still,
And nothing stirr'd within their silent depths;
Ships sailorless lay rotting on the sea,
And their masts fell down piecemeal: as they dropp'd
They slept on the abyss without a surge—
The waves were dead; the tides were in their grave,
The moon, their mistress, had expired before,
The winds were wither'd in the stagnant air,   80
And the clouds perish'd; Darkness had no need
Of aid from them—She was the Universe.

Diodati, July, 1816.

PROMETHEUS

I

TITAN! to whose immortal eyes
  The sufferings of mortality,
    Seen in their sad reality,
Were not as things that gods despise;
What was thy pity's recompense?
A silent suffering, and intense;
The rock, the vulture, and the chain,
All that the proud can feel of pain,
The agony they do not show,
The suffocating sense of woe,   10
    Which speaks but in its loneliness,
And then is jealous lest the sky
Should have a listener, nor will sigh
    Until its voice is echoless.

II

Titan! to thee the strife was given
  Between the suffering and the will,
    Which torture where they cannot kill;
And the inexorable Heaven,
And the deaf tyranny of Fate,
The ruling principle of Hate,   20
Which for its pleasure doth create
The things it may annihilate,
Refused thee even the boon to die:
The wretched gift Eternity
Was thine—and thou hast borne it well.
All that the Thunderer wrung from thee
Was but the menace which flung back
On him the torments of thy rack;
The fate thou didst so well foresee,
But would not to appease him tell;   30
And in thy Silence was his Sentence,
And in his Soul a vain repentance,
And evil dread so ill dissembled,
That in his hand the lightnings trembled.

III

Thy Godlike crime was to be kind,
  To render with thy precepts less
  The sum of human wretchedness,
And strengthen Man with his own mind;
But baffled as thou wert from high,
Still in thy patient energy,   40
In the endurance, and repulse
  Of thine impenetrable Spirit,
Which Earth and Heaven could not convulse,
  A mighty lesson we inherit:
Thou art a symbol and a sign
  To Mortals of their fate and force;
Like thee, Man is in part divine,
  A troubled stream from a pure source;
And Man in portions can foresee
His own funereal destiny;   50
His wretchedness, and his resistance,
And his sad unallied existence:
To which his Spirit may oppose
Itself—and equal to all woes,
  And a firm will, and a deep sense,
Which even in torture can descry
  Its own concenter'd recompense,
Triumphant where it dares defy,
And making Death a Victory.

Diodati, July, 1816

A FRAGMENT

COULD I remount the river of my years
To the first fountain of our smiles and tears,
I would not trace again the stream of hours
Between their outworn banks of wither'd flowers,
But bid it flow as now—until it glides
Into the number of the nameless tides.

   .   .   .   .   .   .

What is this Death?—a quiet of the heart?
The whole of that of which we are a part?
For life is but a vision—what I see
Of all which lives alone is life to me,   10

And being so—the absent are the dead,
Who haunt us from tranquillity, and spread
A dreary shroud around us, and invest
With sad remembrances our hours of rest.

The absent are the dead—for they are cold,
And ne'er can be what once we did behold;
And they are changed, and cheerless,—or if yet
The unforgotten do not all forget,
Since thus divided—equal must it be
If the deep barrier be of earth, or sea;   20
It may be both—but one day end it must
In the dark union of insensate dust.

The under-earth inhabitants—are they
But mingled millions decomposed to clay?
The ashes of a thousand ages spread
Wherever man has trodden or shall tread?
Or do they in their silent cities dwell
Each in his incommunicative cell?
Or have they their own language? and a sense
Of breathless being?—darken'd and intense   30
As midnight in her solitude?—Oh Earth!
Where are the past?—and wherefore had they birth?
The dead are thy inheritors—and we
But bubbles on thy surface; and the key
Of thy profundity is in the grave,
The ebon portal of thy peopled cave,
Where I would walk in spirit, and behold
Our elements resolved to things untold,
And fathom hidden wonders, and explore
The essence of great bosoms now no more.   40

.   .   .   .   .

Diodati, *July*, 1816.

STANZAS FOR MUSIC

I

BRIGHT be the place of thy soul!
  No lovelier spirit than thine
E'er burst from its mortal control,
  In the orbs of the blessed to shine.

On earth thou wert all but divine,
   As thy soul shall immortally be ;
And our sorrow may cease to repine
   When we know that thy God is with thee.

II

Light be the turf of thy tomb !
   May its verdure like emeralds be !   10
There should not be the shadow of gloom
   In aught that reminds us of thee.
Young flowers and an evergreen tree
   May spring from the spot of thy rest :
But nor cypress nor yew let us see ;
   For why should we mourn for the blest ?

STANZAS FOR MUSIC

I

THEY say that Hope is happiness ;
   But genuine Love must prize the past,
And Memory wakes the thoughts that bless :
   They rose the first—they set the last ;

II

And all that Memory loves the most
   Was once our only Hope to be,
And all that Hope adored and lost
   Hath melted into Memory.

III

Alas ! it is delusion all :
   The future cheats us from afar,   10
Nor can we be what we recall,
   Nor dare we think on what we are.

SO, WE'LL GO NO MORE A ROVING

I

So, we'll go no more a roving
   So late into the night,
Though the heart be still as loving,
   And the moon be still as bright.

II

For the sword outwears its sheath,
    And the soul wears out the breast,
And the heart must pause to breathe,
    And love itself have rest.

III

Though the night was made for loving,
    And the day returns too soon,   10
Yet we'll go no more a roving
    By the light of the moon.

1817.

TO THOMAS MOORE

WHAT are you doing now,
    Oh Thomas Moore ?
What are you doing now,
    Oh Thomas Moore ?
Sighing or suing now,
Rhyming or wooing now,
Billing or cooing now,
    Which, Thomas Moore ?

But the Carnival's coming,
    Oh Thomas Moore !   10
The Carnival's coming,
    Oh Thomas Moore !
Masking and humming,
Fifing and drumming,
Guitarring and strumming,
    Oh Thomas Moore !

TO THOMAS MOORE

I

MY boat is on the shore,
    And my bark is on the sea ;
But, before I go, Tom Moore,
    Here's a double health to thee !

II

Here's a sigh to those who love me,
  And a smile to those who hate ;
And, whatever sky's above me,
  Here's a heart for every fate.

III

Though the ocean roar around me,
  Yet it still shall bear me on ;   10
Though a desert should surround me,
  It hath springs that may be won.

IV

Were't the last drop in the well,
  As I gasp'd upon the brink,
Ere my fainting spirit fell,
  'Tis to thee that I would drink.

V

With that water, as this wine,
  The libation I would pour
Should be—peace with thine and mine,
  And a health to thee, Tom Moore.   20

                              July, 1817.

EPISTLE FROM MR. MURRAY TO
DR. POLIDORI

DEAR Doctor, I have read your play,
Which is a good one in its way,—
Purges the eyes and moves the bowels,
And drenches handkerchiefs like towels
With tears, that, in a flux of grief,
Afford hysterical relief
To shatter'd nerves and quicken'd pulses,
Which your catastrophe convulses.

I like your moral and machinery ;
Your plot, too, has such scope for scenery ;   10
Your dialogue is apt and smart :
The play's concoction full of art ;

Your hero raves, your heroine cries,
All stab, and everybody dies.
In short, your tragedy would be
The very thing to hear and see:
And for a piece of publication,
If I decline on this occasion,
It is not that I am not sensible
To merits in themselves ostensible,   20
But—and I grieve to speak it—plays
Are drugs—mere drugs, sir—now-a-days.
I had a heavy loss by "Manuel,"—
Too lucky if it prove not annual,—
And Sotheby, with his "Orestes,"
(Which, by the by, the author's best is,)
Has lain so very long on hand,
That I despair of all demand.
I've advertised, but see my books,
Or only watch my shopman's looks ;—   30
Still Ivan, Ina, and such lumber,
My back-shop glut, my shelves encumber.

There 's Byron too, who once did better,
Has sent me, folded in a letter,
A sort of—it 's no more a drama
Than Darnley, Ivan, or Kehama:
So alter'd since last year his pen is,
I think he 's lost his wits at Venice.
In short, sir, what with one and t'other,
I dare not venture on another.   40
I write in haste ; excuse each blunder ;
The coaches through the streets so thunder !
My room 's so full—we've Gifford here
Reading MS., with Hookham Frere,
Pronouncing on the nouns and particles
Of some of our forthcoming Articles.

The Quarterly—Ah, sir, if you
Had but the genius to review !—
A smart critique upon St. Helena,
Or if you only would but tell in a   50

Short compass what——but to resume:
As I was saying, sir, the room—
The room's so full of wits and bards,
Crabbes, Campbells, Crokers, Freres, and Wards,
And others, neither bards nor wits:—
My humble tenement admits
All persons in the dress of gent,
From Mr. Hammond to Dog Dent.

A party dines with me to-day,
All clever men, who make their way ;   60
Crabbe, Malcolm, Hamilton, and Chantrey,
Are all partakers of my pantry.
They're at this moment in discussion
On poor De Staël's late dissolution.
Her book, they say, was in advance—
Pray Heaven, she tell the truth of France !
Thus run our time and tongues away ;—
But, to return, sir, to your play :
Sorry, sir, but I cannot deal,
Unless 'twere acted by O'Neill ;   70
My hands so full, my head so busy,
I'm almost dead, and always dizzy ;
And so, with endless truth and hurry,
Dear Doctor, I am yours,
                                    JOHN MURRAY.
                              August, 1817.

TO MR. MURRAY

STRAHAN, Tonson, Lintot of the times,
Patron and publisher of rhymes,
For thee the bard up Pindus climbs,
                My Murray.

To thee, with hope and terror dumb,
The unfledged MS. authors come ;
Thou printest all—and sellest some—
                My Murray.

Upon thy table's baize so green
The last new Quarterly is seen,—   10
But where is thy new Magazine,
        My Murray?

Along thy sprucest bookshelves shine
The works thou deemest most divine—
The " Art of Cookery," and mine,
        My Murray.

Tours, Travels, Essays, too, I wist,
And Sermons, to thy mill bring grist;
And then thou hast the " Navy List,"
        My Murray.   20

And Heaven forbid I should conclude
Without " the Board of Longitude,"
Although this narrow paper would,
        My Murray.
        Venice, *March* 25, 1818.

ODE ON VENICE

I

Oh Venice! Venice! when thy marble walls
  Are level with the waters, there shall be
A cry of nations o'er thy sunken halls,
  A loud lament along the sweeping sea!
If I, a northern wanderer, weep for thee,
What should thy sons do?—anything but weep:
And yet they only murmur in their sleep.
In contrast with their fathers—as the slime,
The dull green ooze of the receding deep,
Is with the dashing of the spring-tide foam   10
That drives the sailor shipless to his home,
Are they to those that were; and thus they creep,
Crouching and crab-like, through their sapping streets.
Oh! agony—that centuries should reap
No mellower harvest! Thirteen hundred years
Of wealth and glory turn'd to dust and tears:

And every monument the stranger meets,
Church, palace, pillar, as a mourner greets;
And even the Lion all subdued appears,
And the harsh sound of the barbarian drum,　　　20
With dull and daily dissonance, repeats
The echo of thy tyrant's voice along
The soft waves, once all musical to song,
That heaved beneath the moonlight with the throng
Of gondolas—and to the busy hum
Of cheerful creatures, whose most sinful deeds
Were but the overbeating of the heart,
And flow of too much happiness, which needs
The aid of age to turn its course apart
From the luxuriant and voluptuous flood　　　30
Of sweet sensations, battling with the blood.
But these are better than the gloomy errors,
The weeds of nations in their last decay,
When Vice walks forth with her unsoften'd terrors,
And Mirth is madness, and but smiles to slay;
And Hope is nothing but a false delay,
The sick man's lightning half an hour ere death,
When Faintness, the last mortal birth of Pain,
And apathy of limb, the dull beginning
Of the cold staggering race which Death is winning,
Steals vein by vein and pulse by pulse away;　　　41
Yet so relieving the o'er-tortured clay,
To him appears renewal of his breath,
And freedom the mere numbness of his chain;
And then he talks of life, and how again
He feels his spirit soaring—albeit weak,
And of the fresher air, which he would seek:
And as he whispers knows not that he gasps,
That his thin finger feels not what it clasps,
And so the film comes o'er him, and the dizzy　　　50
Chamber swims round and round, and shadows busy,
At which he vainly catches, flit and gleam,
Till the last rattle chokes the strangled scream,
And all is ice and blackness,—and the earth
That which it was the moment ere our birth.

II

There is no hope for nations!—Search the page
  Of many thousand years—the daily scene,
The flow and ebb of each recurring age,
  The everlasting *to be* which *hath been*,
  Hath taught us nought, or little: still we lean   60
On things that rot beneath our weight, and wear
Our strength away in wrestling with the air:
For 'tis our nature strikes us down: the beasts
Slaughter'd in hourly hecatombs for feasts
Are of as high an order—they must go
Even where their driver goads them, though to
    slaughter.
Ye men, who pour your blood for kings as water,
What have they given your children in return?
A heritage of servitude and woes,
A blindfold bondage, where your hire is blows.   70
What! do not yet the red-hot plough-shares burn,
O'er which you stumble in a false ordeal,
And deem this proof of loyalty the *real*;
Kissing the hand that guides you to your scars,
And glorying as you tread the glowing bars?
All that your sires have left you, all that Time
Bequeaths of free, and History of sublime,
Spring from a different theme! Ye see and read,
Admire and sigh, and then succumb and bleed!
Save the few spirits who, despite of all,   80
And worse than all, the sudden crimes engender'd
By the down-thundering of the prison-wall,
And thirst to swallow the sweet waters tender'd,
Gushing from Freedom's fountains, when the crowd,
Madden'd with centuries of drought, are loud,
And trample on each other to obtain
The cup which brings oblivion of a chain
Heavy and sore, in which long yoked they plough'd
The sand,—or if there sprung the yellow grain,
'Twas not for them, their necks were too much bow'd,
And their dead palates chew'd the cud of pain: 91
Yes! the few spirits,—who, despite of deeds

Which they abhor, confound not with the cause
Those momentary starts from Nature's laws,
Which, like the pestilence and earthquake, smite
But for a term, then pass, and leave the earth
With all her seasons to repair the blight
With a few summers, and again put forth
Cities and generations—fair, when free—
For, Tyranny, there blooms no bud for thee !   100

III

Glory and Empire ! once upon these towers
   With Freedom—godlike Triad ! how ye sate !
The league of mightiest nations, in those hours
   When Venice was an envy, might abate,
   But did not quench her spirit ; in her fate
All were enwrapp'd : the feasted monarchs knew
   And loved their hostess, nor could learn to hate,
Although they humbled—with the kingly few
The many felt, for from all days and climes
She was the voyager's worship ; even her crimes   110
Were of the softer order—born of Love,
She drank no blood, nor fatten'd on the dead,
But gladden'd where her harmless conquests spread ;
For these restored the Cross, that from above
Hallow'd her sheltering banners, which incessant
Flew between earth and the unholy Crescent,
Which, if it waned and dwindled, Earth may thank
The city it has clothed in chains, which clank
Now, creaking in the ears of those who owe
The name of Freedom to her glorious struggles ;   120
Yet she but shares with them a common woe,
And call'd the " kingdom " of a conquering foe,
But knows what all—and, most of all, *we* know—
With what set gilded terms a tyrant juggles !

IV

The name of Commonwealth is past and gone
   O'er the three fractions of the groaning globe ;
Venice is crush'd, and Holland deigns to own
   A sceptre, and endures the purple robe :

If the free Switzer yet bestrides alone
His chainless mountains, 'tis but for a time,   130
For tyranny of late is cunning grown,
And in its own good season tramples down
The sparkles of our ashes.   One great clime,
Whose vigorous offspring by dividing ocean
Are kept apart and nursed in the devotion
Of Freedom, which their fathers fought for, and
Bequeath'd—a heritage of heart and hand,
And proud distinction from each other land,
Whose sons must bow them at a monarch's motion,
As if his senseless sceptre were a wand   140
Full of the magic of exploded science—
Still one great clime, in full and free defiance,
Yet rears her crest, unconquer'd and sublime,
Above the far Atlantic !—She has taught
Her Esau-brethren that the haughty flag,
The floating fence of Albion's feebler crag,
May strike to those whose red right hands have bought
Rights cheaply earn'd with blood.   Still, still, for ever,
Better, though each man's life-blood were a river,
That it should flow, and overflow, than creep   150
Through thousand lazy channels in our veins,
Damm'd like the dull canal with locks and chains,
And moving, as a sick man in his sleep,
Three paces, and then faltering :—better be
Where the extinguish'd Spartans still are free,
In their proud charnel of Thermopylae,
Than stagnate in our marsh,—or o'er the deep
Fly, and one current to the ocean add,
One spirit to the souls our fathers had,
One freeman more, America, to thee !   160

STANZAS TO THE PO

RIVER, that rollest by the ancient walls,
   Where dwells the lady of my love, when she
Walks by thy brink, and there perchance recalls
   A faint and fleeting memory of me :

What if thy deep and ample stream should be
  A mirror of my heart, where she may read
The thousand thoughts I now betray to thee,
  Wild as thy wave, and headlong as thy speed !

What do I say—a mirror of my heart ?
  Are not thy waters sweeping, dark, and strong ?   10
Such as my feelings were and are, thou art ;
  And such as thou art were my passions long.

Time may have somewhat tamed them,—not for ever ;
  Thou overflow'st thy banks, and not for aye
Thy bosom overboils, congenial river !
  Thy floods subside, and mine have sunk away :

But left long wrecks behind, and now again,
  Borne on our old unchanged career, we move :
Thou tendest wildly onwards to the main,
  And I—to loving one I should not love.   20

The current I behold will sweep beneath
  Her native walls, and murmur at her feet ;
Her eyes will look on thee, when she shall breathe
  The twilight air, unharm'd by summer's heat.

She will look on thee,—I have look'd on thee,
  Full of that thought : and, from that moment, ne'er
Thy waters could I dream of, name, or see,
  Without the inseparable sigh for her !

Her bright eyes will be imaged in thy stream,
  Yes ! they will meet the wave I gaze on now :   30
Mine cannot witness, even in a dream,
  That happy wave repass me in its flow !

The wave that bears my tears returns no more :
  Will she return by whom that wave shall sweep ?—
Both tread thy banks, both wander on thy shore,
  I by thy source, she by the dark-blue deep.

But that which keepeth us apart is not
   Distance, nor depth of wave, nor space of earth,
But the distraction of a various lot,
   As various as the climates of our birth.   40

A stranger loves the lady of the land,
   Born far beyond the mountains, but his blood
Is all meridian, as if never fann'd
   By the black wind that chills the polar flood.

My blood is all meridian ; were it not,
   I had not left my clime, nor should I be,
In spite of tortures ne'er to be forgot,
   A slave again of love,—at least of thee.

'Tis vain to struggle—let me perish young—
   Live as I lived, and love as I have loved ;   50
To dust if I return, from dust I sprung,
   And then, at least, my heart can ne'er be moved.
                            April, 1819.

SONNET TO THE PRINCE REGENT,

ON THE REPEAL OF LORD EDWARD FITZGERALD'S FORFEITURE

To be the father of the fatherless,
   To stretch the hand from the throne's height, and raise
His offspring, who expired in other days
To make thy sire's sway by a kingdom less,—
This is to be a monarch, and repress
   Envy into unutterable praise.
   Dismiss thy guard, and trust thee to such traits,
For who would lift a hand, except to bless ?
   Were it not easy, sir, and is't not sweet
   To make thyself beloved ? and to be
Omnipotent by mercy's means ? for thus
   Thy sovereignty would grow but more complete :
A despot thou, and yet thy people free,
   And by the heart, not hand, enslaving us.
                    Bologna, *August* 12, 1819.

STANZAS

COULD Love for ever
Run like a river,
And Time's endeavour
   Be tried in vain—
No other pleasure
With this could measure;
And like a treasure
   We'd hug the chain.
But since our sighing
Ends not in dying,   10
And, form'd for flying,
   Love plumes his wing;
Then for this reason
Let's love a season;
But let that season be only Spring,

When lovers parted
Feel broken-hearted,
And, all hopes thwarted,
   Expect to die;
A few years older,   20
Ah! how much colder
They might behold her
   For whom they sigh!
When link'd together,
In every weather,
They pluck Love's feather
   From out his wing—
He'll stay for ever,
But sadly shiver
Without his plumage, when past the Spring.   30

Like chiefs of Faction,
His life is action—
A formal paction

That curbs his reign,
Obscures his glory,
Despot no more, he
Such territory
    Quits with disdain.
Still, still advancing,
With banners glancing,   40
His power enhancing,
    He must move on—
Repose but cloys him,
Retreat destroys him,
Love brooks not a degraded throne.

Wait not, fond lover !
Till years are over,
And then recover
    As from a dream.
While each bewailing   50
The other's failing,
With wrath and railing,
    All hideous seem—
While first decreasing,
Yet not quite ceasing,
Wait not till teasing
    All passion blight :
If once diminish'd,
Love's reign is finish'd—
Then part in friendship—and bid good-night. 60

So shall Affection
To recollection
The dear connexion
    Bring back with joy :
You had not waited
Till, tired or hated,
Your passions sated
    Began to cloy.
Your last embraces
Leave no cold traces—   70
The same fond faces

As through the past :
And eyes, the mirrors
Of your sweet errors,
Reflect but rapture—not least though last.

True, separations
Ask more than patience ;
What desperations
    From such have risen !
But yet remaining,   80
What is't but chaining
Hearts which, once waning,
    Beat 'gainst their prison ?
Time can but cloy love
And use destroy love :
The winged boy, Love,
    Is but for boys—
You'll find it torture,
Though sharper, shorter,
To wean, and not wear out your joys.   90
                                        1819.

ON MY WEDDING-DAY

HERE 's a happy new year ! but with reason
    I beg you'll permit me to say—
Wish me *many* returns of the *season*,
    But as *few* as you please of the day.
                            January 2, 1820.

EPITAPH FOR WILLIAM PITT

WITH death doom'd to grapple,
    Beneath this cold slab, he
Who lied in the Chapel
    Now lies in the Abbey.
                            January, 1820.

STANZAS

WHEN a man hath no freedom to fight for at home,
  Let him combat for that of his neighbours ;
Let him think of the glories of Greece and of Rome,
  And get knock'd on the head for his labours.

To do good to mankind is the chivalrous plan,
  And is always as nobly requited ;
Then battle for freedom wherever you can,
  And, if not shot or hang'd, you'll get knighted.

November, 1820.

EPIGRAM

  THE world is a bundle of hay,
    Mankind are the asses who pull ;
  Each tugs it a different way,
    And the greatest of all is John Bull.

THE CHARITY BALL

WHAT matter the pangs of a husband and father,
  If his sorrows in exile be great or be small,
So the Pharisee's glories around her she gather,
  And the saint patronizes her " charity ball ! "

What matters—a heart which, though faulty, was feeling,
  Be driven to excesses which once could appal—
That the sinner should suffer is only fair dealing,
  As the saint keeps her charity back for " the ball ! "

EPIGRAM

ON THE BRAZIERS' COMPANY HAVING RESOLVED TO PRESENT AN ADDRESS TO QUEEN CAROLINE

THE braziers, it seems, are preparing to pass
An address, and present it themselves all in brass ;—
A superfluous pageant—for, by the Lord Harry !
They'll find where they're going much more than they
  carry.

EPIGRAM ON MY WEDDING-DAY

TO PENELOPE

THIS day, of all our days, has done
The worst for me and you :—
'Tis just *six* years since we were *one*,
And *five* since we were *two*.

January 2, 1821.

ON MY THIRTY-THIRD BIRTHDAY

JANUARY 22, 1821

THROUGH life's dull road, so dim and dirty,
I have dragg'd to three-and-thirty.
What have these years left to me ?
Nothing—except thirty-three.

EPIGRAMS

So Castlereagh has cut his throat !—The worst
Of this is,—that his own was not the first.

So *He* has cut his throat at last !—He ! Who ?
The man who cut his country's long ago.

JOHN KEATS

WHO kill'd John Keats ?
  " I," says the Quarterly,
  So savage and Tartarly ;
  " 'Twas one of my feats."

Who shot the arrow ?
  " The poet-priest Milman
  (So ready to kill man),
    Or Southey, or Barrow."

July, 1821.

TO MR. MURRAY

For Orford and for Waldegrave
You give much more than me you gave;
Which is not fairly to behave,
> My Murray.

Because if a live dog, 'tis said,
Be worth a lion fairly sped,
A *live lord* must be worth *two* dead,
> My Murray.

And if, as the opinion goes,
Verse hath a better sale than prose,—
Certes, I should have more than those,
> My Murray.   10

But now this sheet is nearly cramm'd,
So, if *you will*, *I* shan't be shamm'd,
And if you *won't*, *you* may be damn'd,
> My Murray.

THE IRISH AVATAR

" And Ireland, like a bastinadoed elephant, kneeling to receive the paltry rider."—Curran.

Ere the daughter of Brunswick is cold in her grave,
  And her ashes still float to their home o'er the tide,
Lo! George the triumphant speeds over the wave,
  To the long-cherish'd isle which he loved like his—
    bride!

True, the great of her bright and brief era are gone,
  The rainbow-like epoch where Freedom could pause
For the few little years, out of centuries won,
  Which betray'd not, or crush'd not, or wept not her
    cause.

True, the chains of the Catholic clank o'er his rags,
    The castle still stands, and the senate's no more, 10
And the famine which dwelt on her freedomless crags
    Is extending its steps to her desolate shore.

To her desolate shore—where the emigrant stands
    For a moment to gaze ere he flies from his hearth;
Tears fall on his chain, though it drops from his hands,
    For the dungeon he quits is the place of his birth.

But he comes! the Messiah of royalty comes!
    Like a goodly Leviathan roll'd from the waves;
Then receive him as best such an advent becomes,
    With a legion of cooks, and an army of slaves! 20

He comes in the promise and bloom of threescore,
    To perform in the pageant the sovereign's part—
But long live the shamrock, which shadows him o'er!
    Could the green in his *hat* be transferr'd to his *heart!*

Could that long-wither'd spot but be verdant again,
    And a new spring of noble affections arise—
Then might freedom forgive thee this dance in thy chain,
    And this shout of thy slavery which saddens the skies.

Is it madness or meanness which clings to thee now?
    Were he God—as he is but the commonest clay, 30
With scarce fewer wrinkles than sins on his brow—
    Such servile devotion might shame him away.

Ay, roar in his train! let thine orators lash
    Their fanciful spirits to pamper his pride—
Not thus did thy Grattan indignantly flash
    His soul o'er the freedom implored and denied.

Ever glorious Grattan! the best of the good!
    So simple in heart, so sublime in the rest!
With all which Demosthenes wanted endued,
    And his rival or victor in all he possess'd. 40

Ere **Tully** arose in the zenith of Rome,
   Though unequall'd, preceded, the task was begun —
But Grattan sprung up like a god from the tomb
   Of ages, the first, last, the saviour, the *one!*

With the skill of an Orpheus to soften the brute;
   With the fire of Prometheus to kindle mankind;
Even Tyranny listening sate melted or mute,
   And Corruption shrunk scorch'd from the glance of
      his mind.

But back to our theme! Back to despots and slaves!
   Feasts furnish'd by Famine! rejoicings by Pain! 50
True freedom but *welcomes*, while slavery still *raves*,
   When a week's saturnalia hath loosen'd her chain.

Let the poor squalid splendour thy wreck can afford
   (As the bankrupt's profusion his ruin would hide),
Gild over the palace, Lo! Erin, thy lord!
   Kiss his foot with thy blessing, his blessings denied!

Or *if* freedom past hope be extorted at last,
   If the idol of brass find his feet are of clay,
Must what terror or policy wring forth be class'd
   With what monarchs ne'er give, but as wolves yield
      their prey?   60

Each brute hath its nature; a king's is to *reign*,—
   To *reign!* in that word see, ye ages, comprised
The cause of the curses all annals contain,
   From Cæsar the dreaded to George the despised!

Wear, Fingal, thy trapping! O'Connell, proclaim
   His accomplishments! *His!!!* and thy country
      convince
Half an age's contempt was an error of fame,
   And that "Hal is the rascaliest, sweetest *young*
      prince!"

Will thy yard of blue riband, poor Fingal, recall
   The fetters from millions of Catholic limbs ?   70
Or, has it not bound thee the fastest of all
   The slaves, who now hail their betrayer with hymns ?

Ay ! " Build him a dwelling ! " let each give his mite !
   Till, like Babel, the new royal dome hath arisen !
Let thy beggars and helots their pittance unite—
   And a palace bestow for a poor-house and prison !

Spread—spread, for Vitellius, the royal repast,
   Till the gluttonous despot be stuff'd to the gorge !
And the roar of his drunkards proclaim him at last
     The fourth of the fools and oppressors call'd
       " George ! "   80

Let the tables be loaded with feasts till they groan !
   Till they *groan* like thy people, through ages of woe !
Let the wine flow around the old Bacchanal's throne,
   Like their blood which has flow'd, and which yet has
     to flow.

But let not *his* name be thine idol alone—
   On his right hand behold a Sejanus appears !
Thine own Castlereagh ! let him still be thine own !
   A wretch never named but with curses and jeers !

Till now, when the isle which should blush for his birth,
   Deep, deep as the gore which he shed on her soil, 90
Seems proud of the reptile which crawl'd from her earth,
   And for murder repays him with shouts and a smile.

Without one single ray of her genius, without
   The fancy, the manhood, the fire of her race—
The miscreant who well might plunge Erin in doubt
   If *she* ever gave birth to a being so base.

If she did—let her long-boasted proverb be hush'd,
   Which proclaims that from Erin no reptile can
     spring—
See the cold-blooded serpent, with venom full flush'd,
   Still warming its folds in the breast of a king !   100

Shout, drink, feast, and flatter! Oh! Erin, how low
  Wert thou sunk by misfortune and tyranny, till
Thy welcome of tyrants hath plunged thee below
  The depth of thy deep in a deeper gulf still!

My voice, though but humble, was raised for thy right,
  My vote, as a freeman's, still voted thee free,
This hand, though but feeble, would arm in thy fight,
  And this heart, though outworn, had a throb still
    for *thee!*

Yes, I loved thee and thine, though thou art not my
    land,
  I have known noble hearts and great souls in thy sons,
And I wept with the world, o'er the patriot band   111
  Who are gone, but I weep them no longer as once.

For happy are they now reposing afar,—
  Thy Grattan, thy Curran, thy Sheridan, all
Who, for years, were the chiefs in the eloquent war,
  And redeem'd, if they have not retarded, thy fall.

Yes, happy are they in their cold English graves!
  Their shades cannot start to thy shouts of to-day—
Nor the steps of enslavers and chain-kissing slaves
  Be stamp'd in the turf o'er their fetterless clay.   120

Till now I had envied thy sons and their shore,
  Though their virtues were hunted, their liberties fled;
There was something so warm and sublime in the core
  Of an Irishman's heart, that I envy—thy *dead.*

Or, if aught in my bosom can quench for an hour
  My contempt for a nation so servile, though sore,
Which though trod like the worm will not turn upon
    power,
  'Tis the glory of Grattan, and genius of Moore!
                                    September, 1821.

STANZAS WRITTEN ON THE ROAD
BETWEEN FLORENCE AND PISA

OH, talk not to me of a name great in story;
The days of our youth are the days of our glory;
And the myrtle and ivy of sweet two-and-twenty
Are worth all your laurels, though ever so plenty.

What are garlands and crowns to the brow that is
    wrinkled?
'Tis but as a dead-flower with May-dew besprinkled.
Then away with all such from the head that is hoary!
What care I for the wreaths that can *only* give glory!

Oh FAME!—if I e'er took delight in thy praises,   9
'Twas less for the sake of thy high-sounding phrases,
Than to see the bright eyes of the dear one discover,
She thought that I was not unworthy to love her.

There chiefly I sought thee, *there* only I found thee;
Her glance was the best of the rays that surround thee;
When it sparkled o'er aught that was bright in my
    story,
I knew it was love, and I felt it was glory.
                          November, 1821.

ON THIS DAY I COMPLETE MY
THIRTY-SIXTH YEAR

                    MISSOLONGHI, Jan. 22, 1824.

'TIS time this heart should be unmoved,
    Since others it hath ceased to move:
Yet, though I cannot be beloved,
    Still let me love!

My days are in the yellow leaf;
    The flowers and fruits of love are gone;
The worm, the canker, and the grief
    Are mine alone!

The fire that on my bosom preys
  Is lone as some volcanic isle ;   10
No torch is kindled at its blaze—
    A funeral pile.

The hope, the fear, the jealous care,
  The exalted portion of the pain
And power of love, I cannot share,
    But wear the chain.

But 'tis not *thus*—and 'tis not *here*—
  Such thoughts should shake my soul, nor *now*,
Where glory decks the hero's bier,
    Or binds his brow.   20

The sword, the banner, and the field,
  Glory and Greece, around me see !
The Spartan, borne upon his shield,
    Was not more free.

Awake ! (not Greece—she *is* awake !)
  Awake, my spirit ! Think through *whom*
Thy life-blood tracks its parent lake,
    And then strike home !

Tread those reviving passions down,
  Unworthy manhood !—unto thee   30
Indifferent should the smile or frown
    Of beauty be.

If thou regrett'st thy youth, *why live ?*
  The land of honourable death
Is here :—up to the field, and give
    Away thy breath !

Seek out—less often sought than found—
  A soldier's grave, for thee the best ;
Then look around, and choose thy ground,
    And take thy rest.   40

ENGLISH BARDS AND SCOTCH REVIEWERS

STILL must I hear ?—shall hoarse Fitzgerald bawl
His creaking couplets in a tavern hall,
And I not sing, lest, haply, Scotch reviews
Should dub me scribbler, and denounce my muse ?
Prepare for rhyme—I'll publish, right or wrong :
Fools are my theme, let satire be my song.

Oh ! nature's noblest gift—my grey goose-quill !
Slave of my thoughts, obedient to my will,
Torn from thy parent bird to form a pen,
That mighty instrument of little men !   10
The pen ! foredoom'd to aid the mental throes
Of brains that labour, big with verse or prose,
Though nymphs forsake, and critics may deride,
The lover's solace, and the author's pride.
What wits, what poets dost thou daily raise !
How frequent is thy use, how small thy praise !
Condemn'd at length to be forgotten quite,
With all the pages which 'twas thine to write.
But thou, at least, mine own especial pen !
Once laid aside, but now assumed again,   20
Our task complete, like Hamet's shall be free ;
Though spurn'd by others, yet beloved by me :
Then let us soar to-day ; no common theme,
No eastern vision, no distemper'd dream
Inspires—our path, though full of thorns, is plain ;
Smooth be the verse, and easy be the strain.

When Vice triumphant holds her sov'reign sway,
Obey'd by all who nought beside obey ;

When Folly, frequent harbinger of crime,
Bedecks her cap with bells of every clime ; 30
When knaves and fools combined o'er all prevail,
And weigh their justice in a golden scale ;
E'en then the boldest start from public sneers,
Afraid of shame, unknown to other fears,
More darkly sin, by satire kept in awe,
And shrink from ridicule, though not from law.

Such is the force of wit ! but not belong
To me the arrows of satiric song ;
The royal vices of our age demand
A keener weapon, and a mightier hand. 40
Still there are follies, e'en for me to chase,
And yield at least amusement in the race :
Laugh when I laugh, I seek no other fame ;
Thy cry is up, and scribblers are my game.
Speed, Pegasus !—ye strains of great and small,
Ode, epic, elegy, have at you all !
I too can scrawl, and once upon a time
I pour'd along the town a flood of rhyme,
A schoolboy freak, unworthy praise or blame ;
I printed—older children do the same. 50
'Tis pleasant, sure, to see one's name in print ;
A book 's a book, although there 's nothing in 't.
Not that a title's sounding charm can save
Or scrawl or scribbler from an equal grave :
This Lambe must own, since his patrician name
Fail'd to preserve the spurious farce from shame.
No matter, George continues still to write,
Though now the name is veil'd from public sight.
Moved by the great example, I pursue
The self-same road, but make my own review · 60
Not seek great Jeffrey's, yet, like him, will be
Self-constituted judge of poesy.

A man must serve his time to every trade
Save censure—critics all are ready made.
Take hackney'd jokes from Miller, got by rote,
With just enough of learning to misquote :

A mind well skill'd to find or forge a fault;
A turn for punning, call it Attic salt;
To Jeffrey go, be silent and discreet,
His pay is just ten sterling pounds per sheet: 70
Fear not to lie, 'twill seem a sharper hit;
Shrink not from blasphemy, 'twill pass for wit;
Care not for feeling—pass your proper jest,
And stand a critic, hated yet caress'd.

And shall we own such judgment? no—as soon
Seek roses in December—ice in June;
Hope constancy in wind, or corn in chaff;
Believe a woman or an epitaph,
Or any other thing that's false, before
You trust in critics, who themselves are sore;   80
Or yield one single thought to be misled
By Jeffrey's heart, or Lambe's Bœotian head.
To these young tyrants, by themselves misplaced,
Combined usurpers on the throne of taste;
To these, when authors bend in humble awe,
And hail their voice as truth, their word as law—
While these are censors, 'twould be sin to spare;
While such are critics, why should I forbear?
But yet, so near all modern worthies run,
'Tis doubtful whom to seek, or whom to shun;   90
Nor know we when to spare, or where to strike,
Our bards and censors are so much alike.

Then should you ask me, why I venture o'er
The path which Pope and Gifford trod before;
If not yet sicken'd, you can still proceed:
Go on; my rhyme will tell you as you read.
" But hold ! " exclaims a friend, " here 's some neglect:
This—that—and t'other line seem incorrect."
What then? the self-same blunder Pope has got,
And careless Dryden—" Ay, but Pye has not: "—
Indeed !—'tis granted, faith !—but what care I?   101
Better to err with Pope, than shine with Pye.

Time was, ere yet in these degenerate days
Ignoble themes obtain'd mistaken praise,

When sense and wit with poesy allied,
No fabled graces, flourish'd side by side ;
From the same fount their inspiration drew,
And, rear'd by taste, bloom'd fairer as they grew.
Then, in this happy isle, a Pope's pure strain
Sought the rapt soul to charm, nor sought in vain ;
A polish'd nation's praise aspired to claim,   111
And raised the people's, as the poet's fame.
Like him great Dryden pour'd the tide of song,
In stream less smooth, indeed, yet doubly strong.
Then Congreve's scenes could cheer, or Otway's
    melt—
For nature then an English audience felt.
But why these names, or greater still, retrace,
When all to feebler bards resign their place ?
Yet to such times our lingering looks are cast,
When taste and reason with those times are past.   120
Now look around, and turn each trifling page,
Survey the precious works that please the age ;
This truth at least let satire's self allow,
No dearth of bards can be complain'd of now.
The loaded press beneath her labour groans,
And printers' devils shake their weary bones ;
While Southey's epics cram the creaking shelves,
And Little's lyrics shine in hot-press'd twelves.
Thus saith the Preacher : "Nought beneath the
    sun
Is new ; " yet still from change to change we run :   130
What varied wonders tempt us as they pass !
The cow-pox, tractors, galvanism, and gas,
In turns appear, to make the vulgar stare,
Till the swoln bubble bursts—and all is air !
Nor less new schools of Poetry arise,
Where dull pretenders grapple for the prize :
O'er taste awhile these pseudo-bards prevail ;
Each country book-club bows the knee to Baal,
And, hurling lawful genius from the throne,
Erects a shrine and idol of its own ;   140
Some leaden calf—but whom it matters not,
From soaring Southey down to grovelling Stott.

Behold! in various throngs the scribbling crew,
For notice eager, pass in long review:
Each spurs his jaded Pegasus apace,
And rhyme and blank maintain an equal race;
Sonnets on sonnets crowd, and ode on ode;
And tales of terror jostle on the road;
Immeasurable measures move along;
For simpering folly loves a varied song,   150
To strange mysterious dulness still the friend,
Admires the strain she cannot comprehend.
Thus Lays of Minstrels—may they be the last!—
On half-strung harps whine mournful to the blast.
While mountain spirits prate to river sprites,
That dames may listen to the sound at nights;
And goblin brats, of Gilpin Horner's brood,
Decoy young border-nobles through the wood,
And skip at every step, Lord knows how high,
And frighten foolish babes, the Lord knows why;   160
While high-born ladies in their magic cell,
Forbidding knights to read who cannot spell,
Despatch a courier to a wizard's grave,
And fight with honest men to shield a knave.

Next view in state, proud prancing on his roan,
The golden-crested haughty Marmion,
Now forging scrolls, now foremost in the fight,
Not quite a felon, yet but half a knight,
The gibbet or the field prepared to grace;
A mighty mixture of the great and base.   170
And think'st thou, Scott! by vain conceit perchance,
On public taste to foist thy stale romance,
Though Murray with his Miller may combine
To yield thy muse just half-a-crown per line?
No! when the sons of song descend to trade,
Their bays are sear, their former laurels fade.
Let such forego the poet's sacred name,
Who rack their brains for lucre, not for fame:
Still for stern Mammon may they toil in vain!
And sadly gaze on gold they cannot gain!   180
Such be their meed, such still the just reward

Of prostituted muse and hireling bard !
For this we spurn Apollo's venal son,
And bid a long " good night to Marmion."

These are the themes that claim our plaudits now ;
These are the bards to whom the muse must bow ;
While Milton, Dryden, Pope, alike forgot,
Resign their hallow'd bays to Walter Scott.

The time has been, when yet the muse was young,
When Homer swept the lyre, and Maro sung,   190
An epic scarce ten centuries could claim,
While awe-struck nations hail'd the magic name :
The work of each immortal bard appears
The single wonder of a thousand years.
Empires have moulder'd from the face of earth,
Tongues have expired with those who gave them birth,
Without the glory such a strain can give,
As even in ruin bids the language live.
Not so with us, though minor bards, content
On one great work a life of labour spent :   200
With eagle pinion soaring to the skies,
Behold the ballad-monger Southey rise !
To him let Camoëns, Milton, Tasso yield,
Whose annual strains, like armies, take the field.
First in the ranks see Joan of Arc advance,
The scourge of England and the boast of France !
Though burnt by wicked Bedford for a witch,
Behold her statue placed in glory's niche ;
Her fetters burst, and just released from prison,
A virgin phoenix from her ashes risen.   210
Next see tremendous Thalaba come on,
Arabia's monstrous, wild, and wondrous son ;
Domdaniel's dread destroyer, who o'erthrew
More mad magicians than the world e'er knew.
Immortal hero ! all thy foes o'ercome,
For ever reign—the rival of Tom Thumb !
Since startled metre fled before thy face,
Well wert thou doom'd the last of all thy race !
Well might triumphant genii bear thee hence,
Illustrious conqueror of common sense !   220

Now, last and greatest, Madoc spreads his sails,
Cacique in Mexico, and prince in Wales;
Tells us strange tales, as other travellers do,
More old than Mandeville's, and not so true.
Oh! Southey! Southey! cease thy varied song!
A bard may chant too often and too long:
As thou art strong in verse, in mercy, spare!
A fourth, alas! were more than we could bear.
But if, in spite of all the world can say,
Thou still wilt verseward plod thy weary way;   230
If still in Berkley ballads most uncivil,
Thou wilt devote old women to the devil,
The babe unborn thy dread intent may rue:
"God help thee," Southey, and thy readers too.

Next comes the dull disciple of thy school,
That mild apostate from poetic rule,
The simple Wordsworth, framer of a lay
As soft as evening in his favourite May,
Who warns his friend "to shake off toil and trouble,
And quit his books, for fear of growing double;"   240
Who, both by precept and example, shows
That prose is verse, and verse is merely prose;
Convincing all, by demonstration plain,
Poetic souls delight in prose insane;
And Christmas stories tortured into rhyme
Contain the essence of the true sublime.
Thus, when he tells the tale of Betty Foy,
The idiot mother of "an idiot boy;"
A moon-struck, silly lad, who lost his way,
And, like his bard, confounded night with day;   250
So close on each pathetic part he dwells,
And each adventure so sublimely tells,
That all who view the "idiot in his glory"
Conceive the bard the hero of the story.

Shall gentle Coleridge pass unnoticed here,
To turgid ode and tumid stanza dear?
Though themes of innocence amuse him best,
Yet still obscurity's a welcome guest.

If Inspiration should her aid refuse
To him who takes a pixy for a muse,   260
Yet none in lofty numbers can surpass
The bard who soars to elegize an ass.
So well the subject suits his noble mind,
He brays, the laureate of the long-ear'd kind.

Oh! wonder-working Lewis! monk, or bard,
Who fain wouldst make Parnassus a churchyard!
Lo! wreaths of yew, not laurel, bind thy brow,
Thy muse a sprite, Apollo's sexton thou!
Whether on ancient tombs thou tak'st thy stand,
By gibb'ring spectres hail'd, thy kindred band;   270
Or tracest chaste descriptions on thy page,
To please the females of our modest age;
All hail, M.P.! from whose infernal brain
Thin-sheeted phantoms glide, a grisly train;
At whose command "grim women" throng in crowds,
And kings of fire, of water, and of clouds,
With "small gray men," "wild yagers," and what not,
To crown with honour thee and Walter Scott;
Again all hail! if tales like thine may please,
St. Luke alone can vanquish the disease;   280
Even Satan's self with thee might dread to dwell,
And in thy skull discern a deeper hell.

Who in soft guise, surrounded by a choir
Of virgins melting, not to Vesta's fire,
With sparkling eyes, and cheek by passion flush'd,
Strikes his wild lyre, whilst listening dames are hush'd?
'Tis Little! young Catullus of his day,
As sweet, but as immoral, in his lay!
Grieved to condemn, the muse must still be just,
Nor spare melodious advocates of lust.   290
Pure is the flame which o'er her altar burns;
From grosser incense with disgust she turns:
Yet kind to youth, this expiation o'er,
She bids thee "mend thy line and sin no more."

For thee, translator of the tinsel song,
To whom such glittering ornaments belong,

Hibernian Strangford ! with thine eyes of blue,
And boasted locks of red or auburn hue,
Whose plaintive strain each love-sick miss admires,
And o'er harmonious fustian half expires,   300
Learn, if thou canst, to yield thine author's sense,
Nor vend thy sonnets on a false pretence.
Think'st thou to gain thy verse a higher place,
By dressing Camoëns in a suit of lace ?
Mend, Strangford ! mend thy morals and thy taste ;
Be warm, but pure ; be amorous, but be chaste ;
Cease to deceive ; thy pilfer'd harp restore,
Nor teach the Lusian bard to copy Moore.

Behold !—ye tarts !—one moment spare the text—
Hayley's last work, and worst—until his next ;   310
Whether he spin poor couplets into plays,
Or damn the dead with purgatorial praise,
His style in youth or age is still the same,
For ever feeble and for ever tame.
Triumphant first see " Temper's Triumphs " shine !
At least I'm sure they triumph'd over mine.
Of " Music's Triumphs," all who read may swear
That luckless music never triumph'd there.

Moravians, rise ! bestow some meet reward
On dull devotion—Lo ! the Sabbath bard,   320
Sepulchral Grahame, pours his notes sublime
In mangled prose, nor e'en aspires to rhyme ;
Breaks into blank the Gospel of St. Luke,
And boldly pilfers from the Pentateuch ;
And, undisturb'd by conscientious qualms,
Perverts the Prophets, and purloins the Psalms.

Hail, Sympathy ! thy soft idea brings
A thousand visions of a thousand things,
And shows, still whimpering through threescore of
    years,
The maudlin prince of mournful sonneteers.   330
And art thou not their prince, harmonious Bowles !
Thou first, great oracle of tender souls ?

Whether thou sing'st with equal ease, and grief,
The fall of empires, or a yellow leaf;
Whether thy muse most lamentably tells
What merry sounds proceed from Oxford bells,
Or, still in bells delighting, finds a friend
In every chime that jingled from Ostend;
Ah! how much juster were thy muse's hap,
If to thy bells thou wouldst but add a cap!   340
Delightful Bowles! still blessing and still blest,
All love thy strain, but children like it best.
'Tis thine, with gentle Little's moral song,
To soothe the mania of the amorous throng!
With thee our nursery damsels shed their tears,
Ere miss as yet completes her infant years:
But in her teens thy whining powers are vain;
She quits poor Bowles for Little's purer strain.
Now to soft themes thou scornest to confine
The lofty numbers of a harp like thine;   350
" Awake a louder and a loftier strain,"
Such as none heard before, or will again!
Where all discoveries jumbled from the flood,
Since first the leaky ark reposed in mud,
By more or less, are sung in every book,
From Captain Noah down to Captain Cook.
Nor this alone; but, pausing on the road,
The bard sighs forth a gentle episode;
And gravely tells—attend, each beauteous miss!—
When first Madeira trembled to a kiss.   360
Bowles! in thy memory let this precept dwell,
Stick to thy sonnets, man!—at least they sell.
But if some new-born whim, or larger bribe,
Prompt thy crude brain, and claim thee for a scribe;
If chance some bard, though once by dunces fear'd,
Now, prone in dust, can only be revered;
If Pope, whose fame and genius, from the first,
Have foil'd the best of critics, needs the worst,
Do thou essay: each fault, each failing scan;
The first of poets was, alas! but man.   370
Rake from each ancient dunghill every pearl,
Consult Lord Fanny, and confide in Curll:

Let all the scandals of a former age
Perch on thy pen, and flutter o'er thy page;
Affect a candour which thou canst not feel,
Clothe envy in the garb of honest zeal;
Write, as if St. John's soul could still inspire,
And do from hate what Mallet did for hire.
Oh! hadst thou lived in that congenial time,
To rave with Dennis, and with Ralph to rhyme;   380
Throng'd with the rest around his living head,
Not raised thy hoof against the lion dead;
A meet reward had crown'd thy glorious gains,
And link'd thee to the Dunciad for thy pains.

Another epic! Who inflicts again
More books of blank upon the sons of men?
Boeotian Cottle, rich Bristowa's boast,
Imports old stories from the Cambrian coast,
And sends his goods to market—all alive!
Lines forty thousand, cantos twenty-five!   390
Fresh fish from Helicon! who'll buy, who'll buy?
The precious bargain 's cheap—in faith, not I.
Your turtle-feeder's verse must needs be flat,
Though Bristol bloat him with the verdant fat;
If Commerce fills the purse, she clogs the brain,
And Amos Cottle strikes the lyre in vain.
In him an author's luckless lot behold,
Condemn'd to make the books which once he sold.
Oh, Amos Cottle!—Phoebus! what a name
To fill the speaking trump of future fame!—   400
Oh, Amos Cottle! for a moment think
What meagre profits spring from pen and ink!
When thus devoted to poetic dreams,
Who will peruse thy prostituted reams?
Oh! pen perverted! paper misapplied!
Had Cottle still adorn'd the counter's side,
Bent o'er the desk, or, born to useful toils,
Been taught to make the paper which he soils,
Plough'd, delved, or plied the oar with lusty limb,
He had not sung of Wales, nor I of him.   410

  As Sisyphus against the infernal steep
Rolls the huge rock whose motions ne'er may sleep,
So up thy hill, ambrosial Richmond, heaves
Dull Maurice all his granite weight of leaves:
Smooth, solid monuments of mental pain!
The petrifactions of a plodding brain,
That, ere they reach the top, fall lumbering back again.

  With broken lyre, and cheek serenely pale,
Lo! sad Alcaeus wanders down the vale;
Though fair they rose, and might have bloom'd at last,
His hopes have perish'd by the northern blast: 421
Nipp'd in the bud by Caledonian gales,
His blossoms wither as the blast prevails!
O'er his lost works let *classic* Sheffield weep;
May no rude hand disturb their early sleep!

  Yet say! why should the bard at once resign
His claim to favour from the sacred Nine?
For ever startled by the mingled howl
Of northern wolves, that still in darkness prowl;
A coward brood, which mangle as they prey,   430
By hellish instinct, all that cross their way;
Aged or young, the living or the dead,
No mercy find—these harpies must be fed.
Why do the injured unresisting yield
The calm possession of their native field?
Why tamely thus before their fangs retreat,
Nor hunt the blood-hounds back to Arthur's Seat?

  Health to immortal Jeffrey! once, in name,
England could boast a judge almost the same;
In soul so like, so merciful, yet just,   440
Some think that Satan has resign'd his trust,
And given the spirit to the world again,
To sentence letters, as he sentenced men.
With hand less mighty, but with heart as black,
With voice as willing to decree the rack;
Bred in the courts betimes, though all that law
As yet hath taught him is to find a flaw;
Since well instructed in the patriot school
To rail at party, though a party tool,

Who knows, if chance his patrons should restore   450
Back to the sway they forfeited before,
His scribbling toils some recompense may meet,
And raise this Daniel to the judgment-seat ?
Let Jeffrey's shade indulge the pious hope,
And greeting thus, present him with a rope :
" Heir to my virtues ! man of equal mind !
Skill'd to condemn as to traduce mankind,
This cord receive, for thee reserved with care,
To wield in judgment, and at length to wear."

    Health to great Jeffrey ! Heaven preserve his life,
To flourish on the fertile shores of Fife,   461
And guard it sacred in its future wars,
Since authors sometimes seek the field of Mars !
Can none remember that eventful day,
That ever-glorious, almost fatal fray,
When Little's leadless pistol met his eye,
And Bow-street myrmidons stood laughing by ?
Oh, day disastrous ! on her firm-set rock,
Dunedin's castle felt a secret shock ;
Dark roll'd the sympathetic waves of Forth,   470
Low groan'd the startled whirlwinds of the north ;
Tweed ruffled half his waves to form a tear,
The other half pursued its calm career ;
Arthur's steep summit nodded to its base,
The surly Tolbooth scarcely kept her place.
The Tolbooth felt—for marble sometimes can,
On such occasions, feel as much as man—
The Tolbooth felt defrauded of his charms,
If Jeffrey died, except within her arms :
Nay last, not least, on that portentous morn,   480
The sixteenth story, where himself was born,
His patrimonial garret, fell to ground,
And pale Edina shudder'd at the sound :
Strew'd were the streets around with milk-white
        reams,
Flow'd all the Canongate with inky streams ;
This of his candour seem'd the sable dew,
That of his valour show'd the bloodless hue ;

And all with justice deem'd the two combined
The mingled emblems of his mighty mind.
But Caledonia's goddess hover'd o'er 490
The field, and saved him from the wrath of Moore ;
From either pistol snatch'd the vengeful lead,
And straight restored it to her favourite's head ;
That head, with greater than magnetic power,
Caught it, as Danaë caught the golden shower,
And, though the thickening dross will scarce refine,
Augments its ore, and is itself a mine.
" My son," she cried, " ne'er thirst for gore again,
Resign the pistol and resume the pen ;
O'er politics and poesy preside, 500
Boast of thy country, and Britannia's guide !
For long as Albion's heedless sons submit,
Or Scottish taste decides on English wit,
So long shall last thine unmolested reign,
Nor any dare to take thy name in vain.
Behold, a chosen band shall aid thy plan,
And own thee chieftain of the critic clan.
First in the oat-fed phalanx shall be seen
The travell'd thane, Athenian Aberdeen.
Herbert shall wield Thor's hammer, and sometimes,
In gratitude, thou'lt praise his rugged rhymes. 511
Smug Sydney too thy bitter page shall seek,
And classic Hallam, much renown'd for Greek ;
Scott may perchance his name and influence lend,
And paltry Pillans shall traduce his friend ;
While gay Thalia's luckless votary, Lambe,
Damn'd like the devil, devil-like will damn.
Known be thy name, unbounded be thy sway !
Thy Holland's banquets shall each toil repay ;
While grateful Britain yields the praise she owes 520
To Holland's hirelings and to learning's foes.
Yet mark one caution ere thy next Review
Spread its light wings of saffron and of blue,
Beware lest blundering Brougham destroy the sale,
Turn beef to bannocks, cauliflowers to kail."
Thus having said, the kilted goddess kiss'd
Her son, and vanish'd in a Scottish mist.

Then prosper, Jeffrey! pertest of the train
Whom Scotland pampers with her fiery grain!
Whatever blessing waits a genuine Scot,   530
In double portion swells thy glorious lot;
For thee Edina culls her evening sweets,
And showers their odours on thy candid sheets,
Whose hue and fragrance to thy work adhere—
This scents its pages, and that gilds its rear.
Lo! blushing Itch, coy nymph, enamour'd grown,
Forsakes the rest, and cleaves to thee alone;
And, too unjust to other Pictish men,
Enjoys thy person, and inspires thy pen!

Illustrious Holland! hard would be his lot,   540
His hirelings mention'd, and himself forgot!
Holland, with Henry Petty at his back,
The whipper-in and huntsman of the pack.
Blest be the banquets spread at Holland House,
Where Scotchmen feed, and critics may carouse!
Long, long beneath that hospitable roof
Shall Grub-street dine, while duns are kept aloof.
See honest Hallam lay aside his fork,
Resume his pen, review his Lordship's work,
And, grateful for the dainties on his plate,   550
Declare his landlord can at least translate!
Dunedin! view thy children with delight,
They write for food—and feed because they write:
And lest, when heated with the unusual grape,
Some glowing thoughts should to the press escape,
And tinge with red the female reader's cheek,
My lady skims the cream of each critique;
Breathes o'er the page her purity of soul,
Reforms each error, and refines the whole.

Now to the Drama turn—Oh! motley sight!   560
What precious scenes the wondering eyes invite!
Puns, and a prince within a barrel pent,
And Dibdin's nonsense yield complete content.
Though now, thank Heaven! the Rosciomania's o'er,
And full-grown actors are endured once more;

Yet what avail their vain attempts to please,
While British critics suffer scenes like these;
While Reynolds vents his " dammes ! " " poohs ! " and
    " zounds ! "
And common-place and common sense confounds ?
While Kenney's " World "—ah ! where is Kenney's
    wit ?—   570
Tires the sad gallery, lulls the listless pit;
And Beaumont's pilfer'd Caratach affords
A tragedy complete in all but words ?
Who but must mourn, while these are all the rage,
The degradation of our vaunted stage ?
Heavens ! is all sense of shame and talent gone ?
Have we no living bard of merit ?—none !
Awake, George Colman ! Cumberland, awake !
Ring the alarum bell ! let folly quake !
Oh, Sheridan ! if aught can move thy pen,   580
Let Comedy assume her throne again ;
Abjure the mummery of the German schools ;
Leave new Pizarros to translating fools ;
Give, as thy last memorial to the age,
One classic drama, and reform the stage.
Gods ! o'er those boards shall Folly rear her head,
Where Garrick trod, and Siddons lives to tread ?
On those shall Farce display Buffoon'ry's mask,
And Hook conceal his heroes in a cask ?
Shall sapient managers new scenes produce   590
From Cherry, Skeffington, and Mother Goose ?
While Shakspeare, Otway, Massinger, forgot,
On stalls must moulder, or in closets rot ?
Lo ! with what pomp the daily prints proclaim
The rival candidates for Attic fame !
In grim array though Lewis' spectres rise,
Still Skeffington and Goose divide the prize.
And sure *great* Skeffington must claim our praise,
For skirtless coats and skeletons of plays
Renown'd alike ; whose genius ne'er confines   600
Her flight to garnish Greenwood's gay designs ;
Nor sleeps with " Sleeping Beauties," but anon
In five facetious acts comes thundering on,

While poor John Bull, bewilder'd with the scene,
Stares, wondering what the devil it can mean ;
But as some hands applaud, a venal few !
Rather than sleep, why John applauds it too.

Such are we now. Ah ! wherefore should we turn
To what our fathers were, unless to mourn ?
Degenerate Britons ! are ye dead to shame,   610
Or, kind to dulness, do you fear to blame ?
Well may the nobles of our present race
Watch each distortion of a Naldi's face ;
Well may they smile on Italy's buffoons,
And worship Catalani's pantaloons,
Since their own drama yields no fairer trace
Of wit than puns, of humour than grimace.

Then let Ausonia, skill'd in every art
To soften manners, but corrupt the heart,
Pour her exotic follies o'er the town,   620
To sanction Vice, and hunt Decorum down :
Let wedded strumpets languish o'er Deshayes,
And bless the promise which his form displays ;
While Gayton bounds before th' enraptured looks
Of hoary marquises and stripling dukes :
Let high-born lechers eye the lively Presle
Twirl her light limbs, that spurn the needless veil ;
Let Angiolini bare her breast of snow,
Wave the white arm, and point the pliant toe ;
Collini trill her love-inspiring song,   630
Strain her fair neck, and charm the listening throng !
Whet not your scythe, suppressors of our vice !
Reforming saints ! too delicately nice !
By whose decrees, our sinful souls to save,
No Sunday tankards foam, no barbers shave ;
And beer undrawn, and beards unmown, display
Your holy reverence for the Sabbath-day.

Or hail at once the patron and the pile
Of vice and folly, Greville and Argyle !
Where yon proud palace, Fashion's hallow'd fane,   640
Spreads wide her portals for the motley train,

Behold the new Petronius of the day,
Our arbiter of pleasure and of play !
There the hired eunuch, the Hesperian choir,
The melting lute, the soft lascivious lyre,
The song from Italy, the step from France,
The midnight orgy, and the mazy dance,
The smile of beauty, and the flush of wine,
For fops, fools, gamesters, knaves, and lords combine :
Each to his humour—Comus all allows ;   650
Champaign, dice, music, or your neighbour's spouse.
Talk not to us, ye starving sons of trade !
Of piteous ruin, which ourselves have made ;
In Plenty's sunshine Fortune's minions bask,
Nor think of poverty, except " en masque,"
When for the night some lately titled ass
Appears the beggar which his grandsire was.
The curtain dropp'd, the gay burletta o'er,
The audience take their turn upon the floor :
Now round the room the circling dow'gers sweep,   660
Now in loose waltz the thin-clad daughters leap ;
The first in lengthen'd line majestic swim,
The last display the free unfetter'd limb !
Those for Hibernia's lusty sons repair
With art the charms which nature could not spare ;
These after husbands wing their eager flight,
Nor leave much mystery for the nuptial night.

Oh ! blest retreats of infamy and ease,
Where, all forgotten but the power to please,
Each maid may give a loose to genial thought,   670
Each swain may teach new systems, or be taught :
There the blithe youngster, just return'd from Spain,
Cuts the light pack, or calls the rattling main ;
The jovial caster's set, and seven 's the nick,
Or—done !—a thousand on the coming trick !
If, mad with loss, existence 'gins to tire,
And all your hope or wish is to expire,
Here 's Powell's pistol ready for your life,
And, kinder still, two Pagets for your wife ;

Fit consummation of an earthly race   680
Begun in folly, ended in disgrace ;
While none but menials o'er the bed of death,
Wash thy red wounds, or watch thy wavering breath,
Traduced by liars, and forgot by all,
The mangled victim of a drunken brawl,
To live like Clodius, and like Falkland fall.

Truth ! rouse some genuine bard, and guide his hand
To drive this pestilence from out the land.
E'en I—least thinking of a thoughtless throng,
Just skill'd to know the right and choose the wrong,
Freed at that age when reason's shield is lost,   691
To fight my course through passion's countless host,
Whom every path of pleasure's flowery way
Has lured in turn, and all have led astray—
E'en I must raise my voice, e'en I must feel
Such scenes, such men, destroy the public weal :
Although some kind, censorious friend will say,
" What art thou better, meddling fool, than they ? "
And every brother rake will smile to see
That miracle, a moralist in me.   700
No matter—when some bard in virtue strong,
Gifford perchance, shall raise the chastening song,
Then sleep my pen for ever ! and my voice
Be only heard to hail him, and rejoice ;
Rejoice, and yield my feeble praise, though I
May feel the lash that Virtue must apply.

As for the smaller fry, who swarm in shoals,
From silly Hafiz up to simple Bowles,
Why should we call them from their dark abode,
In broad St. Giles's or in Tottenham-road ?   710
Or (since some men of fashion nobly dare
To scrawl in verse) from Bond-street or the Square ?
If things of ton their harmless lays indite,
Most wisely doom'd to shun the public sight,
What harm ? in spite of every critic elf,
Sir T. may read his stanzas to himself ;

Miles Andrews still his strength in couplets try,
And live in prologues, though his dramas die :
Lords too are bards, such things at times befall,
And 'tis some praise in peers to write at all.　　720
Yet, did or taste or reason sway the times,
Ah ! who would take their titles with their rhymes ?
Roscommon ! Sheffield ! with your spirits fled,
No future laurels deck a noble head ;
No muse will cheer, with renovating smile,
The paralytic puling of Carlisle.
The puny schoolboy and his early lay
Men pardon, if his follies pass away ;
But who forgives the senior's ceaseless verse,
Whose hairs grow hoary as his rhymes grow worse ?
What heterogeneous honours deck the peer !　　731
Lord, rhymester, petit-maître, and pamphleteer !
So dull in youth, so drivelling in his age,
His scenes alone had damn'd our sinking stage ;
But managers for once cried, " Hold, enough ! "
Nor drugg'd their audience with the tragic stuff.
Yet at their judgment let his lordship laugh,
And case his volumes in congenial calf ;
Yes ! doff that covering, where morocco shines,
And hang a calf-skin on those recreant lines.　　740

With you, ye Druids ! rich in native lead,
Who daily scribble for your daily bread ;
With you I war not : Gifford's heavy hand
Has crush'd, without remorse, your numerous band.
On " all the talents " vent your venal spleen ;
Want is your plea, let pity be your screen.
Let monodies on Fox regale your crew,
And Melville's Mantle prove a blanket too !
One common Lethe waits each hapless bard,
And, peace be with you ! 'tis your best reward.　　750
Such damning fame as Dunciads only give
Could bid your lines beyond a morning live ;
But now at once your fleeting labours close,
With names of greater note in blest repose.

Far be 't from me unkindly to upbraid
The lovely Rosa's prose in masquerade,
Whose strains, the faithful echoes of her mind,
Leave wondering comprehension far behind.
Though Crusca's bards no more our journals fill,
Some stragglers skirmish round the columns still;   760
Last of the howling host which once was Bell's,
Matilda snivels yet, and Hafiz yells;
And Merry's metaphors appear anew,
Chain'd to the signature of O. P. Q.

When some brisk youth, the tenant of a stall,
Employs a pen less pointed than his awl,
Leaves his snug shop, forsakes his store of shoes,
St. Crispin quits, and cobbles for the muse,
Heavens! how the vulgar stare! how crowds applaud!
How ladies read, and literati laud!   770
If chance some wicked wag should pass his jest,
'Tis sheer ill-nature—don't the world know best?
Genius must guide when wits admire the rhyme,
And Capel Lofft declares 'tis quite sublime.
Hear, then, ye happy sons of needless trade!
Swains! quit the plough, resign the useless spade!
Lo! Burns and Bloomfield, nay, a greater far,
Gifford was born beneath an adverse star,
Forsook the labours of a servile state,
Stemm'd the rude storm, and triumph'd over fate:
Then why no more? if Phoebus smiled on you,   781
Bloomfield! why not on brother Nathan too?
Him too the mania, not the muse, has seized;
Not inspiration, but a mind diseased:
And now no boor can seek his last abode,
No common be enclosed without an ode.
Oh! since increased refinement deigns to smile
On Britain's sons, and bless our genial isle,
Let poesy go forth, pervade the whole,
Alike the rustic, and mechanic soul!   790
Ye tuneful cobblers! still your notes prolong,
Compose at once a slipper and a song;

So shall the fair your handywork peruse,
Your sonnets sure shall please—perhaps your shoes.
May Moorland weavers boast Pindaric skill,
And tailors' lays be longer than their bill!
While punctual beaux reward the grateful notes,
And pay for poems—when they pay for coats.

To the famed throng now paid the tribute due,
Neglected genius! let me turn to you.   800
Come forth, oh Campbell! give thy talents scope;
Who dares aspire if thou must cease to hope?
And thou, melodious Rogers! rise at last,
Recall the pleasing memory of the past;
Arise! let blest remembrance still inspire,
And strike to wonted tones thy hallow'd lyre;
Restore Apollo to his vacant throne,
Assert thy country's honour and thine own.
What! must deserted Poesy still weep
Where her last hopes with pious Cowper sleep?   810
Unless, perchance, from his cold bier she turns,
To deck the turf that wraps her minstrel, Burns!
No! though contempt hath mark'd the spurious brood,
The race who rhyme from folly, or for food,
Yet still some genuine sons 'tis hers to boast,
Who, least affecting, still affect the most:
Feel as they write, and write but as they feel—
Bear witness Gifford, Sotheby, Macneil.

" Why slumbers Gifford? " once was ask'd in vain;
Why slumbers Gifford? let us ask again.   820
Are there no follies for his pen to purge?
Are there no fools whose backs demand the scourge?
Are there no sins for satire's bard to greet?
Stalks not gigantic Vice in every street?
Shall peers or princes tread pollution's path,
And 'scape alike the law's and muse's wrath?
Nor blaze with guilty glare through future time,
Eternal beacons of consummate crime?
Arouse thee, Gifford! be thy promise claim'd,
Make bad men better, or at least ashamed.   830

Unhappy White ! while life was in its spring,
And thy young muse just waved her joyous wing,
The spoiler swept that soaring lyre away,
Which else had sounded an immortal lay.
Oh ! what a noble heart was here undone,
When Science' self destroy'd her favourite son !
Yes, she too much indulged thy fond pursuit,
She sow'd the seeds, but death has reap'd the fruit.
'Twas thine own genius gave the final blow,
And help'd to plant the wound that laid thee low :
So the struck eagle, stretch'd upon the plain,   841
No more through rolling clouds to soar again,
View'd his own feather on the fatal dart,
And wing'd the shaft that quiver'd in his heart ;
Keen were his pangs, but keener far to feel
He nursed the pinion which impell'd the steel ;
While the same plumage that had warm'd his nest
Drank the last life-drop of his bleeding breast.

There be who say, in these enlighten'd days,
That splendid lies are all the poet's praise ;   850
That strain'd invention, ever on the wing,
Alone impels the modern bard to sing :
'Tis true, that all who rhyme—nay, all who write,
Shrink from that fatal word to genius—trite ;
Yet Truth sometimes will lend her noblest fires,
And decorate the verse herself inspires :
This fact in Virtue's name let Crabbe attest ;
Though nature's sternest painter, yet the best.

And here let Shee and Genius find a place,
Whose pen and pencil yield an equal grace ;   86c
To guide whose hand the sister arts combine,
And trace the poet's or the painter's line ;
Whose magic touch can bid the canvas glow,
Or pour the easy rhyme's harmonious flow ;
While honours, doubly merited, attend
The poet's rival, but the painter's friend.

Blest is the man who dares approach the bower
Where dwelt the muses at their natal hour ;

Whose steps have press'd, whose eye has mark'd afar,
The clime that nursed the sons of song and war,   870
The scenes which glory still must hover o'er,
Her place of birth, her own Achaian shore.
But doubly blest is he whose heart expands
With hallow'd feelings for those classic lands;
Who rends the veil of ages long gone by,
And views their remnants with a poet's eye!
Wright! 'twas thy happy lot at once to view
Those shores of glory, and to sing them too;
And sure no common muse inspired thy pen
To hail the land of gods and godlike men.   880

    And you, associate bards! who snatch'd to light
Those gems too long withheld from modern sight;
Whose mingling taste combined to cull the wreath
Where Attic flowers Aonion odours breathe,
And all their renovated fragrance flung
To grace the beauties of your native tongue;
Now let those minds, that nobly could transfuse
The glorious spirit of the Grecian muse,
Though soft the echo, scorn a borrow'd tone:
Resign Achaia's lyre, and strike your own.   890

    Let these, or such as these, with just applause,
Restore the muse's violated laws;
But not in flimsy Darwin's pompous chime,
That mighty master of unmeaning rhyme,
Whose gilded cymbals, more adorn'd than clear,
The eye delighted, but fatigued the ear;
In show the simple lyre could once surpass,
But now, worn down, appear in native brass;
While all his train of hovering sylphs around
Evaporate in similes and sound: 900
Him let them shun, with him let tinsel die:
False glare attracts, but more offends the eye.

    Yet let them not to vulgar Wordsworth stoop,
The meanest object of the lowly group,
Whose verse, of all but childish prattle void,
Seems blessed harmony to Lamb and Lloyd:

Let them—but hold, my muse, nor dare to teach
A strain far, far beyond thy humble reach:
The native genius with their being given
Will point the path, and peal their notes to heaven.

And thou, too, Scott! resign to minstrels rude   911
The wilder slogan of a border feud:
Let others spin their meagre lines for hire;
Enough for genius, if itself inspire!
Let Southey sing, although his teeming muse,
Prolific every spring, be too profuse;
Let simple Wordsworth chime his childish verse,
And brother Coleridge lull the babe at nurse;
Let spectre-mongering Lewis aim, at most,
To rouse the galleries, or to raise a ghost;   920
Let Moore still sigh; let Strangford steal from Moore,
And swear that Camoëns sang such notes of yore;
Let Hayley hobble on, Montgomery rave,
And godly Grahame chant a stupid stave:
Let sonneteering Bowles his strains refine,
And whine and whimper to the fourteenth line;
Let Stott, Carlisle, Matilda, and the rest
Of Grub Street, and of Grosvenor Place the best,
Scrawl on, till death release us from the strain,
Or Common Sense assert her rights again.   930
But thou, with powers that mock the aid of praise,
Shouldst leave to humbler bards ignoble lays:
Thy country's voice, the voice of all the Nine,
Demand a hallow'd harp—that harp is thine.
Say! will not Caledonia's annals yield
The glorious record of some nobler field,
Than the wild foray of a plundering clan,
Whose proudest deeds disgrace the name of man?
Or Marmion's acts of darkness, fitter food
For Sherwood's outlaw tales of Robin Hood?   940
Scotland! still proudly claim thy native bard,
And be thy praise his first, his best reward!
Yet not with thee alone his name should live,
But own the vast renown a world can give:

Be known, perchance, when Albion is no more,
And tell the tale of what she was before ;
To future times her faded fame recall,
And save her glory, though his country fall.

Yet what avails the sanguine poet's hope,
To conquer ages, and with time to cope ?   950
New eras spread their wings, new nations rise,
And other victors fill the applauding skies ;
A few brief generations fleet along,
Whose sons forget the poet and his song :
E'en now, what once-loved minstrels scarce may claim
The transient mention of a dubious name !
When fame's loud trump hath blown its noblest blast,
Though long the sound, the echo sleeps at last ;
And glory, like the phoenix midst her fires,
Exhales her odours, blazes, and expires.   960

Shall hoary Granta call her sable sons,
Expert in science, more expert at puns ?
Shall these approach the muse ? ah, no ! she flies,
Even from the tempting ore of Seaton's prize ;
Though printers condescend the press to soil
With rhyme by Hoare, and epic blank by Hoyle :
Not him whose page, if still upheld by whist,
Requires no sacred theme to bid us list.
Ye ! who in Granta's honours would surpass,
Must mount her Pegasus, a full-grown ass ;   970
A foal well worthy of her ancient dam,
Whose Helicon is duller than her Cam.

There Clarke, still striving piteously " to please,"
Forgetting doggrel leads not to degrees,
A would-be satirist, a hired buffoon,
A monthly scribbler of some low lampoon,
Condemn'd to drudge, the meanest of the mean,
And furbish falsehoods for a magazine,
Devotes to scandal his congenial mind ;
Himself a living libel on mankind.   980

Oh ! dark asylum of a Vandal race !
At once the boast of learning, and disgrace !
So lost to Phoebus, that nor Hodgson's verse
Can make thee better, nor poor Hewson's worse.
But where fair Isis rolls her purer wave,
The partial muse delighted loves to lave ;
On her green banks a greener wreath she wove,
To crown the bards that haunt her classic grove :
Where Richards wakes a genuine poet's fires,
And modern Britons glory in their sires.   990

For me, who, thus unask'd, have dared to tell
My country what her sons should know too well,
Zeal for her honour bade me here engage
The host of idiots that infest her age ;
No just applause her honour'd name shall lose,
As first in freedom, dearest to the muse.
Oh ! would thy bards but emulate thy fame,
And rise more worthy, Albion, of thy name !
What Athens was in science, Rome in power,
What Tyre appear'd in her meridian hour,   1000
'Tis thine at once, fair Albion ! to have been—
Earth's chief dictatress, ocean's lovely queen :
But Rome decay'd, and Athens strew'd the plain,
And Tyre's proud piers lie shatter'd in the main ;
Like these, thy strength may sink, in ruin hurl'd,
And Britain fall, the bulwark of the world.
But let me cease, and dread Cassandra's fate,
With warning ever scoff'd at, till too late ;
To themes less lofty still my lay confine,
And urge thy bards to gain a name like thine.   1010

Then, hapless Britain ! be thy rulers blest,
The senate's oracles, the people's jest !
Still hear thy motley orators dispense
The flowers of rhetoric, though not of sense,
While Canning's colleagues hate him for his wit,
And old dame Portland fills the place of Pitt.

Yet once again, adieu ! ere this the sail
That wafts me hence is shivering in the gale ;

And Afric's coast and Calpe's adverse height,
And Stamboul's minarets must greet my sight : 1020
Thence shall I stray through beauty's native clime,
Where Kaff is clad in rocks, and crown'd with snows
    sublime.
But should I back return, no tempting press
Shall drag my journal from the desk's recess ;
Let coxcombs, printing as they come from far,
Snatch his own wreath of ridicule from Carr ;
Let Aberdeen and Elgin still pursue
The shade of fame through regions of virtù ;
Waste useless thousands on their Phidian freaks,
Misshapen monuments and maim'd antiques ; 1030
And make their grand saloons a general mart
For all the mutilated blocks of art :
Of Dardan tours let dilettanti tell,
I leave topography to rapid Gell ;
And, quite content, no more shall interpose
To stun the public ear—at least with prose.

Thus far I've held my undisturb'd career,
Prepared for rancour, steel'd 'gainst selfish fear :
This thing of rhyme I ne'er disdain'd to own—
Though not obtrusive, yet not quite unknown : 1040
My voice was heard again, though not so loud,
My page, though nameless, never disavow'd ;
And now at once I tear the veil away :—
Cheer on the pack ! the quarry stands at bay,
Unscared by all the din of Melbourne House,
By Lambe's resentment, or by Holland's spouse,
By Jeffrey's harmless pistol, Hallam's rage,
Edina's brawny sons and brimstone page.
Our men in buckram shall have blows enough,
And feel they too are " penetrable stuff : " 1050
And though I hope not hence unscathed to go,
Who conquers me shall find a stubborn foe.
The time hath been, when no harsh sound would fall
From lips that now may seem imbued with gall ;
Nor fools nor follies tempt me to despise
The meanest thing that crawl'd beneath my eyes :

But now, so callous grown, so changed since youth,
I've learn'd to think, and sternly speak the truth;
Learn'd to deride the critic's starch decree,
And break him on the wheel he meant for me;   1060
To spurn the rod a scribbler bids me kiss,
Nor care if courts and crowds applaud or hiss:
Nay more, though all my rival rhymesters frown,
I too can hunt a poetaster down;
And, arm'd in proof, the gauntlet cast at once
To Scotch marauder, and to southern dunce.
Thus much I've dared; if my incondite lay
Hath wrong'd these righteous times, let others say;
This, let the world, which knows not how to spare,
Yet rarely blames unjustly, now declare.   1070

TO ATHENS

From 'The Curse of Minerva'

Slow sinks, more lovely ere his race be run,
Along Morea's hills the setting sun;
Not, as in northern climes, obscurely bright,
But one unclouded blaze of living light;
O'er the hush'd deep the yellow beam he throws,
Gilds the green wave that trembles as it glows;
On old Aegina's rock and Hydra's isle
The god of gladness sheds his parting smile;
O'er his own regions lingering loves to shine,
Though there his altars are no more divine.   10
Descending fast, the mountain-shadows kiss
Thy glorious gulf, unconquer'd Salamis!
Their azure arches through the long expanse,
More deeply purpled, meet his mellowing glance,
And tenderest tints, along their summits driven,
Mark his gay course, and own the hues of heaven;
Till, darkly shaded from the land and deep,
Behind his Delphian rock he sinks to sleep.

On such an eve his palest beam he cast
When, Athens! here thy wisest look'd his last.   20
How watch'd thy better sons his farewell ray,
That closed their murder'd sage's latest day!
Not yet—not yet—Sol pauses on the hill,
The precious hour of parting lingers still;
But sad his light to agonizing eyes,
And dark the mountain's once delightful dyes;
Gloom o'er the lovely land he seem'd to pour,
The land where Phoebus never frown'd before;
But ere he sunk below Cithaeron's head,
The cup of woe was quaff'd—the spirit fled;   30
The soul of him that scorn'd to fear or fly,
Who lived and died as none can live or die.

But, lo! from high Hymettus to the plain
The queen of night asserts her silent reign;
No murky vapour, herald of the storm,
Hides her fair face, or girds her glowing form;
With cornice glimmering as the moonbeams play,
There the white column greets her grateful ray,
And bright around, with quivering beams beset,
Her emblem sparkles o'er the minaret: 40
The groves of olive scatter'd dark and wide,
Where meek Cephisus sheds his scanty tide,
The cypress saddening by the sacred mosque,
The gleaming turret of the gay kiosk,
And sad and sombre 'mid the holy calm,
Near Theseus' fane, yon solitary palm;
All, tinged with varied hues, arrest the eye;
And dull were his that passed them heedless by.

Again the Aegean, heard no more afar,
Lulls his chafed breast from elemental war: 50
Again his waves in milder tints unfold
Their long expanse of sapphire and of gold,
Mix'd with the shades of many a distant isle
That frown, where gentler ocean deigns to smile.

 As thus, within the walls of Pallas' fane,
I mark'd the beauties of the land and main,
Alone, and friendless, on the magic shore,
Whose arts and arms but live in poets' lore;
Oft as the matchless dome I turn'd to scan,
Sacred to gods, but not secure from man,   60
The past return'd, the present seem'd to cease,
And Glory knew no clime beyond her Greece!

THE VISION OF JUDGMENT

I

SAINT PETER sat by the celestial gate:
　His keys were rusty, and the lock was dull,
So little trouble had been given of late;
　Not that the place by any means was full,
　But since the Gallic era " eighty-eight "
　The devils had ta'en a longer, stronger pull,
And " a pull altogether," as they say
At sea—which drew most souls another way.

II

The angels all were singing out of tune,
　And hoarse with having little else to do,　　　10
Excepting to wind up the sun and moon,
　Or curb a runaway young star or two,
Or wild colt of a comet, which too soon
　Broke out of bounds o'er the ethereal blue,
Splitting some planet with its playful tail,
As boats are sometimes by a wanton whale.

III

The guardian seraphs had retired on high,
　Finding their charges past all care below;
Terrestrial business fill'd nought in the sky
　Save the recording angel's black bureau;　　　20
Who found, indeed, the facts to multiply
　With such rapidity of vice and woe,
That he had stripp'd off both his wings in quills,
And yet was in arrear of human ills.

IV

His business so augmented of late years,
    That he was forced, against his will no doubt,
(Just like those cherubs, earthly ministers,)
    For some resource to turn himself about,
And claim the help of his celestial peers,
    To aid him ere he should be quite worn out   30
By the increased demand for his remarks :
Six angels and twelve saints were named his clerks.

V

This was a handsome board—at least for heaven ;
    And yet they had even then enough to do,
So many conquerors' cars were daily driven,
    So many kingdoms fitted up anew ;
Each day, too, slew its thousands six or seven,
    Till at the crowning carnage, Waterloo,
They threw their pens down in divine disgust—
The page was so besmear'd with blood and dust.   40

VI

This by the way ; 'tis not mine to record
    What angels shrink from : even the very devil
On this occasion his own worst abhorr'd,
    So surfeited with the infernal revel :
Though he himself had sharpen'd every sword,
    It almost quench'd his innate thirst of evil.
(Here Satan's sole good work deserves insertion—
'Tis, that he has both generals in reversion.)

VII

Let 's skip a few short years of hollow peace,
    Which peopled earth no better, hell as wont,   50
And heaven none—they form the tyrant's lease,
    With nothing but new names subscribed upon 't ;
'Twill one day finish : meantime they increase,
    " With seven heads and ten horns," and all in front,
Like Saint John's foretold beast ; but ours are born
Less formidable in the head than horn.

VIII

In the first year of freedom's second dawn
  Died George the Third ; although no tyrant, one
Who shielded tyrants, till each sense withdrawn
  Left him nor mental nor external sun :   60
A better farmer ne'er brush'd dew from lawn,
  A worse king never left a realm undone !
He died—but left his subjects still behind,
One half as mad—and t'other no less blind.

IX

He died ! his death made no great stir on earth :
  His burial made some pomp ; there was profusion
Of velvet, gilding, brass, and no great dearth
  Of aught but tears—save those shed by collusion.
For these things may be bought at their true worth ;
  Of elegy there was the due infusion—   70
Bought also ; and the torches, cloaks, and banners,
Heralds, and relics of old Gothic manners,

X

Form'd a sepulchral melodrame. Of all
  The fools who flock'd to swell or see the show,
Who cared about the corpse ? The funeral
  Made the attraction, and the black the woe.
There throbb'd not there a thought which pierced the
      pall ;
  And when the gorgeous coffin was laid low,
It seem'd the mockery of hell to fold
The rottenness of eighty years in gold.   80

XI

So mix his body with the dust ! It might
  Return to what it *must* far sooner, were
The natural compound left alone to fight
  Its way back into earth, and fire, and air ;
But the unnatural balsams merely blight
  What nature made him at his birth, as bare
As the mere million's base unmummied clay—
Yet all his spices but prolong decay.

XII

He 's dead—and upper earth with him has done ;
 He 's buried ; save the undertaker's bill, 90
Or lapidary scrawl, the world is gone
 For him, unless he left a German will :
But where 's the proctor who will ask his son ?
 In whom his qualities are reigning still,
Except that household virtue, most uncommon,
Of constancy to a bad, ugly woman.

XIII

" God save the king ! " It is a large economy
 In God to save the like ; but if he will
Be saving, all the better ; for not one am I
 Of those who think damnation better still : 100
I hardly know too if not quite alone am I
 In this small hope of bettering future ill
By circumscribing, with some slight restriction,
The eternity of hell's hot jurisdiction.

XIV

I know this is unpopular ; I know
 'Tis blasphemous ; I know one may be damn'd
For hoping no one else may e'er be so ;
 I know my catechism ; I know we're cramm'd
With the best doctrines till we quite o'erflow ;
 I know that all save England's church have shamm'd,
And that the other twice two hundred churches 111
And synagogues have made a *damn'd* bad purchase.

XV

God help us all ! God help me too ! I am,
 God knows, as helpless as the devil can wish,
And not a whit more difficult to damn,
 Than is to bring to land a late-hook'd fish,
Or to the butcher to purvey the lamb ;
 Not that I'm fit for such a noble dish,
As one day will be that immortal fry
Of almost everybody born to die. 120

XVI

Saint Peter sat by the celestial gate,
    And nodded o'er his keys; when, lo! there came
A wondrous noise he had not heard of late—
    A rushing sound of wind, and stream, and flame;
In short, a roar of things extremely great,
    Which would have made aught save a saint exclaim
But he, with first a start and then a wink,
Said, "There's another star gone out, I think!"

XVII

But ere he could return to his repose,
    A cherub flapp'd his right wing o'er his eyes— 130
At which St. Peter yawn'd, and rubb'd his nose:
    "Saint porter," said the angel, "prithee rise!"
Waving a goodly wing, which glow'd, as glows
    An earthly peacock's tail, with heavenly dyes:
To which the saint replied, "Well, what's the matter?
"Is Lucifer come back with all this clatter?"

XVIII

"No," quoth the cherub; "George the Third is dead."
    "And who *is* George the Third?" replied the apostle:
"*What George? what Third?*" "The king of England,"
        said
    The angel. "Well! he won't find kings to jostle
Him on his way; but does he wear his head? 141
    Because the last we saw here had a tustle,
And ne'er would have got into heaven's good graces,
Had he not flung his head in all our faces.

XIX

"He was, if I remember, king of France;
    That head of his, which could not keep a crown
On earth, yet ventured in my face to advance
    A claim to those of martyrs—like my own:
If I had had my sword, as I had once
    When I cut ears off, I had cut him down; 150
But having but my *keys*, and not my brand,
I only knock'd his head from out his hand.

XX

" And then he set up such a headless howl,
    That all the saints came out and took him in ;
And there he sits by St. Paul, cheek by jowl ;
    That fellow Paul—the parvenù ! The skin
Of St. Bartholomew, which makes his cowl
    In heaven, and upon earth redeem'd his sin,
So as to make a martyr, never sped
Better than did this weak and wooden head.   160

XXI

" But had it come up here upon its shoulders,
    There would have been a different tale to tell :
The fellow-feeling in the saint's beholders
    Seems to have acted on them like a spell ;
And so this very foolish head heaven solders
    Back on its trunk : it may be very well,
And seems the custom here to overthrow
Whatever has been wisely done below."

XXII

The angel answer'd, " Peter ! do not pout :
    The king who comes has head and all entire,   170
And never knew how much it was about—
    He did as doth the puppet—by its wire,
And will be judged like all the rest, no doubt :
    My business and your own is not to inquire
Into such matters, but to mind our cue—
Which is to act as we are bid to do."

XXIII

While thus they spake, the angelic caravan,
    Arriving like a rush of mighty wind,
Cleaving the fields of space, as doth the swan
    Some silver stream (say Ganges, Nile, or Inde,   180
Or Thames, or Tweed), and midst them an old man
    With an old soul, and both extremely blind,
Halted before the gate, and in his shroud
Seated their fellow-traveller on a cloud.

XXIV

But bringing up the rear of this bright host
    A Spirit of a different aspect waved
His wings, like thunder-clouds above some coast
    Whose barren beach with frequent wrecks is paved;
His brow was like the deep when tempest-toss'd;
    Fierce and unfathomable thoughts engraved   190
Eternal wrath on his immortal face,
And *where* he gazed a gloom pervaded space.

XXV

As he drew near, he gazed upon the gate
    Ne'er to be enter'd more by him or Sin,
With such a glance of supernatural hate,
    As made Saint Peter wish himself within;
He patter'd with his keys at a great rate,
    And sweated through his apostolic skin:
Of course his perspiration was but ichor,
Or some such other spiritual liquor.   200

XXVI

The very cherubs huddled all together,
    Like birds when soars the falcon; and they felt
A tingling to the tip of every feather,
    And form'd a circle like Orion's belt
Around their poor old charge; who scarce knew whither
    His guards had led him, though they gently dealt
With royal manes (for by many stories,
And true, we learn the angels all are Tories).

XXVII

As things were in this posture, the gate flew
    Asunder, and the flashing of its hinges   210
Flung over space an universal hue
    Of many-colour'd flame, until its tinges
Reach'd even our speck of earth, and made a new
    Aurora borealis spread its fringes
O'er the North Pole; the same seen, when ice-bound
By Captain Parry's crew, in " Melville's Sound."

XXVIII

And from the gate thrown open issued beaming
   A beautiful and mighty Thing of Light,
Radiant with glory, like a banner streaming
   Victorious from some world-o'erthrowing fight :   220
My poor comparisons must needs be teeming
   With earthly likenesses, for here the night
Of clay obscures our best conceptions, saving
Johanna Southcote, or Bob Southey raving.

XXIX

'Twas the archangel Michael : all men know
   The make of angels and archangels, since
There's scarce a scribbler has not one to show,
   From the fiends' leader to the angels' prince.
There also are some altar-pieces, though
   I really can't say that they much evince   230
One's inner notions of immortal spirits ;
But let the connoisseurs explain *their* merits.

XXX

Michael flew forth in glory and in good ;
   A goodly work of him from whom all glory
And good arise ; the portal past—he stood ;
   Before him the young cherubs and saints hoary—
(I say *young*, begging to be understood
   By looks, not years ; and should be very sorry
To state, they were not older than St. Peter,
But merely that they seem'd a little sweeter).   240

XXXI

The cherubs and the saints bow'd down before
   That arch-angelic hierarch, the first
Of essences angelical, who wore
   The aspect of a god ; but this ne'er nursed
Pride in his heavenly bosom, in whose core
   No thought, save for his Master's service, durst
Intrude, however glorified and high ;
He knew him but the viceroy of the sky.

XXXII

He and the sombre, silent Spirit met—
    They knew each other both for good and ill;   250
Such was their power, that neither could forget
    His former friend and future foe; but still
There was a high, immortal, proud regret
    In either's eye, as if 'twere less their will
Than destiny to make the eternal years
Their date of war, and their " champ clos " the spheres.

XXXIII

But here they were in neutral space: we know
    From Job, that Satan hath the power to pay
A heavenly visit thrice a year or so;
    And that the " sons of God," like those of clay,   260
Must keep him company; and we might show
    From the same book, in how polite a way
The dialogue is held between the Powers
Of Good and Evil—but 'twould take up hours.

XXXIV

And this is not a theologic tract,
    To prove with Hebrew and with Arabic,
If Job be allegory or a fact,
    But a true narrative; and thus I pick
From out the whole but such and such an act
    As sets aside the slightest thought of trick.   270
'Tis every tittle true, beyond suspicion,
And accurate as any other vision.

XXXV

The spirits were in neutral space, before
    The gate of heaven; like eastern thresholds is
The place where Death's grand cause is argued o'er,
    And souls despatch'd to that world or to this;
And therefore Michael and the other wore
    A civil aspect: though they did not kiss,
Yet still between his Darkness and his Brightness
There pass'd a mutual glance of great politeness.   280

XXXVI

The Archangel bow'd, not like a modern beau,
    But with a graceful oriental bend,
Pressing one radiant arm just where below
    The heart in good men is supposed to tend ;
He turn'd as to an equal, not too low,
    But kindly ; Satan met his ancient friend
With more hauteur, as might an old Castilian
Poor noble meet a mushroom rich civilian.

XXXVII

He merely bent his diabolic brow
    An instant ; and then raising it, he stood   290
In act to assert his right or wrong, and show
    Cause why King George by no means could or should
Make out a case to be exempt from woe
    Eternal, more than other kings, endued
With better sense and hearts, whom history mentions,
Who long have " paved hell with their good intentions."

XXXVIII

Michael began : " What wouldst thou with this man,
    Now dead, and brought before the Lord ? What ill
Hath he wrought since his mortal race began,
    That thou canst claim him ? Speak ! and do thy
        will,   300
If it be just : if in this earthly span
    He hath been greatly failing to fulfil
His duties as a king and mortal, say,
And he is thine ; if not, let him have way."

XXXIX

" Michael ! " replied the Prince of Air, " even here
    Before the gate of Him thou servest, must
I claim my subject : and will make appear
    That as he was my worshipper in dust,
So shall he be in spirit, although dear
    To thee and thine, because nor wine nor lust   310
Were of his weaknesses ; yet on the throne
He reign'd o'er millions to serve me alone.

XL

" Look to *our* earth, or rather *mine* ; it was,
 Once, more thy master's : but I triumph not
In this poor planet's conquest ; nor, alas !
 Need he thou servest envy me my lot :
With all the myriads of bright worlds which pass
 In worship round him, he may have forgot
Yon weak creation of such paltry things :
I think few worth damnation save their kings,—   320

XLI

" And these but as a kind of quit-rent, to
 Assert my right as lord : and even had
I such an inclination, 'twere (as you
 Well know) superfluous ; they are grown so bad,
That hell has nothing better left to do
 Than leave them to themselves : so much more mad
And evil by their own internal curse,
Heaven cannot make them better, nor I worse.

XLII

" Look to the earth, I said, and say again :
 When this old, blind, mad, helpless, weak, poor
  worm   330
Began in youth's first bloom and flush to reign,
 The world and he both wore a different form,
And much of earth and all the watery plain
 Of ocean call'd him king : through many a storm
His isles had floated on the abyss of time ;
For the rough virtues chose them for their clime.

XLIII

" He came to his sceptre young ; he leaves it old :
 Look to the state in which he found his realm,
And left it ; and his annals too behold,
 How to a minion first he gave the helm ;   340
How grew upon his heart a thirst for gold,
 The beggar's vice, which can but overwhelm
The meanest hearts ; and for the rest, but glance
Thine eye along America and France.

XLIV

" 'Tis true, he was a tool from first to last
　　(I have the workmen safe) ; but as a tool
So let him be consumed. From out the past
　　Of ages, since mankind have known the rule
Of monarchs—from the bloody rolls amass'd
　　Of sin and slaughter—from the Cæsar's school,　350
Take the worst pupil ; and produce a reign
More drench'd with gore, more cumber'd with the slain.

XLV

" He ever warr'd with freedom and the free :
　　Nations as men, home subjects, foreign foes,
So that they utter'd the word ' Liberty ! '
　　Found George the Third their first opponent. Whose
History was ever stain'd as his will be
　　With national and individual woes ?
I grant his household abstinence ; I grant
His neutral virtues, which most monarchs want ;　360

XLVI

' I know he was a constant consort ; own
　　He was a decent sire, and middling lord.
All this is much, and most upon a throne ;
　　As temperance, if at Apicius' board,
Is more than at an anchorite's supper shown.
　　I grant him all the kindest can accord ;
And this was well for him, but not for those
Millions who found him what oppression chose.

XLVII

" The New World shook him off ; the Old yet groans
　　Beneath what he and his prepared, if not　370
Completed : he leaves heirs on many thrones
　　To all his vices, without what begot
Compassion for him—his tame virtues ; drones
　　Who sleep, or despots who have now forgot
A lesson which shall be re-taught them, wake
Upon the thrones of earth ; but let them quake !

XLVIII

" Five millions of the primitive, who hold
   The faith which makes ye great on earth, implored
A *part* of that vast *all* they held of old,—
   Freedom to worship—not alone your Lord,   380
Michael, but you, and you, Saint Peter ! Cold
   Must be your souls, if you have not abhorr'd
The foe to Catholic participation
In all the license of a Christian nation.

XLIX

" True ! he allowed them to pray God ; but as
   A consequence of prayer, refused the law
Which would have placed them upon the same base
   With those who did not hold the saints in awe."
But here Saint Peter started from his place,
   And cried, " You may the prisoner withdraw :   390
Ere heaven shall ope her portals to this Guelph,
While I am guard, may I be damn'd myself !

L

" Sooner will I with Cerberus exchange
   My office (and *his* is no sinecure)
Than see this royal Bedlam bigot range
   The azure fields of heaven, of that be sure ! "
" Saint ! " replied Satan, " you do well to avenge
   The wrongs he made your satellites endure ;
And if to this exchange you should be given,
I'll try to coax *our* Cerberus up to heaven ! "   400

LI

Here Michael interposed : " Good saint ! and devil !
   Pray, not so fast ; you both outrun discretion.
Saint Peter ! you were wont to be more civil :
   Satan ! excuse this warmth of his expression,
And condescension to the vulgar's level :
   Even saints sometimes forget themselves in session.
Have you got more to say ? "—" No."—" If you please,
I'll trouble you to call your witnesses."

LII

Then Satan turn'd and waved his swarthy hand,
   Which stirr'd with its electric qualities   410
Clouds farther off than we can understand,
   Although we find him sometimes in our skies ;
Infernal thunder shook both sea and land
   In all the planets, and hell's batteries
Let off the artillery, which Milton mentions
As one of Satan's most sublime inventions.

LIII

This was a signal unto such damn'd souls
   As have the privilege of their damnation
Extended far beyond the mere controls
   Of worlds past, present, or to come ; no station   420
Is theirs particularly in the rolls
   Of Hell assign'd ; but where their inclination
Or business carries them in search of game,
They may range freely—being damn'd the same.

LIV

They're proud of this—as very well they may,
   It being a sort of knighthood, or gilt key
Stuck in their loins ; or like to an " entré "
   Up the back stairs, or such free-masonry.
I borrow my comparisons from clay,
   Being clay myself.   Let not those spirits be   430
Offended with such base low likenesses ;
We know their posts are nobler far than these.

LV

When the great signal ran from heaven to hell—
   About ten million times the distance reckon'd
From our sun to its earth, as we can tell
   How much time it takes up, even to a second,
For every ray that travels to dispel
   The fogs of London, through which, dimly beacon'd,
The weathercocks are gilt some thrice a year,
If that the *summer* is not too severe :   440

LVI

I say that I can tell—'twas half a minute;
  I know the solar beams take up more time
Ere, pack'd up for their journey, they begin it;
  But then their telegraph is less sublime,
And if they ran a race, they would not win it
  'Gainst Satan's couriers bound for their own clime.
The sun takes up some years for every ray
To reach its goal—the devil not half a day.

LVII

Upon the verge of space, about the size
  Of half-a-crown, a little speck appear'd   450
(I've seen a something like it in the skies
  In the Ægean, ere a squall); it near'd,
And, growing bigger, took another guise;
  Like an aërial ship it tack'd, and steer'd,
Or *was* steer'd (I am doubtful of the grammar
Of the last phrase, which makes the stanza stammer;—

LVIII

But take your choice): and then it grew a cloud;
  And so it was—a cloud of witnesses.
But such a cloud! No land e'er saw a crowd
  Of locusts numerous as the heavens saw these;   460
They shadow'd with their myriads space; their loud
  And varied cries were like those of wild geese
(If nations may be liken'd to a goose),
And realised the phrase of " hell broke loose."

LIX

Here crash'd a sturdy oath of stout John Bull,
  Who damn'd away his eyes as heretofore :
There Paddy brogued " By Jasus ! "—" What 's your
    wull ? "
  The temperate Scot exclaim'd : the French ghost
    swore
In certain terms I shan't translate in full,
  As the first coachman will ; and 'midst the war,
The voice of Jonathan was heard to express,   471
" *Our* President is going to war, I guess."

LX

Besides there were the Spaniard, Dutch, and Dane ;
  In short, an universal shoal of shades,
From Otaheite's isle to Salisbury Plain,
  Of all climes and professions, years and trades,
Ready to swear against the good king's reign,
  Bitter as clubs in cards are against spades :
All summon'd by this grand " subpœna," to
Try if kings mayn't be damn'd like me or you.   480

LXI

When Michael saw this host, he first grew pale,
  As angels can ; next, like Italian twilight,
He turn'd all colours—as a peacock's tail,
  Or sunset streaming through a Gothic skylight
In some old abbey, or a trout not stale,
  Or distant lightning on the horizon *by night*,
Or a fresh rainbow, or a grand review
Of thirty regiments in red, green, and blue.

LXII

Then he address'd himself to Satan : " Why—
  My good old friend, for such I deem you, though
Our different parties make us fight so shy,   491
  I ne'er mistake you for a *personal* foe ;
Our difference is *political*, and I
  Trust that, whatever may occur below,
You know my great respect for you : and this
Makes me regret whate'er you do amiss—

LXIII

" Why, my dear Lucifer, would you abuse
  My call for witnesses ? I did not mean
That you should half of earth and hell produce ;
  'Tis even superfluous, since two honest, clean,   500
True testimonies are enough : we lose
  Our time, nay, our eternity, between
The accusation and defence : if we
Hear both, 'twill stretch our immortality."

LXIV

Satan replied, " To me the matter is
   Indifferent, in a personal point of view :
I can have fifty better souls than this
   With far less trouble than we have gone through
Already ; and I merely argued his
   Late Majesty of Britain's case with you   510
Upon a point of form : you may dispose
Of him ; I've kings enough below, God knows ! "

LXV

Thus spoke the Demon (late call'd " multifaced "
   By multo-scribbling Southey).   " Then we'll call
One or two persons of the myriads placed
   Around our congress, and dispense with all
The rest," quoth Michael : " Who may be so graced
   As to speak first ? there 's choice enough—who shall
It be ? "   Then Satan answer'd, " There are many ;
But you may choose Jack Wilkes as well as any."   520

LXVI

A merry, cock-eyed, curious-looking sprite
   Upon the instant started from the throng,
Dress'd in a fashion now forgotten quite ;
   For all the fashions of the flesh stick long
By people in the next world ; where unite
   All the costumes since Adam's, right or wrong,
From Eve's fig-leaf down to the petticoat,
Almost as scanty, of days less remote.

LXVII

The spirit look'd around upon the crowds
   Assembled, and exclaim'd, " My friends of all   530
The spheres, we shall catch cold amongst these clouds ;
   So let 's to business : why this general call ?
If those are freeholders I see in shrouds,
   And 'tis for an election that they bawl,
Behold a candidate with unturn'd coat !
Saint Peter, may I count upon your vote ? "

LXVIII

" Sir," replied Michael, " you mistake ; these things
    Are of a former life, and what we do
Above is more august ; to judge of kings
    Is the tribunal met : so now you know."   540
" Then I presume those gentlemen with wings,"
    Said Wilkes, " are cherubs ; and that soul below
Looks much like George the Third, but to my mind
A good deal older—Bless me ! is he blind ?' "

LXIX

" He is what you behold him, and his doom
    Depends upon his deeds," the Angel said ;
" If you have aught to arraign in him, the tomb
    Gives license to the humblest beggar's head
To lift itself against the loftiest."—" Some,"   549
    Said Wilkes, " don't wait to see them laid in lead,
For such a liberty—and I, for one,
Have told them what I thought beneath the sun."

LXX

" *Above* the sun repeat, then, what thou hast
    To urge against him," said the Archangel.   " Why,"
Replied the spirit, " since old scores are past,
    Must I turn evidence ? In faith, not I.
Besides, I beat him hollow at the last,
    With all his Lords and Commons : in the sky
I don't like ripping up old stories, since
His conduct was but natural in a prince.   560

LXXI

" Foolish, no doubt, and wicked, to oppress
    A poor unlucky devil without a shilling ;
But then I blame the man himself much less
    Than Bute and Grafton, and shall be unwilling
To see him punish'd here for their excess,
    Since they were both damn'd long ago, and still in
Their place below : for me, I have forgiven,
And vote his *habeas corpus* into heaven."

LXXII

"Wilkes," said the Devil, "I understand all this;
  You turn'd to half a courtier ere you died,   570
And seem to think it would not be amiss
  To grow a whole one on the other side
Of Charon's ferry; you forget that *his*
  Reign is concluded; whatsoe'er betide,
He won't be sovereign more: you've lost your labour,
For at the best he will but be your neighbour.

LXXIII

"However, I knew what to think of it,
  When I beheld you in your jesting way,
Flitting and whispering round about the spit
  Where Belial, upon duty for the day,   580
With Fox's lard was basting William Pitt,
  His pupil; I knew what to think, I say:
That fellow even in hell breeds farther ills;
I'll have him *gagg'd*—'twas one of his own bills.

LXXIV

"Call Junius!" From the crowd a shadow stalk'd,
  And at the name there was a general squeeze,
So that the very ghosts no longer walk'd
  In comfort, at their own aërial ease,
But were all ramm'd, and jamm'd (but to be balk'd,
  As we shall see), and jostled hands and knees,   590
Like wind compress'd and pent within a bladder,
Or like a human colic, which is sadder.

LXXV

The shadow came—a tall, thin, grey-hair'd figure,
  That look'd as it had been a shade on earth;
Quick in its motions, with an air of vigour,
  But nought to mark its breeding or its birth;
Now it wax'd little, then again grew bigger,
  With now an air of gloom, or savage mirth;
But as you gazed upon its features, they
Changed every instant—to *what*, none could say.   600

LXXVI

The more intently the ghosts gazed, the less
  Could they distinguish whose the features were ;
The Devil himself seem'd puzzled even to guess ;
  They varied like a dream—now here, now there ;
And several people swore from out the press,
  They knew him perfectly ; and one could swear
He was his father : upon which another
Was sure he was his mother's cousin's brother :

LXXVII

Another, that he was a duke, or knight,
  An orator, a lawyer, or a priest,   610
A nabob, a man-midwife ; but the wight
  Mysterious changed his countenance at least
As oft as they their minds : though in full sight
  He stood, the puzzle only was increased ;
The man was a phantasmagoria in
Himself—he was so volatile and thin.

LXXVIII

The moment that you had pronounced him *one*,
  Presto ! his face changed, and he was another ;
And when that change was hardly well put on,
  It varied, till I don't think his own mother 620
(If that he had a mother) would her son
  Have known, he shifted so from one to t'other ;
Till guessing from a pleasure grew a task,
At this epistolary " Iron Mask."

LXXIX

For sometimes he like Cerberus would seem—
  " Three gentlemen at once " (as sagely says
Good Mrs. Malaprop) ; then you might deem
  That he was not even *one* ; now many rays
Were flashing round him ; and now a thick steam
  Hid him from sight—like fogs on London days :
Now Burke, now Tooke, he grew to people's fancies,
And certes often like Sir Philip Francis. 632

LXXX

I've an hypothesis—'tis quite my own;
   I never let it out till now, for fear
Of doing people harm about the throne,
   And injuring some minister or peer,
On whom the stigma might perhaps be blown:
   It is—my gentle public, lend thine ear!
'Tis, that what Junius we are wont to call
Was *really, truly*, nobody at all.   640

LXXXI

I don't see wherefore letters should not be
   Written without hands, since we daily view
Them written without heads; and books, we see,
   Are fill'd as well without the latter too:
And really till we fix on somebody
   For certain sure to claim them as his due,
Their author, like the Niger's mouth, will bother
The world to say if *there* be mouth or author.

LXXXII

" And who and what art thou ? " the Archangel said.
   " For *that* you may consult my title-page,"   650
Replied this mighty shadow of a shade:
   " If I have kept my secret half an age,
I scarce shall tell it now."—" Canst thou upbraid,"
   Continued Michael, " George Rex, or allege
Aught further ? " Junius answer'd, " You had better
First ask him for *his* answer to my letter:

LXXXIII

" My charges upon record will outlast
   The brass of both his epitaph and tomb."
" Repent'st thou not," said Michael, " of some past
   Exaggeration ? something which may doom   660
Thyself if false, as him if true ? Thou wast
   Too bitter—is it not so ?—in thy gloom
Of passion ? "—" Passion ! " cried the phantom dim,
" I loved my country, and I hated him.

LXXXIV

" What I have written, I have written : let
     The rest be on his head or mine ! " So spoke
Old " Nominis Umbra ; " and while speaking yet,
     Away he melted in celestial smoke.
Then Satan said to Michael, " Don't forget   669
     To call George Washington, and John Horne Tooke,
And Franklin ; "—but at this time there was heard
A cry for room, though not a phantom stirr'd.

LXXXV

At length with jostling, elbowing, and the aid
     Of cherubim appointed to that post,
The devil Asmodeus to the circle made
     His way, and look'd as if his journey cost
Some trouble.   When his burden down he laid,
     " What 's this ? " cried Michael ; " why, 'tis not a
          ghost ? "
" I know it," quoth the incubus ; " but he
Shall be one, if you leave the affair to me.   680

LXXXVI

" Confound the renegado ! I have sprain'd
     My left wing, he 's so heavy ; one would think
Some of his works about his neck were chain'd.
     But to the point ; while hovering o'er the brink
Of Skiddaw (where as usual it still rain'd),
     I saw a taper, far below me, wink,
And stooping, caught this fellow at a libel —
No less on history than the Holy Bible.

LXXXVII

" The former is the devil's scripture, and
     The latter yours, good Michael : so the affair   690
Belongs to all of us, you understand.
     I snatch'd him up just as you see him there,
And brought him off for sentence out of hand :
     I 've scarcely been ten minutes in the air—
At least a quarter it can hardly be :
I dare say that his wife is still at tea."

LXXXVIII

Here Satan said, " I know this man of old,
   And have expected him for some time here ;
A sillier fellow you will scarce behold,
   Or more conceited in his petty sphere :   700
But surely it was not worth while to fold
   Such trash below your wing, Asmodeus dear :
We had the poor wretch safe (without being bored
With carriage) coming of his own accord.

LXXXIX

" But since he 's here, let 's see what he has done."
    " Done ! " cried Asmodeus, " he anticipates
The very business you are now upon,
   And scribbles as if head clerk to the Fates.
Who knows to what his ribaldry may run,   709
   When such an ass as this, like Balaam's, prates ? "
" Let 's hear," quoth Michael, " what he has to say :
You know we're bound to that in every way."

XC

Now the bard, glad to get an audience, which
   By no means often was his case below,
Began to cough, and hawk, and hem, and pitch
   His voice into that awful note of woe
To all unhappy hearers within reach
   Of poets when the tide of rhyme 's in flow ;
But stuck fast with his first hexameter,
Not one of all whose gouty feet would stir.   720

XCI

But ere the spavin'd dactyls could be spurr'd
   Into recitative, in great dismay
Both cherubim and seraphim were heard
   To murmur loudly through their long array ;
And Michael rose ere he could get a word
   Of all his founder'd verses under way,
And cried, " For God's sake stop, my friend ! 'twere
     best—
Non Di, non homines—you know the rest."

XCII

A general bustle spread throughout the throng,
  Which seem'd to hold all verse in detestation ;   730
The angels had of course enough of song
  When upon service ; and the generation
Of ghosts had heard too much in life, not long
  Before, to profit by a new occasion :
The monarch, mute till then, exclaim'd, " What !
    what !
Pye come again ? No more—no more of that ! "

XCIII

The tumult grew ; an universal cough
  Convulsed the skies, as during a debate,
When Castlereagh has been up long enough
  (Before he was first minister of state,   740
I mean—the *slaves hear now*) ; some cried " Off, off ! "
  As at a farce ; till, grown quite desperate,
The bard Saint Peter pray'd to interpose
(Himself an author) only for his prose.

XCIV

The varlet was not an ill-favour'd knave ;
  A good deal like a vulture in the face,
With a hook nose and a hawk's eye, which gave
  A smart and sharper-looking sort of grace
To his whole aspect, which, though rather grave,
  Was by no means so ugly as his case ;   750
But that, indeed, was hopeless as can be,
Quite a poetic felony " *de se.*"

XCV

Then Michael blew his trump, and still'd the noise
  With one still greater, as is yet the mode
On earth besides ; except some grumbling voice,
  Which now and then will make a slight inroad
Upon decorous silence, few will twice
  Lift up their lungs when fairly overcrow'd ;
And now the bard could plead his own bad cause,
With all the attitudes of self-applause.   760

XCVI

He said—(I only give the heads)—he said,
 He meant no harm in scribbling; 'twas his way
Upon all topics; 'twas, besides, his bread,
 Of which he butter'd both sides; 'twould delay
Too long the assembly (he was pleased to dread),
 And take up rather more time than a day,
To name his works—he would but cite a few—
"Wat Tyler"—"Rhymes on Blenheim"—"Water-
  loo."

XCVII

He had written praises of a regicide;
 He had written praises of all kings whatever;   770
He had written for republics far and wide,
 And then against them bitterer than ever;
For pantisocracy he once had cried
 Aloud, a scheme less moral than 'twas clever;
Then grew a hearty anti-jacobin—
Had turn'd his coat—and would have turn'd his skin.

XCVIII

He had sung against all battles, and again
 In their high praise and glory; he had call'd
Reviewing "the ungentle craft," and then
 Become as base a critic as e'er crawl'd—   780
Fed, paid, and pamper'd by the very men
 By whom his muse and morals had been maul'd:
He had written much blank verse, and blanker prose,
And more of both than anybody knows.

XCIX

He had written Wesley's life:—here turning round
 To Satan, "Sir, I'm ready to write yours,
In two octavo volumes, nicely bound,
 With notes and preface, all that most allures
The pious purchaser; and there's no ground
 For fear, for I can choose my own reviewers: 790
So let me have the proper documents,
That I may add you to my other saints."

C

Satan bow'd, and was silent. "Well, if you,
　　With amiable modesty, decline
My offer, what says Michael ? There are few
　　Whose memoirs could be render'd more divine.
Mine is a pen of all work ; not so new
　　As it was once, but I would make you shine
Like your own trumpet. By the way, my own
Has more of brass in it, and is as well blown.   800

CI

"But talking about trumpets, here's my Vision !
　　Now you shall judge, all people ; yes, you shall
Judge with my judgment, and by my decision
　　Be guided who shall enter heaven or fall.
I settle all these things by intuition,
　　Times present, past, to come, and all,
Like King Alfonso. When I thus see double,
I save the Deity some worlds of trouble."

CII

He ceased, and drew forth an MS. ; and no
　　Persuasion on the part of devils, saints,   810
Or angels, now could stop the torrent ; so
　　He read the first three lines of the contents ;
But at the fourth, the whole spiritual show
　　Had vanish'd, with variety of scents,
Ambrosial and sulphureous, as they sprang,
Like lightning, off from his "melodious twang."

CIII

Those grand heroics acted as a spell ;
　　The angels stopp'd their ears and plied their pinions ;
The devils ran howling, deafen'd, down to hell ;
　　The ghosts fled, gibbering, for their own dominions—   821
　　(For 'tis not yet decided where they dwell,
　　And I leave every man to his opinions) ;
Michael took refuge in his trump—but, lo !
His teeth were set on edge, he could not blow !

CIV

Saint Peter, who has hitherto been known
    For an impetuous saint, upraised his keys,
And at the fifth line knocked the poet down;
    Who fell like Phæton, but more at ease,
Into his lake, for there he did not drown;
    A different web being by the Destinies   830
Woven for the Laureate's final wreath, whene'er
Reform shall happen either here or there.

CV

He first sank to the bottom—like his works,
    But soon rose to the surface—like himself;
For all corrupted things are buoy'd like corks,
    By their own rottenness, light as an elf,
Or wisp that flits o'er a morass: he lurks,
    It may be, still, like dull books on a shelf,
In his own den, to scrawl some "Life" or "Vision,"
As Welborn says—"the devil turn'd precisian."

CVI

As for the rest, to come to the conclusion   841
    Of this true dream, the telescope is gone
Which kept my optics free from all delusion,
    And show'd me what I in my turn have shown;
All I saw farther, in the last confusion,
    Was, that King George slipp'd into heaven for one;
And when the tumult dwindled to a calm,
I left him practising the hundredth psalm.

FROM 'CHILDE HAROLD'S PILGRIMAGE.'

TO IANTHE

NOT in those climes where I have late been straying,
Though Beauty long hath there been matchless
   deem'd ;
Not in those visions to the heart displaying
Forms which it sighs but to have only dream'd,
Hath aught like thee in truth or fancy seem'd :
Nor, having seen thee, shall I vainly seek
To paint those charms which varied as they beam'd—
To such as see thee not my words were weak ;
To those who gaze on thee what language could they
   speak ?

Ah ! may'st thou ever be what now thou art,   10
Nor unbeseem the promise of thy spring,
As fair in form, as warm yet pure in heart,
Love's image upon earth without his wing,
And guileless beyond Hope's imagining !
And surely she who now so fondly rears
Thy youth, in thee, thus hourly brightening,
Beholds the rainbow of her future years,
Before whose heavenly hues all sorrow disappears.

Young Peri of the West !—'tis well for me
My years already doubly number thine ;   20
My loveless eye unmoved may gaze on thee,
And safely view thy ripening beauties shine ;
Happy, I ne'er shall see them in decline ;
Happier, that while all younger hearts shall bleed,
Mine shall escape the doom thine eyes assign
To those whose admiration shall succeed,
But mix'd with pangs to Love's even loveliest hours
   decreed.

Oh! let that eye, which, wild as the Gazelle's,
Now brightly bold or beautifully shy,
Wins as it wanders, dazzles where it dwells,   30
Glance o'er this page, nor to my verse deny
That smile for which my breast might vainly sigh
Could I to thee be ever more than friend:
This much, dear maid, accord; nor question why
To one so young my strain I would commend,
But bid me with my wreath one matchless lily blend.

Such is thy name with this my verse entwined;
And long as kinder eyes a look shall cast
On Harold's page, Ianthe's here enshrined
Shall thus be first beheld, forgotten last: 40
My days once number'd, should this homage past
Attract thy fairy fingers near the lyre
Of him who hail'd thee, loveliest as thou wast,
Such is the most my memory may desire;
Though more than Hope can claim, could Friendship
    less require?

CHILDE HAROLD

FROM CANTO I, i–xi

OH, thou! in Hellas deem'd of heavenly birth,
Muse! form'd or fabled at the minstrel's will!
Since shamed full oft by later lyres on earth,
Mine dares not call thee from thy sacred hill:
Yet there I've wander'd by thy vaunted rill;
Yes! sigh'd o'er Delphi's long deserted shrine,
Where, save that feeble fountain, all is still;
Nor mote my shell awake the weary Nine
To grace so plain a tale—this lowly lay of mine.

Whilome in Albion's isle there dwelt a youth,   10
Who ne in virtue's ways did take delight;
But spent his days in riot most uncouth,
And vex'd with mirth the drowsy ear of Night.

Ah me! in sooth he was a shameless wight,
Sore given to revel and ungodly glee;
Few earthly things found favour in his sight
Save concubines and carnal companie,
And flaunting wassailers of high and low degree.

Childe Harold was he hight:—but whence his name
And lineage long, it suits me not to say;   20
Suffice it, that perchance they were of fame,
And had been glorious in another day:
But one sad losel soils a name for aye,
However mighty in the olden time;
Nor all that heralds rake from coffin'd clay,
Nor florid prose, nor honeyed lies of rhyme,
Can blazon evil deeds, or consecrate a crime.

Childe Harold bask'd him in the noontide sun,
Disporting there like any other fly;
Nor deem'd before his little day was done   30
One blast might chill him into misery.
But long ere scarce a third of his pass'd by,
Worse than adversity the Childe befell;
He felt the fulness of satiety:
Then loathed he in his native land to dwell,
Which seem'd to him more lone than Eremite's sad cell.

For he through Sin's long labyrinth had run,
Nor made atonement when he did amiss,
Had sigh'd to many though he loved but one,
And that loved one, alas! could ne'er be his.   40
Ah, happy she! to 'scape from him whose kiss
Had been pollution unto aught so chaste;
Who soon had left her charms for vulgar bliss,
And spoil'd her goodly lands to gild his waste,
Nor calm domestic peace had ever deign'd to taste.

And now Childe Harold was sore sick at heart,
And from his fellow bacchanals would flee;
'Tis said, at times the sullen tear would start,
But Pride congeal'd the drop within his ee:

Apart he stalk'd in joyless reverie,   50
And from his native land resolved to go,
And visit scorching climes beyond the sea:
With pleasure drugg'd, he almost long'd for woe,
And e'en for change of scene would seek the shades
    below.

The Childe departed from his father's hall:
It was a vast and venerable pile;
So old, it seemed only not to fall,
Yet strength was pillar'd in each massy aisle.
Monastic dome! condemn'd to uses vile!
Where Superstition once had made her den   60
Now Paphian girls were known to sing and smile;
    And monks might deem their time was come agen,
If ancient tales say true, nor wrong these holy men.

Yet oft-times in his maddest mirthful mood
Strange pangs would flash along Childe Harold's
    brow,
As if the memory of some deadly feud
Or disappointed passion lurk'd below:
But this none knew, nor haply cared to know;
For his was not that open, artless soul
That feels relief by bidding sorrow flow,   70
    Nor sought he friend to counsel or condole,
Whate'er this grief mote be, which he could not control.

And none did love him: though to hall and bower
He gather'd revellers from far and near,
He knew them flatt'rers of the festal hour;
The heartless parasites of present cheer.
Yea! none did love him—not his lemans dear—
But pomp and power alone are woman's care,
And where these are light Eros finds a feere;
Maidens, like moths, are ever caught by glare,   80
And Mammon wins his way where Seraphs might
    despair.

Childe Harold had a mother—not forgot,
Though parting from that mother he did shun;
A sister whom he loved, but saw her not
Before his weary pilgrimage begun:
If friends he had, he bade adieu to none.
Yet deem not thence his breast a breast of steel:
Ye, who have known what 'tis to dote upon
A few dear objects, will in sadness feel
Such partings break the heart they fondly hope to heal.

His house, his home, his heritage, his lands,   91
The laughing dames in whom he did delight,
Whose large blue eyes, fair locks, and snowy hands,
Might shake the saintship of an anchorite,
And long had fed his youthful appetite;
His goblets brimm'd with every costly wine,
And all that mote to luxury invite,
Without a sigh he left, to cross the brine,
And traverse Paynim shores, and pass Earth's central
line.

CHILDE HAROLD'S DEPARTURE

1

ADIEU, adieu! my native shore
    Fades o'er the waters blue;
The night-winds sigh, the breakers roar,
    And shrieks the wild sea-mew.
Yon sun that sets upon the sea
    We follow in his flight;
Farewell awhile to him and thee,
    My native Land—Good Night!

2

A few short hours and he will rise
    To give the morrow birth;   10
And I shall hail the main and skies,
    But not my mother earth.

Deserted is my own good hall,
  Its hearth is desolate;
Wild weeds are gathering on the wall;
  My dog howls at the gate.

3

"Come hither, hither, my little page!
  Why dost thou weep and wail?
Or dost thou dread the billows' rage,
  Or tremble at the gale?   20
But dash the tear-drop from thine eye;
  Our ship is swift and strong:
Our fleetest falcon scarce can fly
  More merrily along."

4

"Let winds be shrill, let waves roll high,
  I fear not wave nor wind:
Yet marvel not, Sir Childe, that I
  Am sorrowful in mind;
For I have from my father gone,
  A mother whom I love,   30
And have no friend, save these alone,
  But thee—and one above.

5

"My father bless'd me fervently,
  Yet did not much complain;
But sorely will my mother sigh
  Till I come back again.'—
"Enough, enough, my little lad!
  Such tears become thine eye;
If I thy guileless bosom had,
  Mine own would not be dry.   40

6

"Come hither, hither, my staunch yeoman,
  Why dost thou look so pale?
Or dost thou dread a French foeman?
  Or shiver at the gale?"—

" Deem'st thou I tremble for my life ?
   Sir Childe, I'm not so weak ;
But thinking on an absent wife
   Will blanch a faithful cheek.

7

" My spouse and boys dwell near thy hall,
   Along the bordering lake,   50
And when they on their father call,
   What answer shall she make ? "—
" Enough, enough, my yeoman good,
   Thy grief let none gainsay ;
But I, who am of lighter mood,
   Will laugh to flee away."

8

For who would trust the seeming sighs
   Of wife or paramour ?
Fresh feeres will dry the bright blue eyes
   We late saw streaming o'er.   60
For pleasures past I do not grieve,
   Nor perils gathering near ;
My greatest grief is that I leave
   No thing that claims a tear.

9

And now I'm in the world alone,
   Upon the wide, wide sea :
But why should I for others groan,
   When none will sigh for me ?
Perchance my dog will whine in vain,
   Till fed by stranger hands ;   70
But long ere I come back again
   He'd tear me where he stands.

10

With thee, my bark, I'll swiftly go
   Athwart the foaming brine ;
Nor care what land thou bear'st me to,
   So not again to mine.

Welcome, welcome, ye dark-blue waves !
  And when you fail my sight,
Welcome, ye deserts and ye caves !
  My native Land—Good Night !   **80**

PARNASSUS

(Canto I, lx–lxii.)

Oh, thou Parnassus ! whom I now survey,
Not in the phrensy of a dreamer's eye,
Not in the fabled landscape of a lay,
But soaring snow-clad through thy native sky,
In the wild pomp of mountain majesty !
What marvel if I thus essay to sing ?
The humblest of thy pilgrims passing by
Would gladly woo thine Echoes with his string,
Though from thy heights no more one Muse will wave
    her wing.   9

Oft have I dream'd of Thee ! whose glorious name
Who knows not, knows not man's divinest lore :
And now I view thee, 'tis, alas ! with shame
That I in feeblest accents must adore.
When I recount thy worshippers of yore
I tremble, and can only bend the knee ;
Nor raise my voice, nor vainly dare to soar,
But gaze beneath thy cloudy canopy
In silent joy to think at last I look on Thee !

Happier in this than mightiest bards have been,
Whose fate to distant homes confined their lot,   **20**
Shall I unmoved behold the hallow'd scene,
Which others rave of, though they know it not ?
Though here no more Apollo haunts his grot,
And thou, the Muses' seat, art now their grave,
Some gentle spirit still pervades the spot,
Sighs in the gale, keeps silence in the cave,
And glides with glassy foot o'er yon melodious wave

TO INEZ

1

NAY, smile not at my sullen brow;
　　Alas! I cannot smile again:
Yet Heaven avert that ever thou
　　Shouldst weep, and haply weep in vain.

2

And dost thou ask what secret woe
　　I bear, corroding joy and youth?
And wilt thou vainly seek to know
　　A pang, ev'n thou must fail to soothe?

3

It is not love, it is not hate,
　　Nor low Ambition's honours lost,
That bids me loathe my present state,
　　And fly from all I prized the most:

4

It is that weariness which springs
　　From all I meet, or hear, or see:
To me no pleasure Beauty brings;
　　Thine eyes have scarce a charm for me.

5

It is that settled, ceaseless gloom
　　The fabled Hebrew wanderer bore;
That will not look beyond the tomb,
　　But cannot hope for rest before.

6

What Exile from himself can flee?
　　To zones though more and more remote,
Still, still pursues, where'er I be,
　　The blight of life—the demon Thought.

7

Yet others rapt in pleasure seem,
  And taste of all that I forsake;
Oh! may they still of transport dream,
  And ne'er, at least like me, awake!

8

Through many a clime 'tis mine to go,
  With many a retrospection curst;   30
And all my solace is to know,
  Whate'er betides, I've known the worst.

9

What is that worst? Nay, do not ask—
  In pity from the search forbear:
Smile on—nor venture to unmask
  Man's heart, and view the Hell that's there.

IMMORTALITY

(Canto II, iii–viii)

Son of the morning, rise! approach you here!
Come—but molest not yon defenceless urn:
Look on this spot—a nation's sepulchre!
Abode of gods, whose shrines no longer burn.
Even gods must yield—religions take their turn:
'Twas Jove's—'tis Mahomet's—and other creeds
Will rise with other years, till man shall learn
Vainly his incense soars, his victim bleeds;
Poor child of Doubt and Death, whose hope is built on
  reeds.

Bound to the earth, he lifts his eye to heaven—   10
Is't not enough, unhappy thing! to know
Thou art? Is this a boon so kindly given,
That being, thou wouldst be again, and go,

Thou know'st not, reck'st not, to what region, so
On earth no more, but mingled with the skies ?
Still wilt thou dream on future joy and woe ?
Regard and weigh yon dust before it flies :
That little urn saith more than thousand homilies.

Or burst the vanish'd Hero's lofty mound ;
Far on the solitary shore he sleeps :   20
He fell, and falling nations mourn'd around ;
But now not one of saddening thousands weeps,
Nor warlike worshipper his vigil keeps
Where demi-gods appear'd, as records tell.
Remove yon skull from out the scatter'd heaps :
Is that a temple where a God may dwell ?
Why ev'n the worm at last disdains her shatter'd cell !

Look on its broken arch, its ruin'd wall,
Its chambers desolate, and portals foul :
Yes, this was once Ambition's airy hall,   30
The dome of Thought, the palace of the Soul :
Behold through each lack-lustre, eyeless hole,
The gay recess of Wisdom and of Wit,
And Passion's host, that never brook'd control :
Can all saint, sage, or sophist ever writ,
People this lonely tower, this tenement refit ?

Well didst thou speak, Athena's wisest son !
" All that we know is, nothing can be known."
Why should we shrink from what we cannot shun ?
Each hath his pang, but feeble sufferers groan   40
With brain-born dreams of evil all their own.
Pursue what Chance or Fate proclaimeth best ;
Peace waits us on the shores of Acheron :
There no forced banquet claims the sated guest,
But Silence spreads the couch of ever welcome rest.

Yet if, as holiest men have deem'd, there be
A land of souls beyond that sable shore,
To shame the doctrine of the Sadducee
And sophists, madly vain of dubious lore :

How sweet it were in concert to adore   50
With those who made our mortal labours light !
To hear each voice we fear'd to hear no more !
Behold each mighty shade reveal'd to sight,
The Bactrian, Samian sage, and all who taught the right!

SAPPHO

(CANTO II, xxxix–xli)

Childe Harold sail'd, and pass'd the barren spot,
Where sad Penelope o'erlook'd the wave ;
And onward view'd the mount, not yet forgot,
The lover's refuge, and the Lesbian's grave.
Dark Sappho ! could not verse immortal save
That breast imbued with such immortal fire ?
Could she not live who life eternal gave ?
If life eternal may await the lyre,
That only Heaven to which Earth's children may aspire.

'Twas on a Grecian autumn's gentle eve   10
Childe Harold hail'd Leucadia's cape afar ;
A spot he longed to see, nor cared to leave :
Oft did he mark the scenes of vanish'd war,
Actium, Lepanto, fatal Trafalgar ;
Mark them unmoved, for he would not delight
(Born beneath some remote inglorious star)
In themes of bloody fray, or gallant fight,
But loathed the bravo's trade, and laughed at martial
        wight.

But when he saw the evening star above
Leucadia's far-projecting rock of woe,   20
And hail'd the last resort of fruitless love,
He felt, or deem'd he felt, no common glow :
And as the stately vessel glided slow
Beneath the shadow of that ancient mount,
He watch'd the billows' melancholy flow,
And, sunk albeit in thought as he was wont,
More placid seem'd his eye, and smooth his pallid front.

GREECE

(CANTO II, lxxiii–lxxvii, lxxxiv–xciii)

Fair Greece ! sad relic of departed worth !
Immortal, though no more ; though fallen, great !
Who now shall lead thy scatter'd children forth,
And long accustom'd bondage uncreate ?
Not such thy sons who whilome did await,
The hopeless warriors of a willing doom,
In bleak Thermopylæ's sepulchral strait—
Oh ! who that gallant spirit shall resume,
Leap from Eurotas' banks, and call thee from the
    tomb ?

Spirit of freedom ! when on Phyle's brow   10
Thou sat'st with Thrasybulus and his train,
Couldst thou forebode the dismal hour which now
Dims the green beauties of thine Attic plain ?
Not thirty tyrants now enforce the chain,
But every carle can lord it o'er thy land ;
Nor rise thy sons, but idly rail in vain,
Trembling beneath the scourge of Turkish hand ;
From birth till death enslaved ; in word, in deed,
    unmann'd.

In all save form alone, how changed ! and who
That marks the fire still sparkling in each eye,   20
Who would but deem their bosoms burn'd anew
With thy unquenched beam, lost Liberty !
And many dream withal the hour is nigh
That gives them back their fathers' heritage :
For foreign arms and aid they fondly sigh,
Nor solely dare encounter hostile rage,
Or tear their name defiled from Slavery's mournful
    page.

Hereditary bondsmen ! know ye not
Who would be free themselves must strike the blow ?
By their right arms the conquest must be wrought ?
Will Gaul or Muscovite redress ye ? no !   31
True, they may lay your proud despoilers low,
But not for you will Freedom's altars flame.
Shades of the Helots ! triumph o'er your foe !
Greece ! change thy lords, thy state is still the same ;
Thy glorious day is o'er, but not thy years of shame.

The city won for Allah from the Giaour,
The Giaour from Othman's race again may wrest ;
And the Serai's impenetrable tower
Receive the fiery Frank, her former guest ;   40
Or Wahab's rebel brood, who dared divest
The prophet's tomb of all its pious spoil,
May wind their path of blood along the West ;
But ne'er will freedom seek this fated soil,
But slave succeed to slave through years of endless toil.

.   .   .   .

When riseth Lacedemon's hardihood,
When Thebes Epaminondas rears again,
When Athens' children are with hearts endued,
When Grecian mothers shall give birth to men,
Then may'st thou be restored ; but not till then.   50
A thousand years scarce serve to form a state ;
An hour may lay it in the dust : and when
Can man its shatter'd splendour renovate,
Recall its virtues back, and vanquish Time and Fate ?

And yet how lovely in thine age of woe,
Land of lost gods and godlike men, art thou !
Thy vales of evergreen, thy hills of snow,
Proclaim thee Nature's varied favourite now :
Thy fanes, thy temples to thy surface bow,
Commingling slowly with heroic earth,   60
Broke by the share of every rustic plough :
So perish monuments of mortal birth,
So perish all in turn, save well-recorded Worth ;

Save where some solitary column mourns
Above its prostrate brethren of the cave;
Save where Tritonia's airy shrine adorns
Colonna's cliff, and gleams along the wave;
Save o'er some warrior's half-forgotten grave,
Where the gray stones and unmolested grass
Ages, but not oblivion, feebly brave;   70
While strangers only not regardless pass,
Lingering like me, perchance, to gaze, and sigh "Alas!"

Yet are thy skies as blue, thy crags as wild;
Sweet are thy groves, and verdant are thy fields,
Thine olive ripe as when Minerva smiled,
And still his honey'd wealth Hymettus yields;
There the blithe bee his fragrant fortress builds,
The freeborn wanderer of thy mountain-air;
Apollo still thy long, long summer gilds,
Still in his beam Mendeli's marbles glare;   80
Art, Glory, Freedom fail, but Nature still is fair.

Where'er we tread 'tis haunted, holy ground;
No earth of thine is lost in vulgar mould,
But one vast realm of wonder spreads around,
And all the Muse's tales seem truly told,
Till the sense aches with gazing to behold
The scenes our earliest dreams have dwelt upon;
Each hill and dale, each deepening glen and wold
Defies the power which crush'd thy temples gone:
Age shakes Athena's tower, but spares gray Marathon.

The sun, the soil, but not the slave, the same;   91
Unchanged in all except its foreign lord;
Preserves alike its bounds and boundless fame
The Battle-field, where Persia's victim horde
First bow'd beneath the brunt of Hellas' sword,
As on the morn to distant Glory dear,
When Marathon became a magic word;
Which utter'd, to the hearer's eye appear
The camp, the host, the fight, the conqueror's career,

The flying Mede, his shaftless broken bow;   100
The fiery Greek, his red pursuing spear;
Mountains above, Earth's, Ocean's plain below;
Death in the front, Destruction in the rear!
Such was the scene—what now remaineth here?
What sacred trophy marks the hallow'd ground,
Recording Freedom's smile and Asia's tear?
The rifled urn, the violated mound,
The dust thy courser's hoof, rude stranger! spurns
    around.

Yet to the remnants of thy splendour past
Shall pilgrims, pensive, but unwearied, throng;   110
Long shall the voyager, with th' Ionian blast,
Hail the bright clime of battle and of song;
Long shall thine annals and immortal tongue
Fill with thy fame the youth of many a shore;
Boast of the aged! lesson of the young!
Which sages venerate and bards adore,
As Pallas and the Muse unveil their awful lore.

The parted bosom clings to wonted home,
If aught that's kindred cheer the welcome hearth;
He that is lonely, hither let him roam,   120
And gaze complacent on congenial earth.
Greece is no lightsome land of social mirth:
But he whom Sadness sootheth may abide,
And scarce regret the region of his birth,
When wandering slow by Delphi's sacred side,
Or gazing o'er the plains where Greek and Persian died.

Let such approach this consecrated land,
And pass in peace along the magic waste;
But spare its relics—let no busy hand
Deface the scenes, already how defaced!   130
Not for such purpose were these altars placed:
Revere the remnants nations once revered:
So may our country's name be undisgraced,
So may'st thou prosper where thy youth was rear'd,
By every honest joy of love and life endear'd!

BEREAVEMENT

(Canto II, xcviii)

What is the worst of woes that wait on age ?
What stamps the wrinkle deeper on the brow ?
To view each loved one blotted from life's page,
And be alone on earth, as I am now.
Before the Chastener humbly let me bow,
O'er hearts divided and o'er hopes destroy'd :
Roll on, vain days ! full reckless may ye flow,
Since Time hath reft whate'er my soul enjoy'd,
And with the ills of Eld mine earlier years alloy'd.

ON LEAVING ENGLAND

(Canto III, i, ii)

Is thy face like thy mother's, my fair child !
ADA ! sole daughter of my house and heart ?
When last I saw thy young blue eyes they smiled,
And then we parted,—not as now we part,
But with a hope.—

> Awaking with a start,
The waters heave around me ; and on high
The winds lift up their voices : I depart,
Whither I know not ; but the hour 's gone by,
When Albion's lessening shores could grieve or glad
mine eye.

Once more upon the waters ! yet once more !   10
And the waves bound beneath me as a steed
That knows his rider.   Welcome to their roar !
Swift be their guidance, wheresoe'er it lead !
Though the strain'd mast should quiver as a reed,
And the rent canvas fluttering strew the gale,
Still must I on ; for I am as a weed,
Flung from the rock, on Ocean's foam to sail
Where'er the surge may sweep, the tempest's breath
prevail.

CONSOLATION

(Canto III, xiii–xv)

Where rose the mountains, there to him were friends ;
Where roll'd the ocean, thereon was his home ;
Where a blue sky, and glowing clime, extends,
He had the passion and the power to roam ;
The desert, forest, cavern, breaker's foam,
Were unto him companionship ; they spake
A mutual language, clearer than the tome
Of his land's tongue, which he would oft forsake
For Nature's pages glass'd by sunbeams on the lake.

Like the Chaldean, he could watch the stars,   10
Till he had peopled them with beings bright
As their own beams ; and earth, and earth-born jars,
And human frailties, were forgotten quite :
Could he have kept his spirit to that flight
He had been happy ; but this clay will sink
Its spark immortal, envying it the light
To which it mounts, as if to break the link
That keeps us from yon heaven which woos us to its brink.

But in Man's dwellings he became a thing
Restless and worn, and stern and wearisome,   20
Droop'd as a wild-born falcon with clipt wing,
To whom the boundless air alone were home :
Then came his fit again, which to o'ercome,
As eagerly the barr'd-up bird will beat
His breast and beak against his wiry dome
Till the blood tinge his plumage, so the heat
Of his impeded soul would through his bosom eat.

WATERLOO

(Canto III, xvii, xxi–xxx)

Stop !—for thy tread is on an Empire's dust !
An Earthquake's spoil is sepulchred below !
Is the spot mark'd with no colossal bust ?
Nor column trophied for triumphal show ?
None ; but the moral's truth tells simpler so,
As the ground was before, thus let it be ;—
How that red rain hath made the harvest grow !
And is this all the world has gain'd by thee,
Thou first and last of fields ! king-making Victory ?

. . . .

There was a sound of revelry by night,   10
And Belgium's capital had gather'd then
Her Beauty and her Chivalry, and bright
The lamps shone o'er fair women and brave men ;
A thousand hearts beat happily ; and when
Music arose with its voluptuous swell,
Soft eyes look'd love to eyes which spake again,
And all went merry as a marriage bell ;
But hush ! hark ! a deep sound strikes like a rising
    knell !

Did ye not hear it ?—No ; 'twas but the wind,
Or the car rattling o'er the stony street ;   20
On with the dance ! let joy be unconfined ;
No sleep till morn, when Youth and Pleasure meet
To chase the glowing Hours with flying feet—
But hark !—that heavy sound breaks in once more,
As if the clouds its echo would repeat ;
And nearer, clearer, deadlier than before !
Arm ! Arm ! it is—it is—the cannon's opening roar !

Within a window'd niche of that high hall
Sate Brunswick's fated chieftain ; he did hear
That sound the first amidst the festival,   30
And caught its tone with Death's prophetic ear ;

And when they smiled because he deem'd it near,
His heart more truly knew that peal too well
Which stretch'd his father on a bloody bier,
And roused the vengeance blood alone could quell;
He rush'd into the field, and, foremost fighting, fell.

Ah! then and there was hurrying to and fro,
And gathering tears, and tremblings of distress,
And cheeks all pale, which but an hour ago
Blush'd at the praise of their own loveliness; 40
And there were sudden partings, such as press
The life from out young hearts, and choking sighs
Which ne'er might be repeated; who could guess
If ever more should meet those mutual eyes,
Since upon night so sweet such awful morn could rise!

And there was mounting in hot haste: the steed,
The mustering squadron, and the clattering car,
Went pouring forward with impetuous speed,
And swiftly forming in the ranks of war;
And the deep thunder peal on peal afar; 50
And near, the beat of the alarming drum
Roused up the soldier ere the morning star;
While throng'd the citizens with terror dumb,
Or whispering, with white lips—"The foe! they
  come! they come!"

And wild and high the "Cameron's gathering" rose!
The war-note of Lochiel, which Albyn's hills
Have heard, and heard, too, have her Saxon foes:—
How in the noon of night that pibroch thrills,
Savage and shrill! But with the breath which fills
Their mountain-pipe, so fill the mountaineers 60
With the fierce native daring which instils
The stirring memory of a thousand years,
And Evan's, Donald's fame rings in each clansman's ears!

And Ardennes waves above them her green leaves,
Dewy with nature's tear-drops as they pass,
Grieving, if aught inanimate e'er grieves,
Over the unreturning brave,—alas!
Ere evening to be trodden like the grass

Which now beneath them, but above shall grow
In its next verdure, when this fiery mass   70
Of living valour, rolling on the foe
And burning with high hope, shall moulder cold and
    low.

Last noon beheld them full of lusty life,
Last eve in Beauty's circle proudly gay,
The midnight brought the signal-sound of strife,
The morn the marshalling in arms,—the day
Battle's magnificently stern array!
The thunder-clouds close o'er it, which when rent
The earth is cover'd thick with other clay,   79
Which her own clay shall cover, heap'd and pent,
Rider and horse,—friend, foe,—in one red burial blent!

Their praise is hymn'd by loftier harps than mine:
Yet one I would select from that proud throng,
Partly because they blend me with his line,
And partly that I did his sire some wrong,
And partly that bright names will hallow song;
And his was of the bravest, and when shower'd
The death-bolts deadliest the thinn'd files along,
Even where the thickest of war's tempest lower'd,
They reach'd no nobler breast than thine, young gallant
    Howard!   90

There have been tears and breaking hearts for thee,
And mine were nothing had I such to give;
But when I stood beneath the fresh green tree,
Which living waves where thou didst cease to live,
And saw around me the wide field revive
With fruits and fertile promise, and the Spring
Come forth her work of gladness to contrive,
With all her reckless birds upon the wing,
I turn'd from all she brought to those she could not
    bring.

NAPOLEON

(Canto III, xxxvi–xliv)

There sunk the greatest, nor the worst of men,
Whose spirit, antithetically mixt,
One moment of the mightiest, and again
On little objects with like firmness fixt;
Extreme in all things! hadst thou been betwixt,
Thy throne had still been thine, or never been;
For daring made thy rise as fall: thou seek'st
Even now to re-assume the imperial mien,
And shake again the world, the Thunderer of the
    scene!

Conqueror and captive of the earth art thou!   10
She trembles at thee still, and thy wild name
Was ne'er more bruited in men's minds than now
That thou art nothing, save the jest of Fame,
Who woo'd thee once, thy vassal, and became
The flatterer of thy fierceness, till thou wert
A god unto thyself; nor less the same
To the astounded kingdoms all inert,
Who deem'd thee for a time whate'er thou didst assert.

Oh, more or less than man—in high or low,
Battling with nations, flying from the field;   20
Now making monarchs' necks thy footstool, now
More than thy meanest soldier taught to yield;
An empire thou couldst crush, command, rebuild,
But govern not thy pettiest passion, nor,
However deeply in men's spirits skill'd,
Look through thine own, nor curb the lust of war,
Nor learn that tempted Fate will leave the loftiest star.

Yet well thy soul hath brook'd the turning tide
With that untaught innate philosophy,
Which, be it wisdom, coldness, or deep pride,   30
Is gall and wormwood to an enemy.
When the whole host of hatred stood hard by,

To watch and mock thee shrinking, thou hast smiled
With a sedate and all-enduring eye ;—
  When Fortune fled her spoil'd and favourite child,
He stood unbow'd beneath the ills upon him piled.

Sager than in thy fortunes ; for in them
Ambition steel'd thee on too far to show
That just habitual scorn, which could contemn
Men and their thoughts ; t'was wise to feel, not so
To wear it ever on thy lip and brow,   41
And spurn the instruments thou wert to use
Till they were turn'd unto thine overthrow :
'Tis but a worthless world to win or lose ;
So hath it proved to thee, and all such lot who choose.

If, like a tower upon a headland rock,
Thou hadst been made to stand or fall alone,
Such scorn of man had help'd to brave the shock ;
But men's thoughts were the steps which paved thy
     throne,
Their admiration thy best weapon shone ;   50
The part of Philip's son was thine, not then
(Unless aside thy purple had been thrown)
Like stern Diogenes to mock at men ;
For sceptred cynics earth were far too wide a den.

But quiet to quick bosoms is a hell,
And _there_ hath been thy bane ; there is a fire
And motion of the soul which will not dwell
In its own narrow being, but aspire
Beyond the fitting medium of desire ,
And, but once kindled, quenchless evermore,   60
Preys upon high adventure, nor can tire
Of aught but rest ; a fever at the core,
Fatal to him who bears, to all who ever bore.

This makes the madmen who have made men mad
By their contagion ; Conquerors and Kings,
Founders of sects and systems, to whom add
Sophists, Bards, Statesmen, all unquiet things

Which stir too strongly the soul's secret springs,
And are themselves the fools to those they fool ;
Envied, yet how unenviable ! what stings   70
Are theirs ! One breast laid open were a school
Which would unteach mankind the lust to shine or rule :

Their breath is agitation, and their life
A storm whereon they ride, to sink at last,
And yet so nursed and bigoted to strife,
That should their days, surviving perils past,
Melt to calm twilight, they feel overcast
With sorrow and supineness, and so die ;
Even as a flame unfed, which runs to waste
With its own flickering, or a sword laid by,   80
Which eats into itself, and rusts ingloriously.

THE DRACHENFELS

1

The castled crag of Drachenfels
Frowns o'er the wide and winding Rhine,
Whose breast of waters broadly swells
Between the banks which bear the vine,
And hills all rich with blossom'd trees,
And fields which promise corn and wine,
And scatter'd cities crowning these,
Whose far white walls along them shine,
Have strew'd a scene, which I should see
With double joy wert *thou* with me.   10

2

And peasant girls, with deep blue eyes,
And hands which offer early flowers,
Walk smiling o'er this paradise ;
Above, the frequent feudal towers
Through green leaves lift their walls of gray ;
And many a rock which steeply lowers,
And noble arch in proud decay,
Look o'er this vale of vintage-bowers ;
But one thing want these banks of Rhine,—
Thy gentle hand to clasp in mine !   20

3

I send the lilies given to me;
Though long before thy hand they touch,
I know that they must wither'd be,
But yet reject them not as such;
For I have cherish'd them as dear,
Because they yet may meet thine eye,
And guide thy soul to mine even here,
When thou behold'st them drooping nigh,
And know'st them gather'd by the Rhine,
And offer'd from my heart to thine!   30

4

The river nobly foams and flows,
The charm of this enchanted ground,
And all its thousand turns disclose
Some fresher beauty varying round:
The haughtiest breast its wish might bound
Through life to dwell delighted here;
Nor could on earth a spot be found
To nature and to me so dear,
Could thy dear eyes in following mine
Still sweeten more these banks of Rhine!   40

NATURE THE CONSOLER

(Canto III, lxviii–lxxv)

Lake Leman woos me with its crystal face,
The mirror where the stars and mountains view
The stillness of their aspect in each trace
Its clear depth yields of their far height and hue:
There is too much of man here, to look through
With a fit mind the might which I behold;
But soon in me shall Loneliness renew
Thoughts hid, but not less cherish'd than of old,
Ere mingling with the herd had penn'd me in their
     fold.

To fly from, need not be to hate, mankind: 10
All are not fit with them to stir and toil,
Nor is it discontent to keep the mind
Deep in its fountain, lest it overboil
In the hot throng, where we become the spoil
Of our infection, till too late and long
We may deplore and struggle with the coil,
In wretched interchange of wrong for wrong
Midst a contentious world, striving where none are
          strong.

There, in a moment we may plunge our years
In fatal penitence, and in the blight   20
Of our own soul turn all our blood to tears,
And colour things to come with hues of Night;
The race of life becomes a hopeless flight
To those that walk in darkness: on the sea
The boldest steer but where their ports invite;
But there are wanderers o'er Eternity
Whose bark drives on and on, and anchor'd ne'er
          shall be.

Is it not better, then, to be alone,
And love Earth only for its earthly sake?
By the blue rushing of the arrowy Rhone,   30
Or the pure bosom of its nursing lake,
Which feeds it as a mother who doth make
A fair but froward infant her own care,
Kissing its cries away as these awake;—
Is it not better thus our lives to wear,
Than join the crushing crowd, doom'd to inflict or
          bear?

I live not in myself, but I become
Portion of that around me; and to me
High mountains are a feeling, but the hum
Of human cities torture: I can see   40

Nothing to loathe in nature, save to be
A link reluctant in a fleshly chain,
Class'd among creatures, when the soul can flee,
And with the sky, the peak, the heaving plain
Of ocean, or the stars, mingle, and not in vain.

And thus I am absorb'd, and this is life:
I look upon the peopled desert past,
As on a place of agony and strife,
Where, for some sin, to Sorrow I was cast,
To act and suffer, but remount at last   50
With a fresh pinion; which I feel to spring,
Though young, yet waxing vigorous as the blast
Which it would cope with, on delighted wing,
Spurning the clay-cold bonds which round our being
          cling.

And when, at length, the mind shall be all free
From what it hates in this degraded form,
Reft of its carnal life, save what shall be
Existent happier in the fly and worm,—
When elements to elements conform,
And dust is as it should be, shall I not   60
Feel all I see, less dazzling, but more warm?
The bodiless thought? the Spirit of each spot?
Of which, even now, I share at times the immortal lot?

Are not the mountains, waves, and skies, a part
Of me and of my soul, as I of them?
Is not the love of these deep in my heart
With a pure passion? should I not contemn
All objects, if compared with these? and stem
A tide of suffering, rather than forego
Such feelings for the hard and worldly phlegm   70
Of those whose eyes are only turn'd below,
Gazing upon the ground, with thoughts which dare not
          glow?

LAKE OF GENEVA

(Canto III, lxxxv–lxxxvii, xcii–xcvii)

Clear, placid Leman! thy contrasted lake,
With the wild world I dwelt in, is a thing
Which warns me, with its stillness, to forsake
Earth's troubled waters for a purer spring.
This quiet sail is as a noiseless wing
To waft me from distraction; once I loved
Torn ocean's roar, but thy soft murmuring
Sounds sweet as if a Sister's voice reproved,
That I with stern delights should e'er have been so
    moved.

It is the hush of night, and all between   10
Thy margin and the mountains, dusk, yet clear,
Mellow'd and mingling, yet distinctly seen,
Save darken'd Jura, whose capt heights appear
Precipitously steep; and drawing near,
There breathes a living fragrance from the shore,
Of flowers yet fresh with childhood; on the ear
Drops the light drip of the suspended oar,
Or chirps the grasshopper one good-night carol more;

He is an evening reveller, who makes
His life an infancy, and sings his fill;   20
At intervals, some bird from out the brakes
Starts into voice a moment, then is still.
There seems a floating whisper on the hill,
But that is fancy, for the starlight dews
All silently their tears of love instil,
Weeping themselves away, till they infuse
Deep into Nature's breast the spirit of her hues.

.   .   .   .   .   .

The sky is changed!—and such a change! Oh night,
And storm, and darkness, ye are wondrous strong,
Yet lovely in your strength, as is the light   30
Of a dark eye in woman! Far along,

From peak to peak, the rattling crags among
Leaps the live thunder ! Not from one lone cloud,
But every mountain now hath found a tongue,
And Jura answers, through her misty shroud,
Back to the joyous Alps, who call to her aloud !

And this is in the night :—Most glorious night !
Thou wert not sent for slumber ! let me be
A sharer in thy fierce and far delight,—
A portion of the tempest and of thee !   40
How the lit lake shines, a phosphoric sea,
And the big rain comes dancing to the earth !
And now again 'tis black,—and now, the glee
Of the loud hills shakes with its mountain-mirth,
As if they did rejoice o'er a young earthquake's birth.

Now, where the swift Rhone cleaves his way between
Heights which appear as lovers who have parted
In hate, whose mining depths so intervene,
That they can meet no more, though broken-hearted ;
Though in their souls, which thus each other
      thwarted,   50
Love was the very root of the fond rage
Which blighted their life's bloom, and then departed :
Itself expired, but leaving them an age
Of years all winters,—war within themselves to wage.

Now, where the quick Rhone thus hath cleft his
      way,
The mightiest of the storms hath ta'en his stand :
For here, not one, but many, make their play,
And fling their thunder-bolts from hand to hand,
Flashing and cast around : of all the band,
The brightest through these parted hills hath fork'd
His lightnings,—as if he did understand,   61
That in such gaps as desolation work'd,
There the hot shaft should blast whatever therein
      lurk'd.

Sky, mountains, river, winds, lake, lightnings! ye!
With night, and clouds, and thunder, and a soul
To make these felt and feeling, well may be
Things that have made me watchful; the far roll
Of your departing voices, is the knoll
Of what in me is sleepless,—if I rest.
But where of ye, O tempests! is the goal?   70
Are ye like those within the human breast?
Or do ye find, at length, like eagles, some high
    nest?

Could I embody and unbosom now
That which is most within me,—could I wreak
My thoughts upon expression, and thus throw
Soul, heart, mind, passions, feelings, strong or weak,
All that I would have sought, and all I seek,
Bear, know, feel, and yet breathe—into *one* word,
And that one word were Lightning, I would speak;
But as it is, I live and die unheard,   80
With a most voiceless thought, sheathing it as a sword.

CLARENS

(Canto III, xcix–civ)

Clarens! sweet Clarens, birthplace of deep Love!
Thine air is the young breath of passionate thought;
Thy trees take root in Love; the snows above
The very Glaciers have his colours caught,
And sun-set into rose-hues sees them wrought
By rays which sleep there lovingly: the rocks,
The permanent crags, tell here of Love, who sought
In them a refuge from the worldly shocks,
Which stir and sting the soul with hope that woos,
    then mocks.

Clarens! by heavenly feet thy paths are trod,—   10
Undying Love's, who here ascends a throne
To which the steps are mountains; where the god
Is a pervading life and light,—so shown

Not on those summits solely, nor alone
In the still cave and forest ; o'er the flower
His eye is sparkling, and his breath hath blown,
His soft and summer breath, whose tender power
Passes the strength of storms in their most desolate
      hour.

All things are here of *him ;* from the black pines,
Which are his shade on high, and the loud roar   20
Of torrents, where he listeneth, to the vines
Which slope his green path downward to the shore,
Where the bow'd waters meet him, and adore,
Kissing his feet with murmurs ; and the wood,
The covert of old trees, with trunks all hoar,
But light leaves, young as joy, stands where it stood,
Offering to him, and his, a populous solitude.

A populous solitude of bees and birds,
And fairy-form'd and many-colour'd things,
Who worship him with notes more sweet than words,
And innocently open their glad wings,   31
Fearless and full of life : the gush of springs,
And fall of lofty fountains, and the bend
Of stirring branches, and the bud which brings
The swiftest thought of beauty, here extend,
Mingling, and made by Love, unto one mighty end.

He who hath loved not, here would learn that lore,
And make his heart a spirit ; he who knows
That tender mystery, will love the more ;
For this is Love's recess, where vain men's woes,   40
And the world's waste, have driven him far from
    those,
For 'tis his nature to advance or die ;
He stands not still, but or decays, or grows
Into a boundless blessing, which may vie
With the immortal lights, in its eternity !

'Twas not for fiction chose Rousseau this spot,
Peopling it with affections ; but he found
It was the scene which Passion must allot
To the mind's purified beings ; 'twas the ground
Where early Love his Psyche's zone unbound,   50
And hallow'd it with loveliness : 'tis lone,
And wonderful, and deep, and hath a sound,
And sense, and sight of sweetness ; here the Rhone
Hath spread himself a couch, the Alps have reared
    a throne.

GIBBON AND VOLTAIRE

(Canto III, cv–cviii)

Lausanne ! and Ferney ! ye have been the abodes
Of names which unto you bequeath'd a name ;
Mortals, who sought and found, by dangerous roads,
A path to perpetuity of fame :
They were gigantic minds, and their steep aim
Was, Titan-like, on daring doubts to pile
Thoughts which should call down thunder, and the
    flame
Of Heaven again assail'd, if Heaven the while
On man and man's research could deign do more than
    smile.

The one was fire and fickleness, a child   10
Most mutable in wishes, but in mind
A wit as various,—gay, grave, sage, or wild,—
Historian, bard, philosopher, combined ;
He multiplied himself among mankind,
The Proteus of their talents : But his own
Breathed most in ridicule,—which, as the wind,
Blew where it listed, laying all things prone,—
Now to o'erthrow a fool, and now to shake a throne.

The other, deep and slow, exhausting thought,
And hiving wisdom with each studious year,   20
In meditation dwelt, with learning wrought,
And shaped his weapon with an edge severe,
Sapping a solemn creed with solemn sneer;
The lord of irony,—that master-spell,
Which stung his foes to wrath, which grew from fear,
And doom'd him to the zealot's ready Hell,
Which answers to all doubts so eloquently well.

Yet, peace be with their ashes,—for by them,
If merited, the penalty is paid;
It is not ours to judge,—far less condemn;   30
The hour must come when such things shall be made
Known unto all,—or hope and dread allay'd
By slumber, on one pillow, in the dust,
Which, thus much we are sure, must lie decay'd;
And when it shall revive, as is our trust,
'Twill be to be forgiven, or suffer what is just.

I HAVE NOT LOVED THE WORLD

(Canto III, cxiii, cxiv)

I have not loved the world, nor the world me;
I have not flatter'd its rank breath, nor bow'd
To its idolatries a patient knee,
Nor coin'd my cheek to smiles,—nor cried aloud
In worship of an echo; in the crowd
They could not deem me one of such; I stood
Among them, but not of them; in a shroud
Of thoughts which were not their thoughts, and still
   could,
Had I not filed my mind, which thus itself subdued.

I have not loved the world, nor the world me,—   10
But let us part fair foes; I do believe,
Though I have found them not, that there may be
Words which are things,—hopes which will not
   deceive,

And virtues which are merciful, nor weave
Snares for the failing ; I would also deem
O'er others' griefs that some sincerely grieve ;
That two, or one, are almost what they seem,—
That goodness is no name, and happiness no dream.

VENICE

(Canto IV, i–iv, xi–xviii)

I stood in Venice, on the Bridge of Sighs ;
A palace and a prison on each hand :
I saw from out the wave her structures rise
As from the stroke of the enchanter's wand :
A thousand years their cloudy wings expand
Around me, and a dying Glory smiles
O'er the far times, when many a subject land
Look'd to the winged Lion's marble piles,
Where Venice sate in state, throned on her hundred isles !

She looks a sea Cybele, fresh from ocean,   10
Rising with her tiara of proud towers
At airy distance, with majestic motion,
A ruler of the waters and their powers :
And such she was ;—her daughters had their dowers
From spoils of nations, and the exhaustless East
Pour'd in her lap all gems in sparkling showers.
In purple was she robed, and of her feast
Monarchs partook, and deem'd their dignity increased.

In Venice Tasso's echoes are no more,
And silent rows the songless gondolier ;   20
Her palaces are crumbling to the shore,
And music meets not always now the ear :
Those days are gone—but Beauty still is here.
States fall, arts fade—but Nature doth not die,
Nor yet forget how Venice once was dear,
The pleasant place of all festivity,
The revel of the earth, the masque of Italy !

But unto us she hath a spell beyond
Her name in story, and her long array
Of mighty shadows, whose dim forms despond   30
Above the dogeless city's vanish'd sway;
Ours is a trophy which will not decay
With the Rialto; Shylock and the Moor,
And Pierre, can not be swept or worn away—
The keystones of the arch! though all were o'er,
For us repeopled were the solitary shore.

.   .   .   .   .   .

The spouseless Adriatic mourns her lord;
And, annual marriage now no more renew'd,
The Bucentaur lies rotting unrestored,
Neglected garment of her widowhood!   40
St. Mark yet sees his lion where he stood
Stand, but in mockery of his wither'd power,
Over the proud Place where an Emperor sued,
And monarchs gazed and envied in the hour
When Venice was a queen with an unequall'd dower.

The Suabian sued, and now the Austrian reigns—
An Emperor tramples where an Emperor knelt;
Kingdoms are shrunk to provinces, and chains
Clank over sceptred cities; nations melt
From power's high pinnacle, when they have felt
The sunshine for a while, and downward go   51
Like lauwine loosen'd from the mountain's belt;
Oh for one hour of blind old Dandolo!
Th' octogenarian chief, Byzantium's conquering foe.

Before St. Mark still glow his steeds of brass,
Their gilded collars glittering in the sun;
But is not Doria's menace come to pass?
Are they not *bridled?*—Venice, lost and won,
Her thirteen hundred years of freedom done,
Sinks, like a sea-weed, into whence she rose!   60
Better be whelm'd beneath the waves, and shun,
Even in destruction's depth, her foreign foes,
From whom submission wrings an infamous repose.

In youth she was all glory,—a new Tyre,—
Her very by-word sprung from victory,
The " Planter of the Lion," which through fire
And blood she bore o'er subject earth and sea ;
Though making many slaves, herself still free,
And Europe's bulwark 'gainst the Ottomite ;
Witness Troy's rival, Candia ! Vouch it, ye   70
Immortal waves that saw Lepanto's fight !
For ye are names no time nor tyranny can blight.

Statues of glass—all shiver'd—the long file
Of her dead Doges are declined to dust ;
But where they dwelt, the vast and sumptuous pile
Bespeaks the pageant of their splendid trust ;
Their sceptre broken, and their sword in rust,
Have yielded to the stranger : empty halls,
Thin streets, and foreign aspects, such as must   80
Too oft remind her who and what enthrals,
Have flung a desolate cloud o'er Venice' lovely walls.

When Athens' armies fell at Syracuse,
And fetter'd thousands bore the yoke of war,
Redemption rose up in the Attic Muse,
Her voice their only ransom from afar :
See ! as they chant the tragic hymn, the car
Of the o'ermaster'd victor stops, the reins
Fall from his hands—his idle scimitar
Starts from its belt—he rends his captive's chains,
And bids him thank the bard for freedom and his
     strains.   90

Thus, Venice, if no stronger claim were thine,
Were all thy proud historic deeds forgot,
Thy choral memory of the Bard divine,
Thy love of Tasso, should have cut the knot
Which ties thee to thy tyrants,—and thy lot
Is shameful to the nations,—most of all,
Albion ! to thee : the Ocean queen should not
Abandon Ocean's children ; in the fall
Of Venice think of thine, despite thy watery wall.

I loved her from my boyhood—she to me   100
Was as a fairy city of the heart,
Rising like water-columns from the sea,
Of joy the sojourn, and of wealth the mart;
And Otway, Radcliffe, Schiller, Shakspeare's art,
Had stamp'd her image in me, and even so,
Although I found her thus, we did not part;
Perchance even dearer in her day of woe,
Than when she was a boast, a marvel, and a show.

AN AUGUST EVENING IN ITALY

(Canto IV, xxvii–xxix)

The Moon is up, and yet it is not night—
Sunset divides the sky with her—a sea
Of glory streams along the Alpine height
Of blue Friuli's mountains; Heaven is free
From clouds, but of all colours seems to be,—
Melted to one vast Iris of the West,—
Where the Day joins the past Eternity;
While, on the other hand, meek Dian's crest
Floats through the azure air—an island of the blest!

A single star is at her side, and reigns   10
With her o'er half the lovely heaven; but still
Yon sunny sea heaves brightly, and remains
Roll'd o'er the peak of the far Rhaetian hill,
As Day and Night contending were, until
Nature reclaim'd her order:—gently flows
The deep-dyed Brenta, where their hues instil
The odorous purple of a new-born rose,
Which streams upon her stream, and glass'd within it
    glows,

Fill'd with the face of heaven, which, from afar,
Comes down upon the waters; all its hues,   20
From the rich sunset to the rising star,
Their magical variety diffuse:

And now they change ; a paler shadow strews
Its mantle o'er the mountains ; parting day
Dies like the dolphin, whom each pang imbues
With a new colour as it gasps away,
The last still loveliest, till—'tis gone—and all is gray.

PETRARCH

(CANTO IV, xxx–xxxii)

There is a tomb in Arqua ;—rear'd in air,
Pillar'd in their sarcophagus, repose
The bones of Laura's lover : here repair
Many familiar with his well-sung woes,
The pilgrims of his genius.   He arose
To raise a language, and his land reclaim
From the dull yoke of her barbaric foes :
Watering the tree which bears his lady's name
With his melodious tears, he gave himself to fame.

They keep his dust in Arqua, where he died ;   10
The mountain-village where his latter days
Went down the vale of years ; and 'tis their pride—
An honest pride—and let it be their praise,
To offer to the passing stranger's gaze
His mansion and his sepulchre ; both plain
And venerably simple, such as raise
A feeling more accordant with his strain
Than if a pyramid form'd his monumental fane.

And the soft quiet hamlet where he dwelt
Is one of that complexion which seems made   20
For those who their mortality have felt,
And sought a refuge from their hopes decay'd
In the deep umbrage of a green hill's shade,
Which shows a distant prospect far away
Of busy cities, now in vain display'd,
For they can lure no further ; and the ray
Of a bright sun can make sufficient holiday.

ITALY

(Canto IV, xlii–xlvii)

Italia ! oh Italia ! thou who hast
The fatal gift of beauty, which became
A funeral dower of present woes and past,
On thy sweet brow is sorrow plough'd by shame,
And annals graved in characters of flame.
Oh, God ! that thou wert in thy nakedness
Less lovely or more powerful, and couldst claim
Thy right, and awe the robbers back, who press
To shed thy blood, and drink the tears of thy distress ;

Then might'st thou more appal ; or, less desired,
Be homely and be peaceful, undeplored   11
For thy destructive charms ; then, still untired,
Would not be seen the armed torrents pour'd
Down the deep Alps ; nor would the hostile horde
Of many-nation'd spoilers from the Po
Quaff blood and water ; nor the stranger's sword
Be thy sad weapon of defence, and so,
Victor or vanquish'd, thou the slave of friend or foe.

Wandering in youth, I traced the path of him,
The Roman friend of Rome's least-mortal mind,   20
The friend of Tully : as my bark did skim
The bright blue waters with a fanning wind,
Came Megara before me, and behind
Aegina lay, Piraeus on the right,
And Corinth on the left ; I lay reclined
Along the prow, and saw all these unite
In ruin, even as he had seen the desolate sight ;

For Time hath not rebuilt them, but uprear'd
Barbaric dwellings on their shatter'd site,
Which only make more mourn'd and more endear'd
The few last rays of their far-scatter'd light,   31

And the crush'd relics of their vanish'd might.
The Roman saw these tombs in his own age,
These sepulchres of cities, which excite
Sad wonder, and his yet surviving page
The moral lesson bears, drawn from such pilgrimage.

That page is now before me, and on mine
His country's ruin added to the mass
Of perish'd states he mourn'd in their decline,
And I in desolation : all that *was*   40
Of then destruction *is ;* and now, alas !
Rome—Rome imperial, bows her to the storm,
In the same dust and blackness, and we pass
The skeleton of her Titanic form,
Wrecks of another world, whose ashes still are warm.

Yet, Italy ! through every other land
Thy wrongs should ring, and shall, from side to side ;
Mother of Arts ! as once of arms : thy hand
Was then our guardian, and is still our guide ;
Parent of our Religion ! whom the wide   50
Nations have knelt to for the keys of heaven !
Europe, repentant of her parricide,
Shall yet redeem thee, and, all backward driven,
Roll the barbarian tide, and sue to be forgiven.

CLITUMNUS

(Canto IV, lxvi, lxvii)

But thou, Clitumnus ! in thy sweetest wave
Of the most living crystal that was e'er
The haunt of river nymph, to gaze and lave
Her limbs where nothing hid them, thou dost rear
Thy grassy banks whereon the milk-white steer
Grazes ; the purest god of gentle waters !
And most serene of aspect, and most clear ;
Surely that stream was unprofaned by slaughters,
A mirror and a bath for Beauty's youngest daughters !

And on thy happy shore a Temple still,   10
Of small and delicate proportion, keeps,
Upon a mild declivity of hill,
Its memory of thee; beneath it sweeps
Thy current's calmness; oft from out it leaps
The finny darter with the glittering scales,
Who dwells and revels in thy glassy deeps;
While, chance, some scatter'd water-lily sails
Down where the shallower wave still tells its bubbling tales.

TERNI

(Canto IV, lxix–lxxii)

The roar of waters!—from the headlong height
Velino cleaves the wave-worn precipice;
The fall of waters! rapid as the light
The flashing mass foams shaking the abyss;
The hell of waters! where they howl and hiss,
And boil in endless torture; while the sweat
Of their great agony, wrung out from this
Their Phlegethon, curls round the rocks of jet
That guard the gulf around, in pitiless horror set.

And mounts in spray the skies, and thence again
Returns in an unceasing shower, which round,   11
With its unemptied cloud of gentle rain,
Is an eternal April to the ground,
Making it all one emerald:—how profound
The gulf! and how the giant element
From rock to rock leaps with delirious bound,
Crushing the cliffs, which, downward worn and rent
With his fierce footsteps, yield in chasms a fearful vent

To the broad column which rolls on, and shows
More like the fountain of an infant sea   20
Torn from the womb of mountains by the throes
Of a new world, than only thus to be

Parent of rivers, which flow gushingly,
With many windings, through the vale:—Look back!
Lo! where it comes like an eternity,
As if to sweep down all things in its track,
Charming the eye with dread,—a matchless cataract,

Horribly beautiful! but on the verge,
From side to side, beneath the glittering morn,
An Iris sits, amidst the infernal surge,   30
Like Hope upon a death-bed, and, unworn
Its steady dyes, while all around is torn
By the distracted waters, bears serene
Its brilliant hues with all their beams unshorn:
Resembling, 'mid the torture of the scene,
Love watching Madness with unalterable mien.

THE APENNINES, AND HORACE

(CANTO IV, lxxiii–lxxvii)

ONCE more upon the woody Apennine,
The infant Alps, which—had I not before
Gazed on their mightier parents, where the pine
Sits on more shaggy summits, and where roar
The thundering lauwine—might be worshipp'd more;
But I have seen the soaring Jungfrau rear
Her never-trodden snow, and seen the hoar
Glaciers of bleak Mont Blanc both far and near,
And in Chimari heard the thunder-hills of fear,

Th' Acroceraunian mountains of old name;   10
And on Parnassus seen the eagles fly
Like spirits of the spot, as 'twere for fame,
For still they soared unutterably high:
I've look'd on Ida with a Trojan's eye;
Athos, Olympus, Aetna, Atlas, made
These hills seem things of lesser dignity,
All, save the lone Soracte's height, display'd
Not *now* in snow, which asks the lyric Roman's aid

For our remembrance, and from out the plain
Heaves like a long-swept wave about to break,   20
And on the curl hangs pausing: not in vain
May he, who will, his recollections rake,
And quote in classic raptures, and awake
The hills with Latian echoes; I abhorr'd
Too much, to conquer for the poet's sake,
The drill'd dull lesson, forced down word by word
In my repugnant youth, with pleasure to record

Aught that recalls the daily drug which turn'd
My sickening memory; and, though Time hath
    taught
My mind to meditate what then it learn'd,   30
Yet such the fix'd inveteracy wrought
By the impatience of my early thought,
That, with the freshness wearing out before
My mind could relish what it might have sought,
If free to choose, I cannot now restore
Its health; but what it then detested, still abhor.

Then farewell, Horace; whom I hated so,
Not for thy faults, but mine; it is a curse
To understand, not feel thy lyric flow,
To comprehend, but never love thy verse: 40
Although no deeper Moralist rehearse
Our little life, nor Bard prescribe his art,
Nor livelier Satirist the conscience pierce,
Awakening without wounding the touch'd heart,
Yet fare thee well—upon Soracte's ridge we part.

ROME

(Canto IV, lxxviii–lxxxii, cvii–cx)

Oh Rome! my country! city of the soul!
The orphans of the heart must turn to thee,
Lone mother of dead empires! and control
In their shut breasts their petty misery.
What are our woes and sufferance? Come and see
The cypress, hear the owl, and plod your way
O'er steps of broken thrones and temples, Ye!
Whose agonies are evils of a day—
A world is at our feet as fragile as our clay.

The Niobe of nations! there she stands,   10
Childless and crownless, in her voiceless woe;
An empty urn within her wither'd hands,
Whose holy dust was scatter'd long ago;
The Scipios' tomb contains no ashes now;
The very sepulchres lie tenantless
Of their heroic dwellers: dost thou flow,
Old Tiber! through a marble wilderness?
Rise, with thy yellow waves, and mantle her distress.

The Goth, the Christian, Time, War, Flood, and Fire,
Have dealt upon the seven-hill'd city's pride;   20
She saw her glories star by star expire,
And up the steep barbarian monarchs ride,
Where the car climb'd the Capitol; far and wide
Temple and tower went down, nor left a site:
Chaos of ruins! who shall trace the void,
O'er the dim fragments cast a lunar light,
And say, 'here was, or is,' where all is doubly night?

The double night of ages, and of her,
Night's daughter, Ignorance, hath wrapt and wrap
All round us; we but feel our way to err: 30
The ocean hath its chart, the stars their map,

And Knowledge spreads them on her ample lap ;
But Rome is as the desert, where we steer
Stumbling o'er recollections ; now we clap
Our hands, and cry ' Eureka ! ' it is clear—
When but some false mirage of ruin rises near.

Alas ! the lofty city ! and alas !
The trebly hundred triumphs ! and the day
When Brutus made the dagger's edge surpass
The conqueror's sword in bearing fame away !   40
Alas, for Tully's voice, and Virgil's lay,
And Livy's pictured page !—but these shall be
Her resurrection ; all beside—decay.
Alas, for Earth, for never shall we see
That brightness in her eye she bore when Rome was
    free !

*   *   *   *   *

Cypress and ivy, weed and wallflower grown
Matted and mass'd together, hillocks heap'd
On what were chambers, arch crush'd, column strown
In fragments, choked up vaults, and frescos steep'd
In subterranean damps, where the owl peep'd,   50
Deeming it midnight :—Temples, baths, or halls ?
Pronounce who can ; for all that Learning reap'd
From her research hath been, that these are walls—
Behold the Imperial Mount ! 'tis thus the mighty falls.

There is the moral of all human tales ;
'Tis but the same rehearsal of the past,
First Freedom, and then Glory—when that fails,
Wealth, vice, corruption,—barbarism at last.
And History, with all her volumes vast,
Hath but *one* page,—'tis better written here   60
Where gorgeous Tyranny hath thus amass'd
All treasures, all delights, that eye or ear,
Heart, soul could seek, tongue ask—Away with words !
    draw near,

Admire, exult, despise, laugh, weep,—for here
There is such matter for all feeling :—Man !
Thou pendulum betwixt a smile and tear,
Ages and realms are crowded in this span,
This mountain, whose obliterated plan
The pyramid of empires pinnacled,
Of Glory's gewgaws shining in the van   70
Till the sun's rays with added flame were fill'd !
Where are its golden roofs ? where those who dared
    to build ?

Tully was not so eloquent as thou,
Thou nameless column with the buried base !
What are the laurels of the Caesar's brow ?
Crown me with ivy from his dwelling-place.
Whose arch or pillar meets me in the face,
Titus or Trajan's ? No—'tis that of Time :
Triumph, arch, pillar, all he doth displace
Scoffing ; and apostolic statues climb   80
To crush the imperial urn, whose ashes slept sublime.

FREEDOM

(Canto IV, xcvi–xcviii)

Can tyrants but by tyrants conquer'd be,
And Freedom find no champion and no child
Such as Columbia saw arise when she
Sprung forth a Pallas, arm'd and undefiled ?
Or must such minds be nourish'd in the wild,
Deep in the unpruned forest, 'midst the roar
Of cataracts, where nursing Nature smiled
On infant Washington ? Has Earth no more
Such seeds within her breast, or Europe no such shore ?

But France got drunk with blood to vomit crime,
And fatal have her Saturnalia been   11
To Freedom's cause, in every age and clime ;
Because the deadly days which we have seen,

And vile Ambition, that built up between
Man and his hopes an adamantine wall,
And the base pageant last upon the scene,
Are grown the pretext for the eternal thrall
Which nips life's tree, and dooms man's worst—his
    second fall.

Yet, Freedom ! yet thy banner, torn, but flying,
Streams like the thunder-storm *against* the wind ;   20
Thy trumpet voice, though broken now and dying,
The loudest still the tempest leaves behind ;
Thy tree hath lost its blossoms, and the rind,
Chopp'd by the axe, looks rough and little worth,
But the sap lasts,—and still the seed we find
Sown deep, even in the bosom of the North ;
So shall a better spring less bitter fruit bring forth.

TOMB OF CECILIA METELLA

(CANTO IV, xcix–ciii)

THERE is a stern round tower of other days,
Firm as a fortress, with its fence of stone,
Such as an army's baffled strength delays,
Standing with half its battlements alone,
And with two thousand years of ivy grown,
The garland of eternity, where wave
The green leaves over all by time o'erthrown ;—
What was this tower of strength ? within its cave
What treasure lay so lock'd, so hid ?—A woman's
    grave.

But who was she, the lady of the dead,   10
Tomb'd in a palace ? Was she chaste and fair ?
Worthy a king's, or more—a Roman's bed ?
What race of chiefs and heroes did she bear ?

What daughter of her beauties was the heir ?
How lived, how loved, how died she ? Was she not
So honoured—and conspicuously there,
Where meaner relics must not dare to rot,
Placed to commemorate a more than mortal lot ?

Was she as those who love their lords, or they
Who love the lords of others ? such have been   20
Even in the olden time, Rome's annals say.
Was she a matron of Cornelia's mien,
Or the light air of Egypt's graceful queen,
Profuse of joy—or 'gainst it did she war
Inveterate in virtue ?   Did she lean
To the soft side of the heart, or wisely bar
Love from amongst her griefs ?—for such the affections
     are.

Perchance she died in youth : it may be, bow'd
With woes far heavier than the ponderous tomb
That weigh'd upon her gentle dust, a cloud   30
Might gather o'er her beauty, and a gloom
In her dark eye, prophetic of the doom
Heaven gives its favourites—early death ; yet shed
A sunset charm around her, and illume
With hectic light, the Hesperus of the dead,
Of her consuming cheek the autumnal leaf-like red.

Perchance she died in age—surviving all,
Charms, kindred, children—with the silver gray
On her long tresses, which might yet recall,
It may be, still a something of the day   40
When they were braided, and her proud array
And lovely form were envied, praised, and eyed
By Rome—But whither would Conjecture stray ?
Thus much alone we know—Metella died,
The wealthiest Roman's wife : Behold his love or pride

GROTTO OF EGERIA

(CANTO IV, cxv–cxxvii)

Egeria ! sweet creation of some heart
Which found no mortal resting-place so fair
As thine ideal breast ; whate'er thou art
Or wert,—a young Aurora of the air,
The nympholepsy of some fond despair ;
Or, it might be, a beauty of the earth,
Who found a more than common votary there
Too much adoring ; whatsoe'er thy birth,
Thou wert a beautiful thought, and softly bodied forth.

The mosses of thy fountain still are sprinkled   10
With thine Elysian water-drops ; the face
Of thy cave-guarded spring with years unwrinkled,
Reflects the meek-eyed genius of the place,
Whose green, wild margin now no more erase
Art's works ; nor must the delicate waters sleep,
Prison'd in marble, bubbling from the base
Of the cleft statue, with a gentle leap
The rill runs o'er, and round fern, flowers, and ivy creep,

Fantastically tangled : the green hills
Are clothed with early blossoms, through the grass
The quick-eyed lizard rustles, and the bills   21
Of summer-birds sing welcome as ye pass ;
Flowers fresh in hue, and many in their class,
Implore the pausing step, and with their dyes,
Dance in the soft breeze in a fairy mass ,
The sweetness of the violet's deep blue eyes,
Kiss'd by the breath of heaven, seems colour'd by its
skies.

Here didst thou dwell, in this enchanted cover,
Egeria ! thy all heavenly bosom beating
For the far footsteps of thy mortal lover ;   30
The purple Midnight veil'd that mystic meeting

With her most starry canopy, and seating
Thyself by thine adorer, what befell ?
This cave was surely shaped out for the greeting
Of an enamour'd Goddess, and the cell
Haunted by holy Love—the earliest oracle !

And didst thou not, thy breast to his replying,
Blend a celestial with a human heart ;
And Love, which dies as it was born, in sighing,
Share with immortal transports ? could thine art
Make them indeed immortal, and impart   41
The purity of heaven to earthly joys,
Expel the venom and not blunt the dart—
The dull satiety which all destroys—
And root from out the soul the deadly weed which cloys ?

Alas ! our young affections run to waste,
Or water but the desert ; whence arise
But weeds of dark luxuriance, tares of haste,
Rank at the core, though tempting to the eyes,
Flowers whose wild odours breathe but agonies,   50
And trees whose gums are poisons ; such the plants
Which spring beneath her steps as Passion flies
O'er the world's wilderness, and vainly pants
For some celestial fruit forbidden to our wants.

Oh Love ! no habitant of earth thou art—
An unseen seraph, we believe in thee,—
A faith whose martyrs are the broken heart,—
But never yet hath seen, nor e'er shall see
The naked eye, thy form, as it should be ;
The mind hath made thee, as it peopled heaven,   60
Even with its own desiring phantasy,
And to a thought such shape and image given,
As haunts the unquench'd soul—parch'd, wearied,
          wrung, and riven.

Of its own beauty is the mind diseased,
And fevers into false creation :—where,
Where are the forms the sculptor's soul hath seiz'd ?
In him alone. Can Nature show so fair ?

Where are the charms and virtues which we dare
Conceive in boyhood and pursue as men,
The unreach'd Paradise of our despair,   70
Which o'er-informs the pencil and the pen,
And overpowers the page where it would bloom again?

Who loves, raves—'tis youth's frenzy—but the cure
Is bitterer still, as charm by charm unwinds
Which robed our idols, and we see too sure
Nor worth nor beauty dwells from out the mind's
Ideal shape of such; yet still it binds
The fatal spell, and still it draws us on,
Reaping the whirlwind from the oft-sown winds;
The stubborn heart, its alchemy begun,   80
Seems ever near the prize—wealthiest when most undone.

We wither from our youth, we gasp away—
Sick—sick; unfound the boon, unslaked the thirst,
Though to the last, in verge of our decay,
Some phantom lures, such as we sought at first—
But all too late,—so are we doubly curst.
Love, fame, ambition, avarice—'tis the same,
Each idle, and all ill, and none the worst—
For all are meteors with a different name,   89
And Death the sable smoke where vanishes the flame.

Few—none—find what they love or could have loved,
Though accident, blind contact, and the strong
Necessity of loving, have removed
Antipathies—but to recur, ere long,
Envenom'd with irrevocable wrong;
And Circumstance, that unspiritual god
And miscreator, makes and helps along
Our coming evils with a crutch-like rod,
Whose touch turns Hope to dust,—the dust we all
          have trod.

Our life is a false nature: 'tis not in   100
The harmony of things,—this hard decree,
This uneradicable taint of sin,
This boundless upas, this all-blasting tree,

Whose root is earth, whose leaves and branches be
The skies which rain their plagues on men like dew—
Disease, death, bondage—all the woes we see,
And worse, the woes we see not—which throb
  through
The immedicable soul, with heart-aches ever new.

Yet let us ponder boldly—'tis a base
Abandonment of reason to resign   110
Our right of thought—our last and only place
Of refuge ; this, at least, shall still be mine :
Though from our birth the faculty divine
Is chain'd and tortured—cabin'd, cribb'd, confined,
And bred in darkness, lest the truth should shine
Too brightly on the unprepared mind,
The beam pours in, for time and skill will couch the
  blind.

THE COLISEUM

(CANTO IV, cxxxix–cxlv)

AND here the buzz of eager nations ran,
In murmur'd pity, or loud-roar'd applause,
As man was slaughter'd by his fellow-man.
And wherefore slaughter'd ? wherefore, but because
Such were the bloody Circus' genial laws,
And the imperial pleasure.—Wherefore not ?
What matters where we fall to fill the maws
Of worms—on battle-plains or listed spot ?
Both are but theatres where the chief actors rot.

I see before me the Gladiator lie :   10
He leans upon his hand—his manly brow
Consents to death, but conquers agony,
And his droop'd head sinks gradually low—
And through his side the last drops, ebbing slow
From the red gash, fall heavy, one by one,
Like the first of a thunder-shower ; and now
The arena swims around him—he is gone,
Ere ceased the inhuman shout which hail'd the wretch
  who won.

He heard it, but he heeded not—his eyes
Were with his heart, and that was far away;   20
He reck'd not of the life he lost nor prize,
But where his rude hut by the Danube lay,
There were his young barbarians all at play,
There was their Dacian mother—he, their sire,
Butcher'd to make a Roman holiday—
All this rush'd with his blood—Shall he expire
And unavenged? Arise! ye Goths, and glut your ire!

But here, where Murder breathed her bloody steam;
And here, where buzzing nations choked the ways,
And roar'd or murmur'd like a mountain stream   30
Dashing or winding as its torrent strays;
Here, where the Roman million's blame or praise
Was death or life, the playthings of a crowd,
My voice sounds much—and fall the stars' faint rays
On the arena void—seats crush'd—walls bow'd—
And galleries, where my steps seem echoes strangely
    loud.

A ruin—yet what ruin! from its mass
Walls, palaces, half-cities, have been rear'd;
Yet oft the enormous skeleton ye pass,
And marvel where the spoil could have appear'd. 40
Hath it indeed been plunder'd, or but clear'd?
Alas! developed, opens the decay,
When the colossal fabric's form is near'd:
It will not bear the brightness of the day,
Which streams too much on all years, man, have reft
    away.

But when the rising moon begins to climb
Its topmost arch, and gently pauses there;
When the stars twinkle through the loops of time,
And the low night-breeze waves along the air
The garland-forest, which the gray walls wear,   50
Like laurels on the bald first Caesar's head;
When the light shines serene but doth not glare,
Then in this magic circle raise the dead:
Heroes have trod this spot—'tis on their dust ye tread.

'While stands the Coliseum, Rome shall stand;
'When falls the Coliseum, Rome shall fall;
'And when Rome falls—the World.' From our
    own land
Thus spake the pilgrims o'er this mighty wall
In Saxon times, which we are wont to call
Ancient; and these three mortal things are still   60
On their foundations, and unalter'd all;
Rome and her Ruin past Redemption's skill,
The World, the same wide den—of thieves, or what ye
    will.

DEATH OF THE PRINCESS CHARLOTTE

(Canto IV, clxvii–clxxii)

Hark! forth from the abyss a voice proceeds,
A long low distant murmur of dread sound,
Such as arises when a nation bleeds
With some deep and immedicable wound;
Through storm and darkness yawns the rending
    ground,
The gulf is thick with phantoms, but the chief
Seems royal still, though with her head discrown'd,
And pale, but lovely, with maternal grief
She clasps a babe, to whom her breast yields no relief.

Scion of chiefs and monarchs, where art thou?   10
Fond hope of many nations, art thou dead?
Could not the grave forget thee, and lay low
Some less majestic, less beloved head?
In the sad midnight, while thy heart still bled,
The mother of a moment, o'er thy boy,
Death hush'd that pang for ever: with thee fled
The present happiness and promised joy
Which fill'd the imperial isles so full it seem'd to cloy.

Peasants bring forth in safety.—Can it be,
Oh thou that wert so happy, so adored!   20
Those who weep not for kings shall weep for thee,
And Freedom's heart, grown heavy, cease to hoard

Her many griefs for ONE; for she had pour'd
Her orisons for thee, and o'er thy head
Beheld her Iris.—Thou, too, lonely lord,
And desolate consort—vainly wert thou wed!
The husband of a year! the father of the dead!

Of sackcloth was thy wedding garment made;
Thy bridal's fruit is ashes: in the dust
The fair-hair'd Daughter of the Isles is laid,   30
The love of millions! How we did intrust
Futurity to her! and, though it must
Darken above our bones, yet fondly deem'd
Our children should obey her child, and bless'd
Her and her hoped-for seed, whose promise seem'd
Like stars to shepherd's eyes:—'twas but a meteor
      beam'd.

Woe unto us, not her; for she sleeps well:
The fickle reek of popular breath, the tongue
Of hollow counsel, the false oracle,
Which from the birth of monarchy hath rung   40
Its knell in princely ears, till the o'erstung
Nations have arm'd in madness, the strange fate
Which tumbles mightiest sovereigns, and hath flung
Against their blind omnipotence a weight
Within the opposing scale, which crushes soon or
      late,—

These might have been her destiny; but no,
Our hearts deny it: and so young, so fair,
Good without effort, great without a foe;
But now a bride and mother—and now *there!*
How many ties did that stern moment tear!   50
From thy Sire's to his humblest subject's breast
Is link'd the electric chain of that despair,
Whose shock was as an earthquake's, and opprest
The land which loved thee so that none could love
      thee best.

I LOVE NOT MAN THE LESS, BUT NATURE MORE

(Canto IV, clxxvii–clxxxiv)

Oh! that the Desert were my dwelling-place,
With one fair Spirit for my minister,
That I might all forget the human race,
And, hating no one, love but only her!
Ye elements!—in whose ennobling stir
I feel myself exalted—Can ye not
Accord me such a being? Do I err
In deeming such inhabit many a spot?
Though with them to converse can rarely be our lot.

There is a pleasure in the pathless woods,   10
There is a rapture on the lonely shore,
There is society, where none intrudes,
By the deep Sea, and music in its roar:
I love not Man the less, but Nature more,
From these our interviews, in which I steal
From all I may be, or have been before,
To mingle with the Universe, and feel
What I can ne'er express, yet cannot all conceal.

Roll on, thou deep and dark blue Ocean—roll!
Ten thousand fleets sweep over thee in vain;   20
Man marks the earth with ruin—his control
Stops with the shore; upon the watery plain
The wrecks are all thy deed, nor doth remain
A shadow of man's ravage, save his own,
When, for a moment, like a drop of rain,
He sinks into thy depths with bubbling groan,
Without a grave, unknell'd, uncoffin'd, and unknown.

His steps are not upon thy paths,—thy fields
Are not a spoil for him,—thou dost arise
And shake him from thee; the vile strength he wields
For earth's destruction thou dost all despise,   31

Spurning him from thy bosom to the skies,
And send'st him, shivering in thy playful spray
And howling, to his Gods, where haply lies
His petty hope in some near port or bay,
And dashest him again to earth :—there let him lay.

The armaments which thunderstrike the walls
Of rock-built cities, bidding nations quake,
And monarchs tremble in their capitals,
The oak leviathans, whose huge ribs make   40
Their clay creator the vain title take
Of lord of thee, and arbiter of war—
These are thy toys, and, as the snowy flake,
They melt into thy yeast of waves, which mar
Alike the Armada's pride or spoils of Trafalgar.

Thy shores are empires, changed in all save thee—
Assyria, Greece, Rome, Carthage, what are they?
Thy waters wash'd them power while they were free,
And many a tyrant since ; their shores obey
The stranger, slave, or savage ; their decay   50
Has dried up realms to deserts :—not so thou ;—
Unchangeable, save to thy wild waves' play,
Time writes no wrinkle on thine azure brow :
Such as creation's dawn beheld, thou rollest now.

Thou glorious mirror, where the Almighty's form
Glasses itself in tempests ; in all time,—
Calm or convulsed, in breeze, or gale, or storm,
Icing the pole, or in the torrid clime
Dark-heaving—boundless, endless, and sublime,
The image of eternity, the throne   60
Of the Invisible ; even from out thy slime
The monsters of the deep are made ; each zone
Obeys thee ; thou goest forth, dread, fathomless, alone.

And I have loved thee, Ocean ! and my joy
Of youthful sports was on thy breast to be
Borne, like thy bubbles, onward : from a boy
I wanton'd with thy breakers—they to me

Were a delight ; and if the freshening sea
Made them a terror—'twas a pleasing fear,
For I was as it were a child of thee,   70
And trusted to thy billows far and near,
And laid my hand upon thy mane—as I do here.

FROM 'THE GIAOUR'

I

No breath of air to break the wave
That rolls below the Athenian's grave,
That tomb which, gleaming o'er the cliff,
First greets the homeward-veering skiff,
High o'er the land he saved in vain ;
When shall such hero live again ?

. . . . . .

Fair clime ! where every season smiles
Benignant o'er those blessed isles,
Which, seen from far Colonna's height,
Make glad the heart that hails the sight,   10
And lend to loneliness delight.
There mildly dimpling, Ocean's cheek
Reflects the tints of many a peak
Caught by the laughing tides that lave
These Edens of the eastern wave :
And if at times a transient breeze
Break the blue crystal of the seas,
Or sweep one blossom from the trees,
How welcome is each gentle air
That wakes and wafts the odours there !   20
For there the Rose, o'er crag or vale,
Sultana of the Nightingale,
The maid for whom his melody,
His thousand songs are heard on high,
Blooms blushing to her lover's tale :
His queen, the garden queen, his Rose,
Unbent by winds, unchill'd by snows,

Far from the winters of the west,
By every breeze and season blest,
Returns the sweets by nature given   30
In softest incense back to heaven ;
And grateful yields that smiling sky
Her fairest hue and fragrant sigh.
And many a summer flower is there,
And many a shade that love might share,
And many a grotto, meant for rest,
That holds the pirate for a guest ;
Whose bark in sheltering cove below
Lurks for the passing peaceful prow,
Till the gay mariner's guitar   40
Is heard, and seen the evening star ;
Then stealing with the muffled oar,
Far shaded by the rocky shore,
Rush the night-prowlers on the prey,
And turn to groans his roundelay.
Strange—that where Nature loved to trace,
As if for Gods, a dwelling-place,
And every charm and grace hath mix'd
Within the paradise she fix'd,
There man, enamour'd of distress,   50
Should mar it into wilderness,
And trample, brute-like, o'er each flower
That tasks not one laborious hour ;
Nor claims the culture of his hand
To bloom along the fairy land,
But springs as to preclude his care,
And sweetly woos him—but to spare !
Strange—that where all is peace beside,
There passion riots in her pride,
And lust and rapine wildly reign   60
To darken o'er the fair domain.
It is as though the fiends prevail'd
Against the seraphs they assail'd,
And, fix'd on heavenly thrones, should dwell
The freed inheritors of hell ;
So soft the scene, so form'd for joy,
So curst the tyrants that destroy !

He who hath bent him o'er the dead
Ere the first day of death is fled,
The first dark day of nothingness,   70
The last of danger and distress,
(Before Decay's effacing fingers
Have swept the lines where beauty lingers,)
And mark'd the mild angelic air,
The rapture of repose that's there,
The fix'd yet tender traits that streak
The languor of the placid cheek,
And—but for that sad shrouded eye,
   That fires not, wins not, weeps not, now,
    And but for that chill, changeless brow,   80
Where cold Obstruction's apathy
Appals the gazing mourner's heart,
As if to him it could impart
The doom he dreads, yet dwells upon;
Yes, but for these and these alone,
Some moments, ay, one treacherous hour,
He still might doubt the tyrant's power;
So fair, so calm, so softly seal'd,
The first, last look by death reveal'd!
Such is the aspect of this shore;   90
'Tis Greece, but living Greece no more!
So coldly sweet, so deadly fair,
We start, for soul is wanting there.
Hers is the loveliness in death,
That parts not quite with parting breath;
But beauty with that fearful bloom,
That hue which haunts it to the tomb,
Expression's last receding ray,
A gilded halo hovering round decay,
The farewell beam of Feeling pass'd away!   100
Spark of that flame, perchance of heavenly birth,
Which gleams, but warms no more its cherish'd
    earth!

Clime of the unforgotten brave!
Whose land from plain to mountain-cave
Was Freedom's home or Glory's grave!

Shrine of the mighty ! can it be,
That this is all remains of thee ?
Approach, thou craven crouching slave :
  Say, is not this Thermopylæ ?
These waters blue that round you lave,—   110
  Oh servile offspring of the free,
Pronounce what sea, what shore is this ?
The gulf, the rock of Salamis !
These scenes, their story not unknown,
Arise, and make again your own ;
Snatch from the ashes of your sires
The embers of their former fires ;
And he who in the strife expires
Will add to theirs a name of fear
That Tyranny shall quake to hear,   120
And leave his sons a hope, a fame,
They too will rather die than shame :
For Freedom's battle once begun,
Bequeathed by bleeding Sire to Son,
Though baffled oft is ever won.
Bear witness, Greece, thy living page !
Attest it many a deathless age !
While kings, in dusty darkness hid,
Have left a nameless pyramid,
Thy heroes, though the general doom   130
Hath swept the column from their tomb,
A mightier monument command,
The mountains of their native land !
There points thy Muse to stranger's eye
The graves of those that cannot die !
'Twere long to tell, and sad to trace,
Each step from splendour to disgrace ;
Enough—no foreign foe could quell
Thy soul, till from itself it fell ;
Yes ! Self-abasement paved the way   140
To villain-bonds and despot sway.

II

As rising on its purple wing
The insect queen of eastern spring,
O'er emerald meadows of Kashmeer
Invites the young pursuer near,
And leads him on from flower to flower
A weary chase and wasted hour,
Then leaves him, as it soars on high,
With panting heart and tearful eye:
So Beauty lures the full-grown child,
With hue as bright, and wing as wild;   10
A chase of idle hopes and fears,
Begun in folly, closed in tears.
If won, to equal ills betray'd,
Woe waits the insect and the maid;
A life of pain, the loss of peace,
From infant's play, and man's caprice:
The lovely toy so fiercely sought
Hath lost its charm by being caught,
For every touch that woo'd its stay
Hath brush'd its brightest hues away,   20
Till charm, and hue, and beauty gone,
'Tis left to fly or fall alone.
With wounded wing, or bleeding breast,
Ah! where shall either victim rest?
Can this with faded pinion soar
From rose to tulip as before?
Or Beauty, blighted in an hour,
Find joy within her broken bower?
No: gayer insects fluttering by
Ne'er droop the wing o'er those that die,   30
And lovelier things have mercy shown
To every failing but their own,
And every woe a tear can claim
Except an erring sister's shame.

.   .   .   .   .   .

The Mind, that broods o'er guilty woes,
   Is like the Scorpion girt by fire;
In circle narrowing as it glows,

The flames around their captive close,
Till inly search'd by thousand throes,
  And maddening in her ire,   40
One sad and sole relief she knows,
The sting she nourish'd for her foes,
Whose venom never yet was vain,
Gives but one pang and cures all pain,
And darts into her desperate brain :
So do the dark in soul expire,
Or live like Scorpion girt by fire ;
So writhes the mind Remorse hath riven,
Unfit for earth, undoomed for heaven,
Darkness above, despair beneath,   50
Around it flame, within it death !

'KNOW YE THE LAND ?'

(From *The Bride of Abydos*.)

KNOW ye the land where the cypress and myrtle
  Are emblems of deeds that are done in their clime ?
Where the rage of the vulture, the love of the turtle,
  Now melt into sorrow, now madden to crime !
Know ye the land of the cedar and vine,
Where the flowers ever blossom, the beams ever shine ;
Where the light wings of Zephyr, oppress'd with
    perfume,
Wax faint o'er the gardens of Gúl in her bloom ;
Where the citron and olive are fairest of fruit,
And the voice of the nightingale never is mute ;   10
Where the tints of the earth, and the hues of the sky,
In colour though varied, in beauty may vie,
And the purple of ocean is deepest in dye ;
Where the virgins are soft as the roses they twine,
And all, save the spirit of man, is divine ?
'Tis the clime of the East ; 'tis the land of the Sun—
Can he smile on such deeds as his children have done ?
Oh ! wild as the accents of lovers' farewell
Are the hearts which they bear, and the tales which
    they tell.

THE HELLESPONT

(The Bride of Abydos, II, i–iv)

I

THE winds are high on Helle's wave,
  As on that night of stormy water
When Love, who sent, forgot to save
The young, the beautiful, the brave,
    The lonely hope of Sestos' daughter.
Oh! when alone along the sky
Her turret-torch was blazing high,
Though rising gale, and breaking foam,
And shrieking sea-birds warn'd him home;
And clouds aloft and tides below,   10
With signs and sounds, forbade to go,
He could not see, he would not hear,
Or sound or sign foreboding fear;
His eye but saw that light of love,
The only star it hail'd above;
His ear but rang with Hero's song,
'Ye waves, divide not lovers long!'—
That tale is old, but love anew
May nerve young hearts to prove as true.

II

The winds are high, and Helle's tide   20
  Rolls darkly heaving to the main;
And Night's descending shadows hide
  That field with blood bedew'd in vain,
    The desert of old Priam's pride;
    The tombs, sole relics of his reign,
All—save immortal dreams that could beguile
The blind old man of Scio's rocky isle!

III

Oh! yet—for there my steps have been;
  These feet have press'd the sacred shore,
These limbs that buoyant wave hath borne—
Minstrel! with thee to muse, to mourn,   31
  To trace again those fields of yore,

Believing every hillock green
  Contains no fabled hero's ashes,
And that around the undoubted scene
  Thine own 'broad Hellespont' still dashes,
Be long my lot! and cold were he
Who there could gaze denying thee!

IV

The night hath closed on Helle's stream,
  Nor yet hath risen on Ida's hill   40
That moon, which shone on his high theme:
No warrior chides her peaceful beam,
  But conscious shepherds bless it still.
Their flocks are grazing on the mound
  Of him who felt the Dardan's arrow:
That mighty heap of gather'd ground
Which Ammon's son ran proudly round,
By nations raised, by monarchs crown'd,
  Is now a lone and nameless barrow!
  Within—thy dwelling-place how narrow!   50
Without—can only strangers breathe
The name of him that *was* beneath:
Dust long outlasts the storied stone;
But Thou—thy very dust is gone!

FROM 'THE CORSAIR'

'O'er the glad waters of the dark blue sea,
Our thoughts as boundless, and our souls as free,
Far as the breeze can bear, the billows foam,
Survey our empire, and behold our home!
These are our realms, no limits to their sway—
Our flag the sceptre all who meet obey.
Ours the wild life in tumult still to range
From toil to rest, and joy in every change.
Oh, who can tell? not thou, luxurious slave!
Whose soul would sicken o'er the heaving wave;   10
Not thou, vain lord of wantonness and ease!
Whom slumber soothes not—pleasure cannot please—

Oh, who can tell, save he whose heart hath tried,
And danced in triumph o'er the waters wide,
The exulting sense—the pulse's maddening play,
That thrills the wanderer of that trackless way?
That for itself can woo the approaching fight,
And turn what some deem danger to delight;
That seeks what cravens shun with more than zeal,
And where the feebler faint can only feel—   20
Feel—to the rising bosom's inmost core,
Its hope awaken and its spirit soar?
No dread of death—if with us die our foes—
Save that it seems even duller than repose:
Come when it will—we snatch the life of life—
When lost—what recks it—by disease or strife?
Let him who crawls enamour'd of decay,
Cling to his couch, and sicken years away:
Heave his thick breath, and shake his palsied hea....
Ours—the fresh turf, and not the feverish bed.   30
While gasp by gasp he falters forth his soul,
Ours with one pang—one bound—escapes control.
His corse may boast its urn and narrow cave,
And they who loathed his life may gild his grave:
Ours are the tears, though few, sincerely shed,
When Ocean shrouds and sepulchres our dead.
For us, even banquets fond regret supply
In the red cup that crowns our memory;
And the brief epitaph in danger's day,
When those who win at length divide the prey,   40
And cry, Remembrance saddening o'er each brow,
How had the brave who fell exulted *now!*

THE SIEGE OF CORINTH

In the year since Jesus died for men,
Eighteen hundred years and ten,
We were a gallant company,
Riding o'er land, and sailing o'er sea.
Oh! but we went merrily!
We forded the river, and clomb the high hill,
Never our steeds for a day stood still;
Whether we lay in the cave or the shed,
Our sleep fell soft on the hardest bed:
Whether we couched in our rough capote,　　10
On the rougher plank of our gliding boat,
Or stretched on the beach, or our saddles spread,
As a pillow beneath the resting head,
Fresh we woke upon the morrow:
　　All our thoughts and words had scope,
　　We had health, and we had hope,
Toil and travel, but no sorrow.
We were of all tongues and creeds;—
Some were those who counted beads,
Some of mosque, and some of church,　　20
　　And some, or I mis-say, of neither;
Yet through the wide world might ye search,
　　Nor find a motlier crew nor blither.
But some are dead, and some are gone,
And some are scattered and alone,
And some are rebels on the hills
　　That look along Epirus' valleys,
　　Where Freedom still at moments rallies,
And pays in blood Oppression's ills;
　　And some are in a far countree,　　30
And some all restlessly at home;
　　But never more, oh! never, we
Shall meet to revel and to roam.

But those hardy days flew cheerily !
And when they now fall drearily,
My thoughts, like swallows, skim the main,
And bear my spirit back again
Over the earth, and through the air,
A wild bird and a wanderer.
'Tis this that ever wakes my strain, 40
And oft, too oft, implores again
The few who may endure my lay,
To follow me so far away.
Stranger, wilt thou follow now,
And sit with me on Acro-Corinth's brow ?

I

Many a vanish'd year and age,
And tempest's breath, and battle's rage,
Have swept o'er Corinth ; yet she stands,
A fortress form'd to Freedom's hands.
The whirlwind's wrath, the earthquake's shock,
Have left untouch'd her hoary rock, 51
The keystone of a land, which still,
Though fall'n, looks proudly on that hill,
The landmark to the double tide
That purpling rolls on either side,
As if their waters chafed to meet,
Yet pause and crouch beneath her feet.
But could the blood before her shed
Since first Timoleon's brother bled,
Or baffled Persia's despot fled, 60
Arise from out the earth which drank
The stream of slaughter as it sank,
That sanguine ocean would o'erflow
Her isthmus idly spread below :
Or could the bones of all the slain,
Who perish'd there, be piled again,
That rival pyramid would rise
More mountain-like, through those clear skies,
Than yon tower-capp'd Acropolis,
Which seems the very clouds to kiss. 70

II

On dun Cithæron's ridge appears
The gleam of twice ten thousand spears;
And downward to the Isthmian plain,
From shore to shore of either main,
The tent is pitch'd, the crescent shines
Along the Moslem's leaguering lines;
And the dusk Spahi's bands advance
Beneath each bearded pacha's glance;
And far and wide as eye can reach
The turban'd cohorts throng the beach;   80
And there the Arab's camel kneels,
And there his steed the Tartar wheels;
The Turcoman hath left his herd,
The sabre round his loins to gird;
And there the volleying thunders pour,
Till waves grow smoother to the roar.
The trench is dug, the cannon's breath
Wings the far hissing globe of death;
Fast whirl the fragments from the wall,
Which crumbles with the ponderous ball;   90
And from that wall the foe replies,
O'er dusty plain and smoky skies,
With fires that answer fast and well
The summons of the Infidel.

III

But near and nearest to the wall
Of those who wish and work its fall,
With deeper skill in war's black art
Than Othman's sons, and high of heart
As any chief that ever stood
Triumphant in the fields of blood;   100
From post to post, and deed to deed,
Fast spurring on his reeking steed,
Where sallying ranks the trench assail,
And make the foremost Moslem quail;

Or where the battery, guarded well,
Remains as yet impregnable,
Alighting cheerly to inspire
The soldier slackening in his fire;
The first and freshest of the host
Which Stamboul's Sultan there can boast,   110
To guide the follower o'er the field,
To point the tube, the lance to wield,
Or whirl around the bickering blade;—
Was Alp, the Adrian renegade!

IV

From Venice—once a race of worth
His gentle sires—he drew his birth;
But late an exile from her shore,
Against his countrymen he bore
The arms they taught to bear; and now
The turban girt his shaven brow.   120
Through many a change had Corinth pass'd
With Greece to Venice' rule at last;
And here, before her walls, with those
To Greece and Venice equal foes,
He stood a foe, with all the zeal
Which young and fiery converts feel,
Within whose heated bosom throngs
The memory of a thousand wrongs.
To him had Venice ceased to be
Her ancient civic boast—'the Free';   130
And in the palace of St. Mark
Unnamed accusers in the dark
Within the 'Lion's mouth' had placed
A charge against him uneffaced:
He fled in time, and saved his life,
To waste his future years in strife,
That taught his land how great her loss
In him who triumph'd o'er the Cross,
'Gainst which he rear'd the Crescent high,
And battled to avenge or die.   140

V

Coumourgi—he whose closing scene
Adorn'd the triumph of Eugene,
When on Carlowitz' bloody plain,
The last and mightiest of the slain,
He sank, regretting not to die,
But cursed the Christian's victory—
Coumourgi—can his glory cease,
That latest conqueror of Greece,
Till Christian hands to Greece restore
The freedom Venice gave of yore?   150
A hundred years have roll'd away
Since he refix'd the Moslem's sway;
And now he led the Mussulman,
And gave the guidance of the van
To Alp, who well repaid the trust
By cities levell'd with the dust;
And proved, by many a deed of death,
How firm his heart in novel faith.

VI

The walls grew weak; and fast and hot
Against them pour'd the ceaseless shot,   160
With unabating fury sent
From battery to battlement;
And thunder-like the pealing din
Rose from each heated culverin;
And here and there some crackling dome
Was fired before the exploding bomb;
And as the fabric sank beneath
The shattering shell's volcanic breath,
In red and wreathing columns flashed
The flame, as loud the ruin crashed,   170
Or into countless meteors driven,
Its earth-stars melted into heaven;
Whose clouds that day grew doubly dun,
Impervious to the hidden sun,
With volumed smoke that slowly grew
To one wide sky of sulphurous hue.

VII

But not for vengeance, long delay'd,
Alone, did Alp, the renegade,
The Moslem warriors sternly teach
His skill to pierce the promised breach .   180
Within these walls a maid was pent
His hope would win, without consent
Of that inexorable sire,
Whose heart refused him in its ire,
When Alp, beneath his Christian name,
Her virgin hand aspired to claim.
In happier mood, and earlier time,
While unimpeach'd for traitorous crime,
Gayest in gondola or hall,
He glitter'd through the Carnival ;   190
And tuned the softest serenade
That e'er on Adria's waters play'd
At midnight to Italian maid.

VIII

And many deem'd her heart was won,
For sought by numbers, given to none,
Had young Francesca's hand remain'd
Still by the church's bonds unchain'd :
And when the Adriatic bore
Lanciotto to the Paynim shore,
Her wonted smiles were seen to fail,   200
And pensive wax'd the maid and pale ;
More constant at confessional,
More rare at masque and festival ;
Or seen at such, with downcast eyes,
Which conquer'd hearts they ceased to prize :
With listless look she seems to gaze :
With humbler care her form arrays ;
Her voice less lively in the song ;
Her step, though light, less fleet among
The pairs, on whom the Morning's glance   210
Breaks, yet unsated with the dance.

IX

Sent by the state to guard the land,
(Which, wrested from the Moslem's hand,
While Sobieski tamed his pride
By Buda's wall and Danube's side,
The chiefs of Venice wrung away
From Patra to Euboea's bay,)
Minotti held in Corinth's towers
The Doge's delegated powers,
While yet the pitying eye of Peace   220
Smiled o'er her long-forgotten Greece:
And ere that faithless truce was broke
Which freed her from the unchristian yoke,
With him his gentle daughter came;
Nor there, since Menelaus' dame
Forsook her lord and land, to prove
What woes await on lawless love,
Had fairer form adorn'd the shore
Than she, the matchless stranger, bore.

X

The wall is rent, the ruins yawn;   230
And with to-morrow's earliest dawn,
O'er the disjointed mass shall vault
The foremost of the fierce assault.
The bands are rank'd; the chosen van
Of Tartar and of Mussulman,
The full of hope, misnamed 'forlorn',
Who hold the thought of death in scorn,
And win their way with falchion's force,
Or pave the path with many a corse,
O'er which the following brave may rise,   240
Their stepping-stone—the last who dies!

XI

'Tis midnight: on the mountains brown
The cold, round moon shines deeply down;
Blue roll the waters, blue the sky
Spreads like an ocean hung on high,

Bespangled with those isles of light,
So wildly, spiritually bright;
Who ever gazed upon them shining
And turn'd to earth without repining.
Nor wish'd for wings to flee away,   250
And mix with their eternal ray?
The waves on either shore lay there
Calm, clear, and azure as the air;
And scarce their foam the pebbles shook,
But murmur'd meekly as the brook.
The winds were pillow'd on the waves;
The banners droop'd along their staves,
And, as they fell around them furling,
Above them shone the crescent curling;
And that deep silence was unbroke,   260
Save where the watch his signal spoke,
Save where the steed neigh'd oft and shrill,
And echo answer'd from the hill,
And the wide hum of that wild host
Rustled like leaves from coast to coast,
As rose the Muezzin's voice in air
In midnight call to wonted prayer;
It rose, that chanted mournful strain,
Like some lone spirit's o'er the plain:
'Twas musical, but sadly sweet,   270
Such as when winds and harp-strings meet,
And take a long unmeasured tone,
To mortal minstrelsy unknown.
It seem'd to those within the wall
A cry prophetic of their fall:
It struck even the besieger's ear
With something ominous and drear,
An undefined and sudden thrill,
Which makes the heart a moment still,
Then beat with quicker pulse, ashamed   280
Of that strange sense its silence framed;
Such as a sudden passing-bell
Wakes, though but for a stranger's knell.

XII

The tent of Alp was on the shore;
The sound was hush'd, the prayer was o'er;
The watch was set, the night-round made,
All mandates issued and obey'd:
'Tis but another anxious night,
His pains the morrow may requite
With all revenge and love can pay,   290
In guerdon for their long delay.
Few hours remain, and he hath need
Of rest, to nerve for many a deed
Of slaughter; but within his soul
The thoughts like troubled waters roll.
He stood alone among the host;
Not his the loud fanatic boast
To plant the Crescent o'er the Cross,
Or risk a life with little loss,
Secure in paradise to be   300
By Houris loved immortally:
Nor his, what burning patriots feel,
The stern exaltedness of zeal,
Profuse of blood, untired in toil,
When battling on the parent soil.
He stood alone—a renegade
Against the country he betray'd;
He stood alone amidst his band,
Without a trusted heart or hand:
They follow'd him, for he was brave,   310
And great the spoil he got and gave;
They crouch'd to him, for he had skill
To warp and wield the vulgar will:
But still his Christian origin
With them was little less than sin.
They envied even the faithless fame
He earn'd beneath a Moslem name;
Since he, their mightiest chief, had been
In youth a bitter Nazarene.
They did not know how pride can stoop,   320
When baffled feelings withering droop;

They did not know how hate can burn
In hearts once changed from soft to stern;
Nor all the false and fatal zeal
The convert of revenge can feel.
He ruled them—man may rule the worst,
By ever daring to be first:
So lions o'er the jackal sway;
The jackal points, he fells the prey,
Then on the vulgar yelling press,   330
To gorge the relics of success.

XIII

His head grows fever'd, and his pulse
The quick successive throbs convulse:
In vain from side to side he throws
His form, in courtship of repose;
Or if he dozed, a sound, a start
Awoke him with a sunken heart.
The turban on his hot brow press'd,
The mail weigh'd lead-like on his breast,
Though oft and long beneath its weight   340
Upon his eyes had slumber sate,
Without or couch or canopy,
Except a rougher field and sky
Than now might yield a warrior's bed,
Than now along the heaven was spread.
He could not rest, he could not stay
Within his tent to wait for day,
But walk'd him forth along the sand,
Where thousand sleepers strew'd the strand.
What pillow'd them? and why should he   350
More wakeful than the humblest be,
Since more their peril, worse their toil?
And yet they fearless dream of spoil;
While he alone, where thousands pass'd
A night of sleep, perchance their last,
In sickly vigil wander'd on,
And envied all he gazed upon.

XIV

He felt his soul become more light
Beneath the freshness of the night.
Cool was the silent sky, though calm,   360
And bathed his brow with airy balm:
Behind, the camp—before him lay,
In many a winding creek and bay,
Lepanto's gulf; and, on the brow
Of Delphi's hill, unshaken snow,
High and eternal, such as shone
Through thousand summers brightly gone,
Along the gulf, the mount, the clime;
It will not melt, like man, to time:
Tyrant and slave are swept away,   370
Less form'd to wear before the ray;
But that white veil, the lightest, frailest,
Which on the mighty mount thou hailest,
While tower and tree are torn and rent,
Shines o'er its craggy battlement;
In form a peak, in height a cloud,
In texture like a hovering shroud,
Thus high by parting Freedom spread,
As from her fond abode she fled,
And linger'd on the spot, where long   380
Her prophet spirit spake in song.
Oh! still her step at moments falters
O'er wither'd fields, and ruin'd altars,
And fain would wake, in souls too broken,
By pointing to each glorious token:
But vain her voice, till better days
Dawn in those yet remember'd rays,
Which shone upon the Persian flying,
And saw the Spartan smile in dying.

XV

Not mindful of these mighty times   390
Was Alp, despite his flight and crimes;
And through this night, as on he wander'd,
And o'er the past and present ponder'd,

And thought upon the glorious dead
Who there in better cause had bled,
He felt how faint and feebly dim
The fame that could accrue to him,
Who cheer'd the band, and waved the sword,
A traitor in a turban'd horde;
And led them to the lawless siege, 400
Whose best success were sacrilege.
Not so had those his fancy number'd,
The chiefs whose dust around him slumber'd;
Their phalanx marshall'd on the plain,
Whose bulwarks were not then in vain.
They fell devoted, but undying;
The very gale their names seem'd sighing;
The waters murmur'd of their name;
The woods were peopled with their fame;
The silent pillar, lone and grey, 410
Claim'd kindred with their sacred clay;
Their spirits wrapped the dusky mountain,
Their memory sparkled o'er the fountain;
The meanest rill, the mightiest river
Roll'd mingling with their fame for ever.
Despite of every yoke she bears,
That land is glory's still and theirs!
'Tis still a watchword to the earth:
When man would do a deed of worth
He points to Greece, and turns to tread, 420
So sanction'd, on the tyrant's head:
He looks to her, and rushes on
Where life is lost, or freedom won.

XVI

Still by the shore Alp mutely mused,
And woo'd the freshness Night diffused.
There shrinks no ebb in that tideless sea,
Which changeless rolls eternally;
So that wildest of waves, in their angriest mood,
Scarce break on the bounds of the land for a rood;
And the powerless moon beholds them flow, 430
Heedless if she come or go:

Calm or high, in main or bay,
On their course she hath no sway.
The rock unworn its base doth bare,
And looks o'er the surf, but it comes not there;
And the fringe of the foam may be seen below,
On the line that it left long ages ago:
A smooth short space of yellow sand
Between it and the greener land.

He wander'd on along the beach,   440
Till within the range of a carbine's reach
Of the leaguer'd wall; but they saw him not,
Or how could he 'scape from the hostile shot?
Did traitors lurk in the Christians' hold?
Were their hands grown stiff, or their hearts wax'd cold?
I know not, in sooth; but from yonder wall
There flash'd no fire, and there hiss'd no ball,
Though he stood beneath the bastion's frown,
That flank'd the seaward gate of the town;
Though he heard the sound, and could almost tell   450
The sullen words of the sentinel,
As his measured step on the stone below
Clank'd, as he paced it to and fro;
And he saw the lean dogs beneath the wall
Hold o'er the dead their carnival,
Gorging and growling o'er carcass and limb;
They were too busy to bark at him!
From a Tartar's skull they had stripp'd the flesh,
As ye peel the fig when its fruit is fresh;
And their white tusks crunch'd o'er the whiter skull,
As it slipp'd through their jaws, when their edge grew
        dull,   461
As they lazily mumbled the bones of the dead,
When they scarce could rise from the spot where they
        fed;
So well had they broken a lingering fast
With those who had fallen for that night's repast.
And Alp knew, by the turbans that roll'd on the sand,
The foremost of these were the best of his band:
Crimson and green were the shawls of their wear,

And each scalp had a single long tuft of hair,
All the rest was shaven and bare.   470
The scalps were in the wild dog's maw,
The hair was tangled round his jaw:
But close by the shore, on the edge of the gulf,
There sat a vulture flapping a wolf,
Who had stolen from the hills, but kept away,
Scared by the dogs, from the human prey;
But he seized on his share of a steed that lay,
Pick'd by the birds, on the sands of the bay.

XVII

Alp turn'd him from the sickening sight:
Never had shaken his nerves in fight;   480
But he better could brook to behold the dying,
Deep in the tide of their warm blood lying,
Scorch'd with the death-thirst, and writhing in vain,
Than the perishing dead who are past all pain.
There is something of pride in the perilous hour,
Whate'er be the shape in which death may lower;
For Fame is there to say who bleeds,
And Honour's eye on daring deeds!
But when all is past, it is humbling to tread
O'er the weltering field of the tombless dead,   490
And see worms of the earth, and fowls of the air,
Beasts of the forest, all gathering there;
All regarding man as their prey,
All rejoicing in his decay.

XVIII

There is a temple in ruin stands,
Fashion'd by long forgotten hands;
Two or three columns, and many a stone,
Marble and granite, with grass o'ergrown!
Out upon Time! it will leave no more
Of the things to come than the things before!   500
Out upon Time! who for ever will leave
But enough of the past for the future to grieve

O'er that which hath been, and o'er that which must be:
What we have seen, our sons shall see;
Remnants of things that have pass'd away,
Fragments of stone, reared by creatures of clay!

XIX

He sate him down at a pillar's base,
And pass'd his hand athwart his face;
Like one in dreary musing mood,
Declining was his attitude;   510
His head was drooping on his breast,
Fever'd, throbbing, and oppressed;
And o'er his brow, so downward bent,
Oft his beating fingers went,
Hurriedly, as you may see
Your own run over the ivory key,
Ere the measured tone is taken
By the chords you would awaken.
There he sate all heavily,
As he heard the night-wind sigh.   520
Was it the wind through some hollow stone
Sent that soft and tender moan?
He lifted his head, and he look'd on the sea,
But it was unrippled as glass may be;
He look'd on the long grass—it waved not a blade;
How was that gentle sound convey'd?
He look'd to the banners—each flag lay still,
So did the leaves on Cithæron's hill,
And he felt not a breath come over his cheek;
What did that sudden sound bespeak?   530
He turn'd to the left—is he sure of sight?
There sate a lady, youthful and bright!

XX

He started up with more of fear
Than if an armed foe were near.
'God of my fathers! what is here?
Who art thou? and wherefore sent
So near a hostile armament?'
His trembling hands refused to sign

The cross he deem'd no more divine :
He had resumed it in that hour, 540
But conscience wrung away the power.
He gazed, he saw : he knew the face
Of beauty, and the form of grace ;
It was Francesca by his side,
The maid who might have been his bride !

The rose was yet upon her cheek,
But mellow'd with a tenderer streak :
Where was the play of her soft lips fled ?
Gone was the smile that enliven'd their red.
The ocean's calm within their view, 550
Beside her eye had less of blue ;
But like that cold wave it stood still,
And its glance, though clear, was chill.
Around her form a thin robe twining,
Nought conceal'd her bosom shining ;
Through the parting of her hair,
Floating darkly downward there,
Her rounded arm show'd white and bare :
And ere yet she made reply,
Once she raised her hand on high ; 560
It was so wan, and transparent of hue,
You might have seen the moon shine through.

XXI

' I come from my rest to him I love best,
That I may be happy, and he may be blessed,
I have pass'd the guards, the gate, the wall ;
Sought thee in safety through foes and all.
'Tis said the lion will turn and flee
From a maid in the pride of her purity ;
And the Power on high, that can shield the good
Thus from the tyrant of the wood, 570
Hath extended its mercy to guard me as well
From the hands of the leaguering infidel.
I come—and if I come in vain,
Never, oh never, we meet again !

Thou hast done a fearful deed
In falling away from thy fathers' creed :
But dash that turban to earth, and sign
The sign of the cross, and for ever be mine ;
Wring the black drop from thy heart,
And to-morrow unites us no more to part.'   580

' And where should our bridal couch be spread ?
In the midst of the dying and the dead ?
For to-morrow we give to the slaughter and flame
The sons and the shrines of the Christian name.
None, save thou and thine, I've sworn,
Shall be left upon the morn :
But thee will I bear to a lovely spot,
Where our hands shall be join'd, and our sorrow
          forgot.
There thou yet shalt be my bride,
When once again I've quell'd the pride   590
Of Venice ; and her hated race
Have felt the arm they would debase
Scourge, with a whip of scorpions, those
Whom vice and envy made my foes.'

Upon his hand she laid her own—
Light was the touch, but it thrill'd to the bone,
And shot a chillness to his heart,
Which fix'd him beyond the power to start.
Though slight was that grasp so mortal cold,
He could not loose him from its hold ;   600
But never did clasp of one so dear
Strike on the pulse with such feeling of fear,
As those thin fingers, long and white,
Froze through his blood by their touch that night.
The feverish glow of his brow was gone,
And his heart sank so still that it felt like stone,
As he look'd on the face, and beheld its hue,
So deeply changed from what he knew :
Fair but faint—without the ray
Of mind, that made each feature play   610
Like sparkling waves on a sunny day ;

And her motionless lips lay still as death,
And her words came forth without her breath,
And there rose not a heave o'er her bosom's swell,
And there seem'd not a pulse in her veins to dwell.
Though her eye shone out, yet the lids were fix'd,
And the glance that it gave was wild and unmix'd
With aught of change, as the eyes may seem
Of the restless who walk in a troubled dream;
Like the figures on arras, that gloomily glare,   620
Stirr'd by the breath of the wintry air,
So seen by the dying lamp's fitful light,
Lifeless, but life-like, and awful to sight;
As they seem, through the dimness, about to come down
From the shadowy wall where their images frown;
Fearfully flitting to and fro,
As the gusts on the tapestry come and go.

'If not for love of me be given
Thus much, then, for the love of Heaven,—
Again I say—that turban tear   630
From off thy faithless brow, and swear
Thine injured country's sons to spare,
Or thou art lost; and never shalt see—
Not earth—that's past—but heaven or me.
If this thou dost accord, albeit
A heavy doom 'tis thine to meet,
That doom shall half absolve thy sin,
And mercy's gate may receive thee within:
But pause one moment more, and take
The curse of Him thou didst forsake;   640
And look once more to heaven, and see
Its love for ever shut from thee.
There is a light cloud by the moon—
'Tis passing, and will pass full soon—
If, by the time its vapoury sail
Hath ceased her shaded orb to veil,
Thy heart within thee is not changed,
Then God and man are both avenged;
Dark will thy doom be, darker still
Thine immortality of ill.'   650

Alp look'd to heaven, and saw on high
The sign she spake of in the sky;
But his heart was swollen, and turn'd aside,
By deep interminable pride.
This first false passion of his breast
Roll'd like a torrent o'er the rest.
He sue for mercy! *He* dismay'd
By wild words of a timid maid!
He, wrong'd by Venice, vow to save
Her sons, devoted to the grave!   660
No—though that cloud were thunder's worst,
And charged to crush him—let it burst!

He look'd upon it earnestly,
Without an accent of reply;
He watch'd it passing; it is flown:
Full on his eye the clear moon shone,
And thus he spake—'Whate'er my fate,
I am no changeling—'tis too late:
The reed in storms may bow and quiver,
Then rise again; the tree must shiver.   670
What Venice made me, I must be,
Her foe in all, save love to thee:
But thou art safe: oh, fly with me!'
He turn'd, but she is gone!
Nothing is there but the column stone.
Hath she sunk in the earth, or melted in air?
He saw not—he knew not—but nothing is there.

XXII

The night is past, and shines the sun
As if that morn were a jocund one.
Lightly and brightly breaks away   680
The Morning from her mantle grey,
And the Noon will look on a sultry day.
Hark to the trump, and the drum,
And the mournful sound of the barbarous horn,
And the flap of the banners, that flit as they're borne,

And the neigh of the steed, and the multitude's hum,
And the clash, and the shout, 'They come! they come!'
The horsetails are pluck'd from the ground, and the sword
From its sheath; and they form, and but wait for the word.
Tartar, and Spahi, and Turcoman,   690
Strike your tents, and throng to the van;
Mount ye, spur ye, skirr the plain,
That the fugitive may flee in vain,
When he breaks from the town; and none escape,
Aged or young, in the Christian shape;
While your fellows on foot, in a fiery mass,
Bloodstain the breach through which they pass.
The steeds are all bridled, and snort to the rein;
Curved is each neck, and flowing each mane;
White is the foam of their champ on the bit;   700
The spears are uplifted; the matches are lit;
The cannon are pointed, and ready to roar,
And crush the wall they have crumbled before:
Forms in his phalanx each janizar;
Alp at their head; his right arm is bare,
So is the blade of his scimitar;
The khan and the pachas are all at their post;
The vizier himself at the head of the host.
When the culverin's signal is fired, then on;
Leave not in Corinth a living one—   710
A priest at her altars, a chief in her halls,
A hearth in her mansions, a stone on her walls.
God and the prophet—Alla Hu!
Up to the skies with that wild halloo!
'There the breach lies for passage, the ladder to scale;
And your hands on your sabres, and how should ye fail?
He who first downs with the red cross may crave
His heart's dearest wish; let him ask it, and have!'
Thus utter'd Coumourgi, the dauntless vizier;
The reply was the brandish of sabre and spear,   720
And the shout of fierce thousands in joyous ire:—
Silence—hark to the signal—fire!

XXIII

As the wolves, that headlong go
On the stately buffalo,
Though with fiery eyes, and angry roar,
And hoofs that stamp, and horns that gore,
He tramples on earth, or tosses on high
The foremost, who rush on his strength but to die:
Thus against the wall they went,
Thus the first were backward bent;   730
Many a bosom, sheathed in brass,
Strew'd the earth like broken glass,
Shiver'd by the shot, that tore
The ground whereon they moved no more:
Even as they fell, in files they lay,
Like the mower's grass at the close of day,
When his work is done on the levell'd plain;
Such was the fall of the foremost slain.

XXIV

As the spring-tides, with heavy plash,
From the cliffs invading dash
Huge fragments, sapp'd by the ceaseless flow,   740
Till white and thundering down they go,
Like the avalanche's snow
On the Alpine vales below;
Thus at length, outbreathed and worn,
Corinth's sons were downward borne
By the long and oft renew'd
Charge of the Moslem multitude.
In firmness they stood, and in masses they fell,
Heaped by the host of the infidel,   750
Hand to hand, and foot to foot:
Nothing there, save death, was mute:
Stroke, and thrust, and flash, and cry
For quarter, or for victory,
Mingle there with the volleying thunder,
Which makes the distant cities wonder
How the sounding battle goes,
If with them, or for their foes;

If they must mourn, or may rejoice
In that annihilating voice,   760
Which pierces the deep hills through and through
With an echo dread and new:
You might have heard it, on that day,
O'er Salamis and Megara;
(We have heard the hearers say,)
Even unto Piræus' bay.

XXV

From the point of encountering blades to the hilt,
Sabres and swords with blood were gilt;
But the rampart is won, and the spoil begun,
And all but the after carnage done.   770
Shriller shrieks now mingling come
From within the plunder'd dome:
Hark to the haste of flying feet,
That splash in the blood of the slippery street;
But here and there, where 'vantage ground
Against the foe may still be found,
Desperate groups, of twelve or ten,
Make a pause, and turn again—
With banded backs against the wall,
Fiercely stand, or fighting fall.   780

There stood an old man—his hairs were white,
But his veteran arm was full of might:
So gallantly bore he the brunt of the fray,
The dead before him, on that day,
In a semicircle lay;
Still he combated unwounded,
Though retreating, unsurrounded.
Many a scar of former fight
Lurk'd beneath his corslet bright;
But of every wound his body bore,   790
Each and all had been ta'en before:
Though aged, he was so iron of limb,
Few of our youth could cope with him,
And the foes, whom he singly kept at bay,
Outnumber'd his thin hairs of silver grey.

From right to left his sabre swept ;
Many an Othman mother wept
Sons that were unborn, when dipp'd
His weapon first in Moslem gore,
Ere his years could count a score.   800
Of all he might have been the sire
Who fell that day beneath his ire :
For, sonless left long years ago,
His wrath made many a childless foe ;
And since the day, when in the strait
His only boy had met his fate,
His parent's iron hand did doom
More than a human hecatomb.
If shades by carnage be appeased,
Patroclus' spirit less was pleased   810
Than his, Minotti's son, who died
Where Asia's bounds and ours divide.
Buried he lay, where thousands before
For thousands of years were inhumed on the shore ;
What of them is left, to tell
Where they lie, and how they fell ?
Not a stone on their turf, nor a bone in their graves ;
But they live in the verse that immortally saves.

XXVI

Hark to the Allah shout ! a band
Of the Mussulman bravest and best is at hand ;   820
Their leader's nervous arm is bare,
Swifter to smite, and never to spare—
Unclothed to the shoulder it waves them on ;
Thus in the fight is he ever known :
Others a gaudier garb may show,
To tempt the spoil of the greedy foe ;
Many a hand's on a richer hilt,
But none on a steel more ruddily gilt ;
Many a loftier turban may wear,—
Alp is but known by the white arm bare ;   830
Look through the thick of the fight, 'tis there !
There is not a standard on that shore

So well advanced the ranks before;
There is not a banner in Moslem war
Will lure the Delhis half so far;
It glances like a falling star!
Where'er that mighty arm is seen,
The bravest be, or late have been;
There the craven cries for quarter
Vainly to the vengeful Tartar;   840
Or the hero, silent lying,
Scorns to yield a groan in dying;
Mustering his last feeble blow
'Gainst the nearest levell'd foe,
Though faint beneath the mutual wound,
Grappling on the gory ground.

XXVII

Still the old man stood erect,
And Alp's career a moment check'd.
' Yield thee, Minotti; quarter take,
For thine own, thy daughter's sake.'   850

' Never, renegado, never!
Though the life of thy gift would last for ever.'

' Francesca!—Oh, my promised bride!
Must she too perish by thy pride?'

' She is safe.'—' Where? where?'—' In heaven;
From whence thy traitor soul is driven—
Far from thee, and undefiled.'
Grimly then Minotti smiled,
As he saw Alp staggering bow
Before his words, as with a blow.   860
' Oh God! when died she?'—' Yesternight—
Nor weep I for her spirit's flight:
None of my pure race shall be
Slaves to Mahomet and thee—
Come on!'—That challenge is in vain—
Alp's already with the slain!

While Minotti's words were wreaking
More revenge in bitter speaking
Than his falchion's point had found,
Had the time allow'd to wound,   870
From within the neighbouring porch
Of a long defended church,
Where the last and desperate few
Would the failing fight renew,
The sharp shot dash'd Alp to the ground;
Ere an eye could view the wound
That crash'd through the brain of the infidel,
Round he spun, and down he fell;
A flash like fire within his eyes
Blazed, as he bent no more to rise,   880
And then eternal darkness sunk
Through all the palpitating trunk;
Nought of life left, save a quivering
Where his limbs were slightly shivering:
They turn'd him on his back; his breast
And brow were stain'd with gore and dust,
And through his lips the life-blood oozed,
From its deep veins lately loosed:
But in his pulse there was no throb,
Nor on his lips one dying sob;   890
Sigh, nor word, nor struggling breath
Heralded his way to death;
Ere his very thought could pray,
Unanel'd he pass'd away,
Without a hope from mercy's aid,—
To the last a Renegade.

XXVIII

Fearfully the yell arose
Of his followers, and his foes;
These in joy, in fury those:
Then again in conflict mixing,   900
Clashing swords, and spears transfixing,
Interchanged the blow and thrust,
Hurling warriors in the dust.

Street by street, and foot by foot,
Still Minotti dares dispute
The latest portion of the land
Left beneath his high command;
With him, aiding heart and hand,
The remnant of his gallant band.
Still the church is tenable,   910
   Whence issued late the fated ball
   That half avenged the city's fall,
When Alp, her fierce assailant, fell:
Thither bending sternly back,
They leave before a bloody track;
And, with their faces to the foe,
Dealing wounds with every blow,
The chief, and his retreating train,
Join to those within the fane;
There they yet may breathe awhile,   920
Shelter'd by the massy pile.

XXIX

Brief breathing-time! the turban'd host,
With added ranks and raging boast,
Press onwards with such strength and heat,
Their numbers balk their own retreat;
For narrow the way that led to the spot
Where still the Christians yielded not;
And the foremost, if fearful, may vainly try
Through the massy column to turn and fly;
They perforce must do or die.   930
They die; but ere their eyes could close,
Avengers o'er their bodies rose;
Fresh and furious, fast they fill
The ranks unthinn'd, though slaughter'd still;
And faint the weary Christians wax
Before the still renew'd attacks:
And now the Othmans gain the gate;
Still resists its iron weight,
And still, all deadly aim'd and hot,
From every crevice comes the shot;   940

From every shatter'd window pour
The volleys of the sulphurous shower:
But the portal wavering grows and weak—
The iron yields, the hinges creak—
It bends—it falls—and all is o'er;
Lost Corinth may resist no more!

XXX

Darkly, sternly, and all alone,
Minotti stood o'er the altar-stone:
Madonna's face upon him shone,
Painted in heavenly hues above,   950
With eyes of light and looks of love;
And placed upon that holy shrine
To fix our thoughts on things divine,
When pictured there, we kneeling see
Her, and the boy-God on her knee,
Smiling sweetly on each prayer
To heaven, as if to waft it there.
Still she smiled; even now she smiles,
Though slaughter streams along her aisles:
Minotti lifted his aged eye,   960
And made the sign of a cross with a sigh,
Then seized a torch which blazed thereby;
And still he stood, while with steel and flame,
Inward and onward the Mussulman came.

XXXI

The vaults beneath the mosaic stone
Contain'd the dead of ages gone;
Their names were on the graven floor,
But now illegible with gore;
The carved crests, and curious hues
The varied marble's vein diffuse,   970
Were smear'd, and slippery,—stain'd, and strown
With broken swords, and helms o'erthrown:
There were dead above, and the dead below
Lay cold in many a coffin'd row;

You might see them piled in sable state,
By a pale light through a gloomy grate;
But War had enter'd their dark caves,
And stored along the vaulted graves
Her sulphurous treasures, thickly spread
In masses by the fleshless dead: 980
  Here, throughout the siege, had been
  The Christians' chiefest magazine;
To these a late form'd train now led,
Minotti's last and stern resource
Against the foe's o'erwhelming force.

XXXII

The foe came on, and few remain
To strive, and those must strive in vain:
For lack of further lives, to slake
The thirst of vengeance now awake,
With barbarous blows they gash the dead,   990
And lop the already lifeless head,
And fell the statues from their niche,
And spoil the shrines of offerings rich,
And from each other's rude hands wrest
The silver vessels saints had bless'd.
To the high altar on they go;
Oh, but it made a glorious show!
On its table still behold
The cup of consecrated gold;
Massy and deep, a glittering prize,   1000
Brightly it sparkles to plunderers' eyes:
That morn it held the holy wine,
Converted by Christ to his blood so divine,
Which his worshippers drank at the break of day,
To shrive their souls ere they join'd in the fray.
Still a few drops within it lay:
And round the sacred table glow
Twelve lofty lamps, in splendid row,
From the purest metal cast;
A spoil—the richest, and the last.   1010

XXXIII

So near they came, the nearest stretch'd
To grasp the spoil he almost reach'd,
   When old Minotti's hand
Touch'd with the torch the train—
   'Tis fired !
Spire, vaults, the shrine, the spoil, the slain,
   The turban'd victors, the Christian band,
All that of living or dead remain,
Hurl'd on high with the shiver'd fane,
   In one wild roar expired !   1020
The shatter'd town—the walls thrown down—
The waves a moment backward bent—
The hills that shake, although unrent,
   As if an earthquake pass'd—
The thousand shapeless things all driven
In cloud and flame athwart the heaven,
   By that tremendous blast—
Proclaim'd the desperate conflict o'er
On that too long afflicted shore :
Up to the sky like rockets go   1030
All that mingled there below :
Many a tall and goodly man,
Scorch'd and shrivell'd to a span,
When he fell to earth again
Like a cinder strew'd the plain ;
Down the ashes shower like rain ;
Some fell in the gulf, which received the sprinkles
With a thousand circling wrinkles ;
Some fell on the shore, but, far away,
Scatter'd o'er the isthmus lay ;   1040
Christian or Moslem, which be they ?
Let their mothers see and say !
When in cradled rest they lay,
And each nursing mother smiled
On the sweet sleep of her child,
Little deem'd she such a day
Would rend those tender limbs away.
Not the matrons that them bore
Could discern their offspring more ;

That one moment left no trace   1050
More of human form or face
Save a scatter'd scalp or bone:
And down came blazing rafters, strown
Around, and many a falling stone,
Deeply dinted in the clay,
All blacken'd there and reeking lay.
All the living things that heard
That deadly earth-shock disappear'd:
The wild birds flew; the wild dogs fled,
And howling left the unburied dead;   1060
The camels from their keepers broke;
The distant steer forsook the yoke—
The nearer steed plunged o'er the plain,
And burst his girth, and tore his rein;
The bull-frog's note, from out the marsh,
Deep-mouth'd arose, and doubly harsh;
The wolves yell'd on the cavern'd hill
Where echo roll'd in thunder still;
The jackal's troop, in gather'd cry,
Bay'd from afar complainingly,   1070
With a mix'd and mournful sound,
Like crying babe, and beaten hound:
With sudden wing, and ruffled breast,
The eagle left his rocky nest,
And mounted nearer to the sun,
The clouds beneath him seem'd so dun;
Their smoke assail'd his startled beak,
And made him higher soar and shriek—
　　　Thus was Corinth lost and won!

SONNET ON CHILLON

ETERNAL Spirit of the chainless Mind !
  Brightest in dungeons, Liberty ! thou art :
  For there thy habitation is the heart—
The heart which love of thee alone can bind ;
And when thy sons to fetters are consign'd—
  To fetters, and the damp vault's dayless gloom,
  Their country conquers with their martyrdom,
And Freedom's fame finds wings on every wind.
Chillon ! thy prison is a holy place,
  And thy sad floor an altar—for 'twas trod,
Until his very steps have left a trace
  Worn, as if thy cold pavement were a sod,
By Bonnivard ! May none those marks efface !
  For they appeal from tyranny to God.

THE PRISONER OF CHILLON

I

MY hair is grey, but not with years,
    Nor grew it white
    In a single night,
As men's have grown from sudden fears :
My limbs are bow'd, though not with toil,
  But rusted with a vile repose,
For they have been a dungeon's spoil,
  And mine has been the fate of those
To whom the goodly earth and air
Are bann'd, and barr'd—forbidden fare :   10
But this was for my father's faith
I suffer'd chains and courted death ;
That father perish'd at the stake
For tenets he would not forsake ;
And for the same his lineal race
In darkness found a dwelling place ;

We were seven—who now are one,
  Six in youth, and one in age,
Finish'd as they had begun,
  Proud of Persecution's rage ;   20
One in fire, and two in field,
Their belief with blood have seal'd,
Dying as their father died,
For the God their foes denied ;
Three were in a dungeon cast,
Of whom this wreck is left the last.

II

There are seven pillars of Gothic mould,
In Chillon's dungeons deep and old,
There are seven columns, massy and grey,
Dim with a dull imprison'd ray,   30
A sunbeam which hath lost its way,
And through the crevice and the cleft
Of the thick wall is fallen and left ;
Creeping o'er the floor so damp,
Like a marsh's meteor lamp :
And in each pillar there is a ring,
  And in each ring there is a chain ;
That iron is a cankering thing,
  For in these limbs its teeth remain,
With marks that will not wear away,   40
Till I have done with this new day,
Which now is painful to these eyes,
Which have not seen the sun so rise
For years—I cannot count them o'er,
I lost their long and heavy score
When my last brother droop'd and died,
And I lay living by his side.

III

They chain'd us each to a column stone,
And we were three—yet, each alone ;
We could not move a single pace,   50
We could not see each other's face,
But with that pale and livid light
That made us strangers in our sight :

And thus together—yet apart,
Fetter'd in hand, but join'd in heart,
'Twas still some solace in the dearth
Of the pure elements of earth,
To hearken to each other's speech,
And each turn comforter to each
With some new hope, or legend old,   60
Or song heroically bold ;
But even these at length grew cold.
Our voices took a dreary tone,
An echo of the dungeon stone,
   A grating sound, not full and free,
   As they of yore were wont to be :
   It might be fancy—but to me
They never sounded like our own.

IV

I was the eldest of the three,
   And to uphold and cheer the rest   70
   I ought to do—and did my best—
And each did well in his degree.
   The youngest, whom my father loved,
Because our mother's brow was given
To him, with eyes as blue as heaven—
   For him my soul was sorely moved ;
And truly might it be distressed
To see such bird in such a nest ;
For he was beautiful as day—
   (When day was beautiful to me   80
   As to young eagles, being free)—
   A polar day, which will not see
A sunset till its summer's gone,
   Its sleepless summer of long light,
The snow-clad offspring of the sun :
   And thus he was as pure and bright,
And in his natural spirit gay,
With tears for nought but others' ills,
And then they flow'd like mountain rills,
Unless he could assuage the woe   90
Which he abhorr'd to view below.

V

The other was as pure of mind,
But form'd to combat with his kind;
Strong in his frame, and of a mood
Which 'gainst the world in war had stood,
And perish'd in the foremost rank
    With joy:—but not in chains to pine:
His spirit wither'd with their clank,
    I saw it silently decline—
        And so perchance in sooth did mine: 100
But yet I forced it on to cheer
Those relics of a home so dear.
He was a hunter of the hills,
    Had follow'd there the deer and wolf;
    To him this dungeon was a gulf,
And fetter'd feet the worst of ills.

VI

Lake Leman lies by Chillon's walls:
A thousand feet in depth below
Its massy waters meet and flow;
Thus much the fathom-line was sent   110
From Chillon's snow-white battlement,
    Which round about the wave inthrals:
A double dungeon wall and wave
Have made—and like a living grave.
Below the surface of the lake
The dark vault lies wherein we lay,
We heard it ripple night and day;
    Sounding o'er our heads it knock'd;
And I have felt the winter's spray
Wash through the bars when winds were high
And wanton in the happy sky;   121
    And then the very rock hath rock'd,
    And I have felt it shake, unshock'd,
Because I could have smiled to see
The death that would have set me free.

VII

I said my nearer brother pined,
I said his mighty heart declined,
He loathed and put away his food;
It was not that 'twas coarse and rude,
For we were used to hunter's fare,   130
And for the like had little care:
The milk drawn from the mountain goat
Was changed for water from the moat,
Our bread was such as captives' tears
Have moisten'd many a thousand years,
Since man first pent his fellow men
Like brutes within an iron den;
But what were these to us or him?
These wasted not his heart or limb;
My brother's soul was of that mould   140
Which in a palace had grown cold,
Had his free breathing been denied
The range of the steep mountain's side;
But why delay the truth?—he died.
I saw, and could not hold his head,
Nor reach his dying hand—nor dead,—
Though hard I strove, but strove in vain,
To rend and gnash my bonds in twain.
He died, and they unlock'd his chain,
And scoop'd for him a shallow grave   150
Even from the cold earth of our cave.
I begg'd them, as a boon, to lay
His corse in dust whereon the day
Might shine—it was a foolish thought,
But then within my brain it wrought,
That even in death his freeborn breast
In such a dungeon could not rest.
I might have spared my idle prayer—
They coldly laugh'd, and laid him there:
The flat and turfless earth above   160
The being we so much did love;
His empty chain above it leant,
Such murder's fitting monument!

VIII

But he, the favourite and the flower,
Most cherish'd since his natal hour,
His mother's image in fair face,
The infant love of all his race,
His martyr'd father's dearest thought,
My latest care, for whom I sought
To hoard my life, that his might be   170
Less wretched now, and one day free;
He, too, who yet had held untired
A spirit natural or inspired—
He, too, was struck, and day by day
Was wither'd on the stalk away.
Oh, God! it is a fearful thing
To see the human soul take wing
In any shape, in any mood:
I've seen it rushing forth in blood,
I've seen it on the breaking ocean   180
Strive with a swoln convulsive motion,
I've seen the sick and ghastly bed
Of Sin delirious with its dread;
But these were horrors—this was woe
Unmix'd with such—but sure and slow:
He faded, and so calm and meek,
So softly worn, so sweetly weak,
So tearless, yet so tender—kind,
And grieved for those he left behind;
With all the while a cheek whose bloom   190
Was as a mockery of the tomb,
Whose tints as gently sunk away
As a departing rainbow's ray;
An eye of most transparent light,
That almost made the dungeon bright,
And not a word of murmur—not
A groan o'er his untimely lot,—
A little talk of better days,
A little hope my own to raise,
For I was sunk in silence—lost   200
In this last loss, of all the most;

And then the sighs he would suppress
Of fainting nature's feebleness,
More slowly drawn, grew less and less:
I listen'd, but I could not hear;
I call'd, for I was wild with fear;
I knew 'twas hopeless, but my dread
Would not be thus admonishéd;
I call'd, and thought I heard a sound—
I burst my chain with one strong bound,   210
And rush'd to him:—I found him not,
I only stirr'd in this black spot,
I only lived, *I* only drew
The accursed breath of dungeon-dew;
The last, the sole, the dearest link
Between me and the eternal brink,
Which bound me to my failing race,
Was broken in this fatal place.
One on the earth, and one beneath—
My brothers—both had ceased to breathe: 220
I took that hand which lay so still,
Alas! my own was full as chill;
I had not strength to stir, or strive,
But felt that I was still alive—
A frantic feeling, when we know
That what we love shall ne'er be so.
     I know not why
     I could not die,
I had no earthly hope but—faith,
And that forbade a selfish death.   230

IX

What next befell me then and there
    I know not well—I never knew—
First came the loss of light, and air,
    And then of darkness too:
I had no thought, no feeling—none—
Among the stones I stood a stone,
And was, scarce conscious what I wist,
As shrubless crags within the mist;

For all was blank, and bleak, and grey;
It was not night—it was not day;   240
It was not even the dungeon-light,
So hateful to my heavy sight,
But vacancy absorbing space,
And fixedness—without a place;
There were no stars—no earth—no time,
No check—no change—no good—no crime,
But silence, and a stirless breath
Which neither was of life nor death;
A sea of stagnant idleness,
Blind, boundless, mute, and motionless!   250

X

A light broke in upon my brain,—
    It was the carol of a bird;
It ceased, and then it came again,
    The sweetest song ear ever heard,
And mine was thankful till my eyes
Ran over with the glad surprise,
And they that moment could not see
I was the mate of misery;
But then by dull degrees came back
My senses to their wonted track;   260
I saw the dungeon walls and floor
Close slowly round me as before,
I saw the glimmer of the sun
Creeping as it before had done,
But through the crevice where it came
That bird was perch'd, as fond and tame,
    And tamer than upon the tree;
A lovely bird, with azure wings,
And song that said a thousand things,
    And seem'd to say them all for me!   270
I never saw its like before,
I ne'er shall see its likeness more:
It seem'd like me to want a mate,
But was not half so desolate,
And it was come to love me when
None lived to love me so again,

And cheering from my dungeon's brink,
Had brought me back to feel and think.
I know not if it late were free,
 Or broke its cage to perch on mine,   280
But knowing well captivity,
 Sweet bird ! I could not wish for thine !
Or if it were, in wingèd guise,
A visitant from Paradise ;
For—Heaven forgive that thought ! the while
Which made me both to weep and smile—
I sometimes deem'd that it might be
My brother's soul come down to me ;
But then at last away it flew,
And then 'twas mortal well I knew,   290
For he would never thus have flown,
And left me twice so doubly lone,
Lone—as the corse within its shroud,
Lone—as a solitary cloud,
 A single cloud on a sunny day,
While all the rest of heaven is clear,
 A frown upon the atmosphere,
That hath no business to appear
 When skies are blue, and earth is gay

XI

A kind of change came in my fate,   300
My keepers grew compassionate ;
I know not what had made them so,
They were inured to sights of woe,
But so it was :—my broken chain
With links unfasten'd did remain,
And it was liberty to stride
Along my cell from side to side,
And up and down, and then athwart,
And tread it over every part ;
And round the pillars one by one,   310
Returning where my walk begun,
Avoiding only, as I trod,
My brothers' graves without a sod ;

For if I thought with heedless tread
My step profaned their lowly bed,
My breath came gaspingly and thick,
And my crush'd heart fell blind and sick.

XII

I made a footing in the wall,
  It was not therefrom to escape,
For I had buried one and all,   320
  Who loved me in a human shape;
And the whole earth would henceforth be
A wider prison unto me:
No child—no sire—no kin had I,
No partner in my misery;
I thought of this, and I was glad,
For thought of them had made me mad;
But I was curious to ascend
To my barr'd windows, and to bend
Once more, upon the mountains high,   330
The quiet of a loving eye.

XIII

I saw them—and they were the same,
They were not changed like me in frame;
I saw their thousand years of snow
On high—their wide long lake below,
And the blue Rhone in fullest flow;
I heard the torrents leap and gush
O'er channell'd rock and broken bush;
I saw the white-wall'd distant town,
And whiter sails go skimming down;   340
And then there was a little isle,
Which in my very face did smile,
  The only one in view;
A small green isle, it seem'd no more,
Scarce broader than my dungeon floor,
But in it there were three tall trees,
And o'er it blew the mountain breeze,

And by it there were waters flowing,
And on it there were young flowers growing,
    Of gentle breath and hue.   350
The fish swam by the castle wall,
And they seem'd joyous each and all;
The eagle rode the rising blast,
Methought he never flew so fast
As then to me he seem'd to fly;
And then new tears came in my eye,
And I felt troubled—and would fain
I had not left my recent chain.
And when I did descend again,
The darkness of my dim abode   360
Fell on me as a heavy load;
It was as is a new-dug grave,
Closing o'er one we sought to save,—
And yet my glance, too much opprest,
Had almost need of such a rest.

                    XIV

It might be months, or years, or days,
    I kept no count, I took no note,
I had no hope my eyes to raise,
    And clear them of their dreary mote;
At last men came to set me free;   370
    I ask'd not why, and reck'd not where;
It was at length the same to me,
Fetter'd or fetterless to be,
    I learn'd to love despair.
And thus when they appear'd at last,
And all my bonds aside were cast,
These heavy walls to me had grown
A hermitage—and all my own!
And half I felt as they were come
To tear me from a second home: 380
With spiders I had friendship made,
And watch'd them in their sullen trade,
Had seen the mice by moonlight play,
And why should I feel less than they?

We were all inmates of one place,
And I, the monarch of each race,
Had power to kill—yet, strange to tell!
In quiet we had learn'd to dwell;
My very chains and I grew friends,
So much a long communion tends   390
To make us what we are:—even **I**
Regain'd my freedom with a sigh.

THE PRISONER OF CHILLON

MAZEPPA

I

'Twas after dread Pultowa's day,
   When fortune left the royal Swede,
Around a slaughter'd army lay,
   No more to combat and to bleed.
The power and glory of the war,
   Faithless as their vain votaries, men,
Had pass'd to the triumphant Czar,
   And Moscow's walls were safe again,
Until a day more dark and drear,
And a more memorable year,   10
Should give to slaughter and to shame
A mightier host and haughtier name;
A greater wreck, a deeper fall,
A shock to one—a thunderbolt to all.

II

Such was the hazard of the die;
The wounded Charles was taught to fly
By day and night through field and flood,
Stain'd with his own and subjects' blood;
For thousands fell that flight to aid:
And not a voice was heard t' upbraid   20
Ambition in his humbled hour,
When truth had nought to dread from power.
His horse was slain, and Gieta gave
His own—and died the Russians' slave.
This too sinks after many a league
Of well sustained, but vain fatigue;
And in the depth of forests, darkling
The watch-fires in the distance sparkling—
   The beacons of surrounding foes—
A king must lay his limbs at length.   30
   Are these the laurels and repose
For which the nations strain their strength?

They laid him by a savage tree,
In outworn nature's agony;
His wounds were stiff, his limbs were stark;
The heavy hour was chill and dark;
The fever in his blood forbade
A transient slumber's fitful aid:
And thus it was; but yet through all,
Kinglike the monarch bore his fall,　　　　40
And made, in this extreme of ill,
His pangs the vassals of his will:
All silent and subdued were they,
As once the nations round him lay.

III

A band of chiefs!—alas! how few,
　　Since but the fleeting of a day
Had thinn'd it; but this wreck was true
　　And chivalrous: upon the clay
Each sate him down, all sad and mute,
　　Beside his monarch and his steed;　　50
For danger levels man and brute,
　　And all are fellows in their need.
Among the rest, Mazeppa made
His pillow in an old oak's shade—
Himself as rough, and scarce less old,
The Ukraine's Hetman, calm and bold;
But first, outspent with this long course,
The Cossack prince rubb'd down his horse,
　　And smooth'd his fetlocks and his mane,　　60
　　And slack'd his girth, and stripp'd his rein,
And joy'd to see how well he fed;
For until now he had the dread
His wearied courser might refuse
To browse beneath the midnight dews:
But he was hardy as his lord,
And little cared for bed and board;
But spirited and docile too.
Whate'er was to be done, would do.

Shaggy and swift, and strong of limb,   70
All Tartar-like he carried him ;
Obey'd his voice, and came to call,
And knew him in the midst of all :
Though thousands were around,—and Night,
Without a star, pursued her flight,—
That steed from sunset until dawn
His chief would follow like a fawn.

                        IV

This done, Mazeppa spread his cloak,
And laid his lance beneath his oak,
Felt if his arms in order good   80
The long day's march had well withstood—
If still the powder fill'd the pan,
    And flints unloosen'd kept their lock—
His sabre's hilt and scabbard felt,
And whether they had chafed his belt ;
And next the venerable man,
From out his havresack and can,
    Prepared and spread his slender stock ;
And to the monarch and his men
The whole or portion offer'd then   90
With far less of inquietude
Than courtiers at a banquet would.
And Charles of this his slender share
With smiles partook a moment there,
To force of cheer a greater show,
And seem above both wounds and woe ;
And then he said—" Of all our band,
Though firm of heart and strong of hand,
In skirmish, march, or forage, none
Can less have said or more have done   100
Than thee, Mazeppa ! On the earth
So fit a pair had never birth,
Since Alexander's days till now,
As thy Bucephalus and thou :
All Scythia's fame to thine should yield
For pricking on o'er flood and field."

Mazeppa answer'd—" Ill betide
The school wherein I learn'd to ride ! "
Quoth Charles—" Old Hetman, wherefore so,
Since thou hast learn'd the art so well ? "   110
Mazeppa said—" 'Twere long to tell ;
And we have many a league to go,
With every now and then a blow,
And ten to one at least the foe,
Before our steeds may graze at ease
Beyond the swift Borysthenes :
And, Sire, your limbs have need of rest,
    And I will be the sentinel
Of this your troop."—" But I request,"
    Said Sweden's monarch, " thou wilt tell   120
This tale of thine, and I may reap,
Perchance, from this the boon of sleep ;
For at this moment from my eyes
The hope of present slumber flies."

" Well, Sire, with such a hope, I'll track
My seventy years of memory back :
I think 'twas in my twentieth spring,—
Aye 'twas,—when Casimir was king—
John Casimir,—I was his page
Six summers, in my earlier age :   130
A learned monarch, faith ! was he,
And most unlike your majesty ;
He made no wars, and did not gain
New realms to lose them back again ;
And (save debates in Warsaw's diet)
He reign'd in most unseemly quiet ;
Not that he had no cares to vex ;
He loved the muses and the sex ;
And sometimes these so froward are,
They made him wish himself at war ;   140
But soon his wrath being o'er, he took
Another mistress, or new book :
And then he gave prodigious fêtes—
All Warsaw gather'd round his gates
To gaze upon his splendid court,
    And dames, and chiefs, of princely port.

He was the Polish Solomon,
So sung his poets, all but one,
Who, being unpension'd, made a satire,
And boasted that he could not flatter.   150
It was a court of jousts and mimes,
Where every courtier tried at rhymes;
Even I for once produced some verses,
And signed my odes ' Despairing Thyrsis.'
There was a certain Palatine,
    A count of far and high descent,
Rich as a salt or silver mine;
    And he was proud, ye may divine,
        As if from heaven he had been sent:
He had such wealth in blood and ore   160
    As few could match beneath the throne;
And he would gaze upon his store,
And o'er his pedigree would pore,
Until by some confusion led,
Which almost look'd like want of head,
    He thought their merits were his own.
His wife was not of his opinion;
    His junior she by thirty years,
Grew daily tired of his dominion;
    And, after wishes, hopes, and fears,   170
    To virtue a few farewell tears,
A restless dream or two, some glances
At Warsaw's youth, some songs, and dances,
Awaited but the usual chances,
Those happy accidents which render
The coldest dames so very tender,
To deck her Count with titles given,
'Tis said, as passports into heaven;
But, strange to say, they rarely boast
Of these, who have deserved them most.   180

V

" I was a goodly stripling then;
    At seventy years I so may say,
That there were few, or boys or men,
    Who, in my dawning time of day,

Of vassal or of knight's degree,
Could vie in vanities with me ;
For I had strength, youth, gaiety,
A port, not like to this ye see,
But smooth, as all is rugged now ;
For time, and care, and war, have plough'd   190
My very soul from out my brow ;
 And thus I should be disavow'd
By all my kind and kin, could they
Compare my day and yesterday ;
This change was wrought, too, long ere age
Had ta'en my features for his page ;
With years, ye know, have not declined
My strength, my courage, or my mind,
Or at this hour I should not be
Telling old tales beneath a tree,   200
With starless skies my canopy.
 But let me on : Theresa's form—
Methinks it glides before me now,
Between me and yon chestnut's bough,
 The memory is so quick and warm ;
And yet I find no words to tell
The shape of her I loved so well :
She had the Asiatic eye,
 Such as our Turkish neighbourhood
Hath mingled with our Polish blood,   210
Dark as above us is the sky ;
But through it stole a tender light,
Like the first moonrise of midnight ;
Large, dark, and swimming in the stream,
Which seem'd to melt to its own beam ;
All love, half languor, and half fire,
Like saints that at the stake expire,
And lift their raptured looks on high,
As though it were a joy to die.
A brow like a midsummer lake,   220
 Transparent with the sun therein,
When waves no murmur dare to make,
 And heaven beholds her face within,
A cheek and lip—but why proceed ?

I loved her then, I love her still;
And such as I am, love indeed
  In fierce extremes—in good and ill.
But still we love even in our rage,
And haunted to our very age
With the vain shadow of the past,   230
As is Mazeppa to the last.

VI

"We met—we gazed—I saw, and sigh'd;
She did not speak, and yet replied;
There are ten thousand tones and signs
We hear and see, but none defines—
Involuntary sparks of thought,
Which strike from out the heart o'erwrought,
And form a strange intelligence,
Alike mysterious and intense,
Which link the burning chain that binds,   240
Without their will, young hearts and minds:
Conveying, as the electric wire,
We know not how, the absorbing fire.
I saw, and sigh'd—in silence wept,
And still reluctant distance kept,
Until I was made known to her,
And we might then and there confer
Without suspicion—then, even then,
  I long'd, and was resolved to speak;
But on my lips they died again,   250
  The accents tremulous and weak,
Until one hour.—There is a game,
  A frivolous and foolish play,
    Wherewith we while away the day;
It is—I have forgot the name—
And we to this, it seems, were set,
By some strange chance, which I forget:
I reck'd not if I won or lost,
  It was enough for me to be
So near to hear, and oh! to see   260
The being whom I loved the most.

I watch'd her as a sentinel,
(May ours this dark night watch as well !)
   Until I saw, and thus it was,
That she was pensive, nor perceived
Her occupation, nor was grieved
Nor glad to lose or gain ; but still
Play'd on for hours, as if her will
Yet bound her to the place, though not
That hers might be the winning lot.   270
   Then through my brain the thought did pass
Even as a flash of lightning there,
That there was something in her air
Which would not doom me to despair ;
And on the thought my words broke forth,
   All incoherent as they were ;
Their eloquence was little worth,
But yet she listen'd—'tis enough—
   Who listens once will listen twice ;
   Her heart, be sure, is not of ice,   280
And one refusal no rebuff.

VII

" I loved, and was beloved again—
   They tell me, Sire, you never knew
   Those gentle frailties ; if 'tis true,
I shorten all my joy or pain ;
To you 'twould seem absurd as vain ;
But all men are not born to reign,
Or o'er their passions, or as you
Thus o'er themselves and nations too.
I am—or rather *was*—a prince,   290
   A chief of thousands, and could lead
   Them on where each would foremost bleed ;
But could not o'er myself evince
The like control—But to resume :
   I loved, and was beloved again ;
In sooth, it is a happy doom,
   But yet where happiest ends in pain.
We met in secret, and the hour
Which led me to that lady's bower

Was fiery Expectation's dower.   300
My days and nights were nothing—all
Except that hour which doth recall,
In the long lapse from youth to age,
    No other like itself : I'd give
    The Ukraine back again to live
It o'er once more, and be a page,
The happy page, who was the lord
Of one soft heart, and his own sword,
And had no other gem nor wealth
Save nature's gift of youth and health.   310
We met in secret—doubly sweet,
Some say, they find it so to meet ;
I know not that—I would have given
    My life but to have call'd her mine
In the full view of earth and heaven ;
    For I did oft and long repine
That we could only meet by stealth.

VIII

" For lovers there are many eyes,
    And such there were on us ; the devil
On such occasions should be civil—   320
The devil !—I'm loth to do him wrong,
    It might be some untoward saint,
Who would not be at rest too long,
    But to his pious bile gave vent—
But one fair night, some lurking spies
Surprised and seized us both.
The Count was something more than wroth—
I was unarm'd ; but if in steel,
All cap-à-pie from head to heel,
What 'gainst their numbers could I do ?   330
'Twas near his castle, far away
    From city or from succour near,
And almost on the break of day ;
I did not think to see another,
    My moments seem'd reduced to few ;
And with one prayer to Mary Mother,
    And, it may be, a saint or two,

As I resign'd me to my fate,
They led me to the castle gate :
   Theresa's doom I never knew,   340
Our lot was henceforth separate.
An angry man, ye may opine,
Was he, the proud Count Palatine ;
And he had reason good to be,
   But he was most enraged lest such
   An accident should chance to touch
Upon his future pedigree ;
Nor less amazed, that such a blot
His noble 'scutcheon should have got,
While he was highest of his line ;   350
   Because unto himself he seem'd
   The first of men, nor less he deem'd
In others' eyes, and most in mine.
'Sdeath ! with a *page*—perchance a king
Had reconciled him to the thing ;
But with a stripling of a page—
I felt but cannot paint—his rage.

IX

" ' Bring forth the horse ! '—the horse was brought ;
   In truth, he was a noble steed,
   A Tartar of the Ukraine breed,   360
Who look'd as though the speed of thought
Were in his limbs ; but he was wild,
   Wild as the wild deer, and untaught,
With spur and bridle undefiled—
   'Twas but a day he had been caught ;
And snorting, with erected mane,
And struggling fiercely, but in vain,
In the full foam of wrath and dread
To me the desert-born was led :
They bound me on, that menial throng ;   370
Upon his back with many a thong
Then loosed him with a sudden lash—
Away !—away !—and on we dash !
Torrents less rapid and less rash.

x

" Away !—away !—My breath was gone,
I saw not where he hurried on :
'Twas scarcely yet the break of day,
And on he foam'd—away !—away !
The last of human sounds which rose,
As I was darted from my foes,   380
Was the wild shout of savage laughter,
Which on the wind came roaring after
A moment from that rabble rout :
With sudden wrath I wrench'd my head,
    And snapp'd the cord, which to the mane
    Had bound my neck in lieu of rein,
And, writhing half my form about,
Howl'd back my curse ; but 'midst the tread,
The thunder of my courser's speed,
Perchance they did not hear nor heed :   390
It vexes me—for I would fain
Have paid their insult back again.
I paid it well in after days :
There is not of that castle gate,
Its drawbridge and portcullis' weight,
Stone, bar, moat, bridge, or barrier left ;
Nor of its fields a blade of grass,
    Save what grows on a ridge of wall,
    Where stood the hearth-stone of the hall ;
And many a time ye there might pass,   400
Nor dream that e'er that fortress was.
I saw its turrets in a blaze,
Their crackling battlements all cleft,
    And the hot lead pour down like rain
From off the scorch'd and blackening roof,
Whose thickness was not vengeance-proof.
    They little thought that day of pain,
When launch'd, as on the lightning's flash,
They bade me to destruction dash,
    That one day I should come again,   410
With twice five thousand horse, to thank
    The Count for his uncourteous ride.

They play'd me then a bitter prank,
   When, with the wild horse for my guide,
They bound me to his foaming flank:
At length I play'd them one as frank—
For time at last sets all things even—
   And if we do but watch the hour,
   There never yet was human power
Which could evade, if unforgiven,   420
The patient search and vigil long
Of him who treasures up a wrong.

XI

" Away, away, my steed and I,
   Upon the pinions of the wind,
   All human dwellings left behind;
We sped like meteors through the sky,
When with its crackling sound the night
Is chequer'd with the northern light:
Town—village—none were on our track,
   But a wild plain of far extent,   430
And bounded by a forest black;
   And, save the scarce seen battlement
On distant heights of some strong hold,
Against the Tartars built of old,
No trace of man. The year before
A Turkish army had march'd o'er;
And where the Spahi's hoof hath trod,
The verdure flies the bloody sod:
The sky was dull, and dim, and gray,
   And a low breeze crept moaning by—   440
I could have answer'd with a sigh—
But fast we fled,—away!—away!—
And I could neither sigh nor pray;
And my cold sweat-drops fell like rain
Upon the courser's bristling mane;
But, snorting still with rage and fear,
He flew upon his far career:
At times I almost thought, indeed,
He must have slacken'd in his speed;

But no—my bound and slender frame   450
  Was nothing to his angry might,
And merely like a spur became :
Each motion which I made to free
My swoln limbs from their agony
  Increased his fury and affright :
I tried my voice,—'twas faint and low,
But yet he swerved as from a blow ;
And, starting to each accent, sprang
As from a sudden trumpet's clang :
Meantime my cords were wet with gore,   460
Which, oozing through my limbs, ran o'er ;
And in my tongue the thirst became
A something fierier far than flame.

XII

" We near'd the wild wood—'twas so wide,
I saw no bounds on either side ;
'Twas studded with old sturdy trees,
That bent not to the roughest breeze
Which howls down from Siberia's waste,
And strips the forest in its haste,—
But these were few and far between,   470
Set thick with shrubs more young and green,
Luxuriant with their annual leaves,
Ere strown by those autumnal eves
That nip the forest's foliage dead,
Discolour'd with a lifeless red,
Which stands thereon like stiffen'd gore
Upon the slain when battle's o'er,
And some long winter's night hath shed
Its frost o'er every tombless head,
So cold and stark the raven's beak   480
May peck unpierced each frozen cheek :
'Twas a wild waste of underwood,
And here and there a chestnut stood,
The strong oak, and the hardy pine :
  But far apart—and well it were,
Or else a different lot were mine—

The boughs gave way, and did not tear
My limbs ; and I found strength to bear
My wounds, already scarr'd with cold ;
My bonds forbade to loose my hold.   490
We rustled through the leaves like wind,
Left shrubs, and trees, and wolves behind ;
By night I heard them on the track,
Their troop came hard upon our back,
With their long gallop, which can tire
The hound's deep hate, and hunter's fire :
Where'er we flew they follow'd on,
Nor left us with the morning sun ;
Behind I saw them, scarce a rood,
At day-break winding through the wood,   500
And through the night had heard their feet
Their stealing, rustling step repeat.
Oh ! how I wish'd for spear or sword,
At least to die amidst the horde,
And perish—if it must be so—
At bay, destroying many a foe !
When first my courser's race begun,
I wish'd the goal already won ;
But now I doubted strength and speed.
Vain doubt ! his swift and savage breed   510
Had nerved him like the mountain-roe ;
Nor faster falls the blinding snow
Which whelms the peasant near the door
Whose threshold he shall cross no more,
Bewilder'd with the dazzling blast,
Than through the forest-paths he passed—
Untired, untamed, and worse than wild ;
All furious as a favour'd child
Balk'd of its wish : or fiercer still—
A woman piqued—who has her will.   520

XIII

" The wood was passed ; 'twas more than noon,
But chill the air, although in June ;
Or it might be my veins ran cold—
Prolong'd endurance tames the bold ;

And I was then not what I seem,
But headlong as a wintry stream,
And wore my feelings out before
I well could count their causes o'er:
And what with fury, fear, and wrath,
The tortures which beset my path,   530
Cold, hunger, sorrow, shame, distress,
Thus bound in nature's nakedness;
Sprung from a race whose rising blood,
When stirred beyond its calmer mood,
And trodden hard upon, is like
The rattle-snake's, in act to strike,
What marvel if this worn-out trunk
Beneath its woes a moment sunk?
The earth gave way, the skies roll'd round,
I seem'd to sink upon the ground;   540
But err'd, for I was fastly bound.
My heart turn'd sick, my brain grew sore,
And throbb'd awhile, then beat no more:
The skies spun like a mighty wheel;
I saw the trees like drunkards reel,
And a slight flash sprang o'er my eyes,
Which saw no farther. He who dies
Can die no more than then I died.
O'ertortured by that ghastly ride,
I felt the blackness come and go,   550
    And strove to wake; but could not make
My senses climb up from below:
I felt as on a plank at sea,
When all the waves that dash o'er thee,
At the same time upheave and whelm,
And hurl thee towards a desert realm.
My undulating life was as
The fancied lights that flitting pass
Our shut eyes in deep midnight, when
Fever begins upon the brain;   560
But soon it pass'd, with little pain,
    But a confusion worse than such:
    I own that I should deem it much,
Dying, to feel the same again;

And yet I do suppose we must
Feel far more ere we turn to dust :
No matter ; I have bared my brow
Full in Death's face—before—and now.

XIV

" My thoughts came back ; where was I ? Cold,
   And numb, and giddy : pulse by pulse   570
Life reassumed its lingering hold,
And throb by throb,—till grown a pang
   Which for a moment would convulse,
   My blood reflow'd, though thick and chill ;
My ear with uncouth noises rang,
   My heart began once more to thrill ;
My sight return'd, though dim ; alas !
And thicken'd, as it were, with glass.
Methought the dash of waves was nigh ;
There was a gleam too of the sky,   580
Studded with stars ;—it is no dream ;
The wild horse swims the wilder stream :
The bright broad river's gushing tide
Sweeps, winding onward, far and wide,
And we are half-way, struggling o'er
To yon unknown and silent shore.
The waters broke my hollow trance,
And with a temporary strength
   My stiffen'd limbs were rebaptized.
My courser's broad breast proudly braves,   590
And dashes off the ascending waves,
   And onward we advance !
We reach the slippery shore at length,
   A haven I but little prized,
For all behind was dark and drear,
And all before was night and fear.
How many hours of night or day
In those suspended pangs I lay,
I could not tell ; I scarcely knew
If this were human breath I drew.   600

XV

"With glossy skin, and dripping mane,
    And reeling limbs, and reeking flank,
The wild steed's sinewy nerves still strain
    Up the repelling bank.
We gain the top: a boundless plain
Spreads through the shadow of the night,
    And onward, onward, onward, seems,
    Like precipices in our dreams,
To stretch beyond the sight;
And here and there a speck of white,   610
    Or scatter'd spot of dusky green,
In masses broke into the light,
    As rose the moon upon my right:
But nought distinctly seen
In the dim waste would indicate
The omen of a cottage gate;
No twinkling taper from afar
Stood like a hospitable star;
Not even an ignis-fatuus rose
To make him merry with my woes: 620
    That very cheat had cheer'd me then!
Although detected, welcome still,
Reminding me, through every ill,
    Of the abodes of men.

XVI

"Onward we went—but slack and slow;
    His savage force at length o'erspent,
The drooping courser, faint and low,
    All feebly foaming went.
A sickly infant had had power
To guide him forward in that hour: 630
    But useless all to me:
His new-born tameness nought avail'd—
My limbs were bound; my force had fail'd,
    Perchance, had they been free.

With feeble effort still I tried
To rend the bonds so starkly tied,
　　But still it was in vain ;
My limbs were only wrung the more,
And soon the idle strife gave o'er,
　　Which but prolong'd their pain :　　640
The dizzy race seem'd almost done,
Although no goal was nearly won :
Some streaks announced the coming sun—
　　How slow, alas ! he came !
Methought that mist of dawning gray
Would never dapple into day ;
How heavily it roll'd away—
　　Before the eastern flame
Rose crimson, and deposed the stars,
And call'd the radiance from their cars,　　650
And fill'd the earth, from his deep throne,
With lonely lustre, all his own.

XVII

" Up rose the sun ; the mists were curl'd
Back from the solitary world
Which lay around, behind, before.
What booted it to traverse o'er
Plain, forest, river ? Man nor brute,
Nor dint of hoof, nor print of foot,
Lay in the wild luxuriant soil ;
No sign of travel, none of toil ;　　660
The very air was mute ;
And not an insect's shrill small horn,
Nor matin bird's new voice was borne
From herb nor thicket. Many a werst,
Panting as if his heart would burst,
The weary brute still stagger'd on ;
And still we were—or seem'd—alone.
At length, while reeling on our way,
Methought I heard a courser neigh,
From out yon tuft of blackening firs.　　670
Is it the wind those branches stirs ?

No, no! from out the forest prance
   A trampling troop; I see them come!
In one vast squadron they advance!
   I strove to cry—my lips were dumb.
The steeds rush on in plunging pride;
But where are they the reins to guide?
A thousand horse, and none to ride!
With flowing tail, and flying mane,
Wide nostrils never stretch'd by pain,   680
Mouths bloodless to the bit or rein,
And feet that iron never shod,
And flanks unscarr'd by spur or rod,
A thousand horse, the wild, the free,
Like waves that follow o'er the sea,
   Came thickly thundering on,
As if our faint approach to meet;
The sight re-nerved my courser's feet,
A moment staggering, feebly fleet,
A moment, with a faint low neigh,   690
   He answer'd, and then fell!
With gasps and glazing eyes he lay,
   And reeking limbs immoveable,
      His first and last career is done!
On came the troop—they saw him stoop,
   They saw me strangely bound along
   His back with many a bloody thong:
They stop—they start—they snuff the air,
Gallop a moment here and there,
Approach, retire, wheel round and round,   700
Then plunging back with sudden bound,
Headed by one black mighty steed,
Who seem'd the patriarch of his breed,
   Without a single speck or hair
Of white upon his shaggy hide;
They snort, they foam, neigh, swerve aside,
And backward to the forest fly,
By instinct, from a human eye.
   They left me there to my despair,
Linked to the dead and stiffening wretch,   710
Whose lifeless limbs beneath me stretch,

Relieved from that unwonted weight,
From whence I could not extricate
Nor him nor me—and there we lay,
   The dying on the dead !
I little deem'd another day
   Would see my houseless, helpless head.

" And there from morn to twilight bound,
I felt the heavy hours toil round,
With just enough of life to see   720
My last of suns go down on me,
In hopeless certainty of mind,
That makes us feel at length resign'd
To that which our foreboding years
Present the worst and last of fears :
Inevitable—even a boon,
Nor more unkind for coming soon,
Yet shunn'd and dreaded with such care,
As if it only were a snare
   That prudence might escape :   730
At times both wish'd for and implored,
At times sought with self-pointed sword,
Yet still a dark and hideous close
To even intolerable woes,
   And welcome in no shape.
And, strange to say, the sons of pleasure,
They who have revell'd beyond measure
In beauty, wassail, wine, and treasure,
Die calm, or calmer, oft than he
Whose heritage was misery :   740
For he who hath in turn run through
All that was beautiful and new,
   Hath nought to hope, and nought to leave ;
And, save the future, (which is view'd
Not quite as men are base or good,
But as their nerves may be endued,)
   With nought perhaps to grieve :
The wretch still hopes his woes must end,
And Death, whom he should deem his friend,

Appears, to his distemper'd eyes,   750
Arrived to rob him of his prize,
The tree of his new Paradise.
To-morrow would have given him all,
Repaid his pangs, repair'd his fall ;
To-morrow would have been the first
Of days no more deplored or curst,
But bright, and long, and beckoning years,
Seen dazzling through the mist of tears,
Guerdon of many a painful hour ;
To-morrow would have given him power   760
To rule, to shine, to smite, to save—
And must it dawn upon his grave ?

                    XVIII

" The sun was sinking—still I lay
    Chain'd to the chill and stiffening steed ;
I thought to mingle there our clay,
    And my dim eyes of death had need,
    No hope arose of being freed :
I cast my last looks up the sky,
    And there between me and the sun
I saw the expecting raven fly,   770
    Who scarce would wait till both should die,
    Ere his repast begun ;
He flew, and perch'd, then flew once more,
And each time nearer than before ;
I saw his wing through twilight flit,
And once so near me he alit
    I could have smote, but lack'd the strength ;
But the slight motion of my hand,
And feeble scratching of the sand,
The exerted throat's faint struggling noise,   780
Which scarcely could be called a voice,
    Together scared him off at length.
I know no more—my latest dream
    Is something of a lovely star
    Which fix'd my dull eyes from afar,

And went and came with wandering beam,
And of the cold, dull, swimming, dense
Sensation of recurring sense,
And then subsiding back to death,
And then again a little breath,   790
A little thrill, a short suspense,
　　An icy sickness curdling o'er
My heart, and sparks that cross'd my brain—
A gasp, a throb, a start of pain,
　　A sigh, and nothing more.

XIX

" I woke—where was I ?—Do I see
A human face look down on me ?
And doth a roof above me close ?
Do these limbs on a couch repose ?
Is this a chamber where I lie ?   800
And is it mortal yon bright eye,
That watches me with gentle glance ?
　　I closed my own again once more,
As doubtful that my former trance
　　Could not as yet be o'er.
A slender girl, long-hair'd, and tall,
Sate watching by the cottage wall ;
The sparkle of her eye I caught,
Even with my first return of thought ;
For ever and anon she threw   810
　　A prying, pitying glance on me
　　With her black eyes so wild and free :
I gazed, and gazed, until I knew
　　No vision it could be,—
But that I lived, and was released
From adding to the vulture's feast :
And when the Cossack maid beheld
My heavy eyes at length unseal'd,
She smiled—and I essay'd to speak,
　　But fail'd—and she approach'd, and made   820
　　With lip and finger signs that said,
I must not strive as yet to break

The silence, till my strength should be
Enough to leave my accents free ;
And then her hand on mine she laid,
And smooth'd the pillow for my head,
And stole along on tiptoe tread,
   And gently oped the door, and spake
In whispers—ne'er was voice so sweet !
Even music follow'd her light feet.   830
   But those she call'd were not awake,
And she went forth ; but, ere she pass'd,
Another look on me she cast,
   Another sign she made, to say,
That I had nought to fear, that all
Were near, at my command or call,
   And she would not delay
Her due return :—while she was gone,
Methought I felt too much alone.

XX

" She came with mother and with sire—   840
What need of more ?—I will not tire
With long recital of the rest,
Since I became the Cossack's guest.
They found me senseless on the plain,
   They bore me to the nearest hut,
They brought me into life again—
Me—one day o'er their realm to reign !
   Thus the vain fool who strove to glut
His rage, refining on my pain,
   Sent me forth to the wilderness,   850
Bound, naked, bleeding, and alone,
To pass the desert to a throne,—
   What mortal his own doom may guess ?
Let none despond, let none despair !
To-morrow the Borysthenes
May see our coursers graze at ease
Upon his Turkish bank,—and never
Had I such welcome for a river
   As I shall yield when safely there.

Comrades, good night!"—The Hetman threw
   His length beneath the oak-tree shade,   861
   With leafy couch already made,
A bed nor comfortless nor new
To him, who took his rest whene'er
The hour arrived, no matter where:
   His eyes the hastening slumbers steep.
And if ye marvel Charles forgot
To thank his tale, *he* wondered not,—
   The king had been an hour asleep.

THE LAMENT OF TASSO

I

LONG years !—It tries the thrilling frame to bear
And eagle-spirit of a child of Song—
Long years of outrage, calumny, and wrong ;
Imputed madness, prison'd solitude,
And the mind's canker in its savage mood,
When the impatient thirst of light and air
Parches the heart ; and the abhorred grate,
Marring the sunbeams with its hideous shade,
Works through the throbbing eyeball to the brain,
With a hot sense of heaviness and pain ;   10
And bare, at once, Captivity display'd
Stands scoffing through the never-open'd gate,
Which nothing through its bars admits, save day,
And tasteless food, which I have eat alone
Till its unsocial bitterness is gone ;
And I can banquet like a beast of prey,
Sullen and lonely, couching in the cave
Which is my lair, and—it may be—my grave.
All this hath somewhat worn me, and may wear,
But must be borne.   I stoop not to despair ;   20
For I have battled with mine agony,
And made me wings wherewith to overfly
The narrow circus of my dungeon wall,
And freed the Holy Sepulchre from thrall ;
And revell'd among men and things divine,
And pour'd my spirit over Palestine,
In honour of the sacred war for Him,
The God who was on earth and is in heaven,
For he has strengthen'd me in heart and limb.
That through this sufferance I might be forgiven,   30
I have employ'd my penance to record
How Salem's shrine was won, and how adored.

II

But this is o'er—my pleasant task is done:—
My long-sustaining friend of many years!
If I do blot thy final page with tears,
Know, that my sorrows have wrung from me none.
But thou, my young creation! my soul's child!
Which ever playing round me came and smiled,
And woo'd me from myself with thy sweet sight,
Thou too art gone—and so is my delight: 40
And therefore do I weep and inly bleed
With this last bruise upon a broken reed.
Thou too art ended—what is left me now?
For I have anguish yet to bear—and how?
I know not that—but in the innate force
Of my own spirit shall be found resource.
I have not sunk, for I had no remorse,
Nor cause for such: they call'd me mad—and why?
Oh Leonora! wilt not *thou* reply?
I was indeed delirious in my heart   50
To lift my love so lofty as thou art;
But still my frenzy was not of the mind:
I knew my fault, and feel my punishment
Not less because I suffer it unbent.
That thou wert beautiful, and I not blind,
Hath been the sin which shuts me from mankind;
But let them go, or torture as they will,
My heart can multiply thine image still;
Successful love may sate itself away;
The wretched are the faithful; 'tis their fate   60
To have all feeling, save the one, decay,
And every passion into one dilate,
As rapid rivers into ocean pour;
But ours is fathomless, and hath no shore.

III

Above me, hark! the long and maniac cry
Of minds and bodies in captivity.
And hark! the lash and the increasing howl,
And the half-inarticulate blasphemy!
There be some here with worse than frenzy foul,

Some who do still goad on the o'er-labour'd mind,
And dim the little light that 's left behind   71
With needless torture, as their tyrant will
Is wound up to the lust of doing ill:
With these and with their victims am I class'd,
'Mid sounds and sights like these long years have pass'd;
'Mid sights and sounds like these my life may close:
So let it be—for then I shall repose.

IV

I have been patient, let me be so yet;
I had forgotten half I would forget,
But it revives—Oh! would it were my lot   80
To be forgetful as I am forgot!—
Feel I not wroth with those who bade me dwell
In this vast lazar-house of many woes?
Where laughter is not mirth, nor thought the mind,
Nor words a language, nor ev'n men mankind;
Where cries reply to curses, shrieks to blows,
And each is tortured in his separate hell—
For we are crowded in our solitudes—
Many, but each divided by the wall,
Which echoes Madness in her babbling moods;   90
While all can hear, none heed his neighbour's call—
None! save that One, the veriest wretch of all,
Who was not made to be the mate of these,
Nor bound between Distraction and Disease.
Feel I not wroth with those who placed me here?
Who have debased me in the minds of men,
Debarring me the usage of my own,
Blighting my life in best of its career,
Branding my thoughts as things to shun and fear?
Would I not pay them back these pangs again,   100
And teach them inward Sorrow's stifled groan?
The struggle to be calm, and cold distress,
Which undermines our Stoical success?
No!—still too proud to be vindictive—I
Have pardon'd princes' insults, and would die.
Yes, Sister of my Sovereign! for thy sake

I weed all bitterness from out my breast,
It hath no business where *thou* art a guest :
Thy brother hates—but I cannot detest ;
Thou pitiest not—but I cannot forsake.   110

V

Look on a love which knows not to despair,
But all unquench'd is still my better part,
Dwelling deep in my shut and silent heart,
As dwells the gather'd lightning in its cloud,
Encompass'd with its dark and rolling shroud,
Till struck,—forth flies the all-ethereal dart !
And thus at the collision of thy name
The vivid thought still flashes through my frame,
And for a moment all things as they were
Flit by me ; they are gone—I am the same.   120
And yet my love without ambition grew ;
I knew thy state, my station, and I knew
A Princess was no love-mate for a bard ;
I told it not, I breathed it not, it was
Sufficient to itself, its own reward ;
And if my eyes reveal'd it, they, alas !
Were punish'd by the silentness of thine,
And yet I did not venture to repine.
Thou wert to me a crystal-girded shrine,
Worshipp'd at holy distance, and around   130
Hallow'd and meekly kiss'd the saintly ground ;
Not for thou wert a princess, but that Love
Had robed thee with a glory, and array'd
Thy lineaments in beauty that dismay'd—
Oh ! not dismay'd—but awed, like One above !
And in that sweet severity there was
A something which all softness did surpass—
I know not how—thy genius master'd mine—
My star stood still before thee : if it were
Presumptuous thus to love without design,   140
That sad fatality hath cost me dear ;
But thou art dearest still, and I should be
Fit for this cell, which wrongs me—but for *thee.*
The very love which lock'd me to my chain

Hath lighten'd half its weight; and for the rest,
Though heavy, lent me vigour to sustain,
And look to thee with undivided breast,
And foil the ingenuity of Pain.

VI

It is no marvel—from my very birth
My soul was drunk with love, which did pervade   150
And mingle with whate'er I saw on earth:
Of objects all inanimate I made
Idols, and out of wild and lonely flowers,
And rocks, whereby they grew, a paradise,
Where I did lay me down within the shade
Of waving trees, and dreamed uncounted hours,
Though I was chid for wandering; and the Wise
Shook their white aged heads o'er me, and said,
Of such materials wretched men were made,
And such a truant boy would end in woe,   160
And that the only lesson was a blow;
And then they smote me, and I did not weep,
But cursed them in my heart, and to my haunt
Return'd and wept alone, and dream'd again
The visions which arise without a sleep,
And with my years my soul began to pant
With feelings of strange tumult and soft pain;
And the whole heart exhaled into One Want,
But undefined and wandering, till the day
I found the thing I sought—and that was thee;   170
And then I lost my being, all to be
Absorb'd in thine—the world was past away—
Thou didst annihilate the earth to me!

VII

I loved all Solitude, but little thought
To spend I know not what of life, remote
From all communion with existence, save
The maniac and his tyrant; had I been
Their fellow, many years ere this had seen
My mind like theirs corrupted to its grave.
But who hath seen me writhe, or heard me rave?   180

Perchance in such a cell we suffer more
Than the wreck'd sailor on his desert shore;
The world is all before him—*mine* is *here*,
Scarce twice the space they must accord my bier.
What though *he* perish, he may lift his eye,
And with a dying glance upbraid the sky;
I will not raise my own in such reproof,
Although 'tis clouded by my dungeon roof.

VIII

Yet do I feel at times my mind decline,
But with a sense of its decay: I see   190
Unwonted lights along my prison shine,
And a strange demon, who is vexing me
With pilfering pranks and petty pains, below
The feeling of the healthful and the free;
But much to One, who long hath suffer'd so,
Sickness of heart, and narrowness of place,
And all that may be borne, or can debase.
I thought mine enemies had been but Man,
But Spirits may be leagued with them; all Earth
Abandons, Heaven forgets me: in the dearth   200
Of such defence the Powers of Evil can,
It may be, tempt me further,—and prevail
Against the outworn creature they assail.
Why in this furnace is my spirit proved,
Like steel in tempering fire? because I loved?
Because I loved what not to love, and see,
Was more or less than mortal, and than me.

IX

I once was quick in feeling—that is o'er:
My scars are callous, or I should have dash'd
My brain against these bars, as the sun flash'd   210
In mockery through them: If I bear and bore
The much I have recounted, and the more
Which hath no words,—'tis that I would not die
And sanction with self-slaughter the dull lie
Which snared me here, and with the brand of shame
Stamp Madness deep into my memory,
And woo Compassion to a blighted name,

Sealing the sentence which my foes proclaim.
No—it shall be immortal! and I make
A future temple of my present cell,   220
Which nations yet shall visit for my sake.
While thou, Ferrara! when no longer dwell
The ducal chiefs within thee, shalt fall down,
And crumbling piecemeal view thy heartless halls,
A poet's wreath shall be thine only crown,—
A poet's dungeon thy most far renown,
While strangers wonder o'er thy unpeopled walls!
And thou, Leonora! thou—who wert ashamed
That such as I could love—who blush'd to hear
To less than monarchs that thou couldst be dear,
Go! tell thy brother, that my heart, untamed   231
By grief—years—weariness—and it may be
A taint of that he would impute to me—
From long infection of a den like this,
Where the mind rots congenial with the abyss,—
Adores thee still; and add—that when the towers
And battlements which guard his joyous hours
Of banquet, dance, and revel, are forgot,
Or left untended in a dull repose,—
This, this, shall be a consecrated spot!   240
But *Thou*—when all that Birth and Beauty throws
Of magic round thee is extinct—shalt have
One half the laurel which o'ershades my grave.
No power in death can tear our names apart,
As none in life could rend thee from my heart.
Yes, Leonora! it shall be our fate
To be entwined for ever—but too late!

THE PROPHECY OF DANTE

DEDICATION

LADY ! if for the cold and cloudy clime,
 Where I was born, but where I would not die,
 Of the great Poet-Sire of Italy
I dare to build the imitative rhyme,
Harsh Runic copy of the South's sublime,
 THOU art the cause ; and howsoever I
 Fall short of his immortal harmony,
Thy gentle heart will pardon me the crime.
Thou, in the pride of Beauty and of Youth,
 Spakest ; and for thee to speak and be obey'd   10
Are one ; but only in the sunny South
 Such sounds are uttered, and such charms display'd,
So sweet a language from so fair a mouth—
 Ah ! to what effort would it not persuade ?

RAVENNA, *June* 21, 1819.

THE PROPHECY OF DANTE

CANTO THE FIRST

ONCE more in man's frail world ! which I had left
 So long that 'twas forgotten ; and I feel
 The weight of clay again,—too soon bereft
Of the immortal vision which could heal
 My earthly sorrows, and to God's own skies
 Lift me from that deep gulf without repeal,
Where late my ears rung with the damned cries
 Of souls in hopeless bale ; and from that place
 Of lesser torment, whence men may arise
Pure from the fire to join the angelic race ;   10

Midst whom my own bright Beatrice bless'd
 My spirit with her light ; and to the base
Of the eternal Triad ! first, last, best,
 Mysterious, three, sole, infinite, great God !
 Soul universal ! led the mortal guest,
Unblasted by the glory, though he trod
 From star to star to reach the almighty throne.
 Oh Beatrice ! whose sweet limbs the sod
So long hath press'd, and the cold marble stone,
 Thou sole pure seraph of my earliest love,   20
 Love so ineffable, and so alone,
That nought on earth could more my bosom move,
 And meeting thee in heaven was but to meet
 That without which my soul, like the arkless dove,
Had wander'd still in search of, nor her feet
 Relieved her wing till found : without thy light
 My paradise had still been incomplete.
Since my tenth sun gave summer to my sight
 Thou wert my life, the essence of my thought,
 Loved ere I knew the name of love, and bright   30
Still in these dim old eyes, now overwrought
 With the world's war, and years, and banishment,
 And tears for thee, by other woes untaught ;
For mine is not a nature to be bent
 By tyrannous faction, and the brawling crowd,
 And though the long, long conflict hath been spent
In vain,—and never more, save when the cloud
 Which overhangs the Apennine my mind's eye
 Pierces to fancy Florence, once so proud
Of me, can I return, though but to die,   40
 Unto my native soil,—they have not yet
 Quench'd the old exile's spirit, stern and high.
But the sun, though not overcast, must set,
 And the night cometh ; I am old in days,
 And deeds, and contemplation, and have met
Destruction face to face in all his ways.
 The world hath left me, what it found me, pure,
 And if I have not gather'd yet its praise,
I sought it not by any baser lure ;
 Man wrongs, and Time avenges, and my name   50

May form a monument not all obscure,
Though such was not my ambition's end or aim,
　To add to the vain-glorious list of those
　Who dabble in the pettiness of fame,
And make men's fickle breath the wind that blows
　Their sail, and deem it glory to be class'd
　With conquerors, and virtue's other foes,
In bloody chronicles of ages past.
　I would have had my Florence great and free;
　Oh Florence! Florence! unto me thou wast　　60
Like that Jerusalem which the Almighty He
　Wept over, 'but thou wouldst not;' as the bird
　Gathers its young, I would have gather'd thee
Beneath a parent pinion, hadst thou heard
　My voice; but as the adder, deaf and fierce,
　Against the breast that cherish'd thee was stirr'd
Thy venom, and my state thou didst amerce,
　And doom this body forfeit to the fire.
　Alas! how bitter is his country's curse
To him who *for* that country would expire,　　70
　But did not merit to expire *by* her,
　And loves her, loves her even in her ire!
The day may come when she will cease to err,
　The day may come she would be proud to have
　The dust she dooms to scatter, and transfer
Of him, whom she denied a home, the grave.
　But this shall not be granted; let my dust
　Lie where it falls; nor shall the soil which gave
Me breath, but in her sudden fury thrust
　Me forth to breathe elsewhere, so reassume　　80
　My indignant bones, because her angry gust
Forsooth is over, and repeal'd her doom;
　No,—she denied me what was mine—my roof,
　And shall not have what is not hers—my tomb.
Too long her armed wrath hath kept aloof
　The breast which would have bled for her, the heart
　That beat, the mind that was temptation proof,
The man who fought, toil'd, travell'd, and each part
　Of a true citizen fulfill'd, and saw
　For his reward the Guelf's ascendant art　　90

Pass his destruction even into a law.
  These things are not made for forgetfulness,
  Florence shall be forgotten first; too raw
The wound, too deep the wrong, and the distress
  Of such endurance too prolong'd to make
  My pardon greater, her injustice less,
Though late repented; yet—yet for her sake
  I feel some fonder yearnings, and for thine,
  My own Beatrice, I would hardly take
Vengeance upon the land which once was mine,   100
  And still is hallow'd by thy dust's return,
  Which would protect the murderess like a shrine,
And save ten thousand foes by thy sole urn.
  Though, like old Marius from Minturnæ's marsh
  And Carthage ruins, my lone breast may burn
At times with evil feelings hot and harsh,
  And sometimes the last pangs of a vile foe
  Writhe in a dream before me, and o'erarch
My brow with hopes of triumph,—let them go!
  Such are the last infirmities of those   110
  Who long have suffer'd more than mortal woe,
And yet being mortal still have no repose
  But on the pillow of Revenge—Revenge,
  Who sleeps to dream of blood, and waking glows
With the oft-baffled slakeless thirst of change,
  When we shall mount again, and they that trod
  Be trampled on, while Death and Até range
O'er humbled heads and sever'd necks——Great God!
  Take these thoughts from me—to thy hands I yield
  My many wrongs, and thine Almighty rod   120
Will fall on those who smote me,—be my shield!
  As thou hast been in peril, and in pain,
  In turbulent cities, and the tented field—
In toil, and many troubles borne in vain
  For Florence,—I appeal from her to Thee!
  Thee whom I late saw in thy loftiest reign,
Even in that glorious vision, which to see
  And live was never granted until now,
  And yet thou hast permitted this to me.
Alas! with what a weight upon my brow   130

The sense of earth and earthly things come back,
   Corrosive passions, feelings dull and low,
The heart's quick throb upon the mental rack,
   Long day, and dreary night; the retrospect
   Of half a century bloody and black,
And the frail few years I may yet expect
   Hoary and hopeless, but less hard to bear,
   For I have been too long and deeply wreck'd
On the lone rock of desolate Despair,
   To lift my eyes more to the passing sail   140
   Which shuns that reef so horrible and bare;
Nor raise my voice—for who would heed my wail?
   I am not of this people, nor this age,
   And yet my harpings will unfold a tale
Which shall preserve these times when not a page
   Of their perturbed annals could attract
   An eye to gaze upon their civil rage,
Did not my verse embalm full many an act
   Worthless as they who wrought it: 'tis the doom
   Of spirits of my order to be rack'd   150
In life, to wear their hearts out, and consume
   Their days in endless strife, and die alone;
   Then future thousands crowd around their tomb,
And pilgrims come from climes where they have known
   The name of him—who now is but a name,
   And wasting homage o'er the sullen stone,
Spread his—by him unheard, unheeded, fame;
   And mine at least hath cost me dear: to die
   Is nothing; but to wither thus—to tame
My mind down from its own infinity—   160
   To live in narrow ways with little men,
   A common sight to every common eye,
A wanderer, while even wolves can find a den,
   Ripp'd from all kindred, from all home, all things
   That make communion sweet, and soften pain—
To feel me in the solitude of kings
   Without the power that makes them bear a crown—
   To envy every dove his nest and wings
Which waft him where the Apennine looks down
   On Arno, till he perches, it may be,   170

Within my all inexorable town,
Where yet my boys are, and that fatal she,
    Their mother, the cold partner who hath brought
    Destruction for a dowry—this to see
And feel, and know without repair, hath taught
    A bitter lesson ; but it leaves me free :
    I have not vilely found, nor basely sought,
They made an Exile—not a slave of me.

CANTO THE SECOND

THE Spirit of the fervent days of Old,
    When words were things that came to pass, and
        thought
    Flash'd o'er the future, bidding men behold
Their children's children's doom already brought
    Forth from the abyss of time which is to be,
    The chaos of events, where lie half-wrought
Shapes that must undergo mortality ;
    What the great Seers of Israel wore within,
    That spirit was on them, and is on me,
And if, Cassandra-like, amidst the din   10
    Of conflict none will hear, or hearing heed
    This voice from out the Wilderness, the sin
Be theirs, and my own feelings be my meed,
    The only guerdon I have ever known.
    Hast thou not bled ? and hast thou still to bleed,
Italia ? Ah ! to me such things, foreshown
    With dim sepulchral light, bid me forget
    In thine irreparable wrongs my own ;
We can have but one country, and even yet
    Thou'rt mine—my bones shall be within thy breast,
    My soul within thy language, which once set   21
With our old Roman sway in the wide West ;
    But I will make another tongue arise
    As lofty and more sweet, in which express'd
The hero's ardour, or the lover's sighs,
    Shall find alike such sounds for every theme
    That every word, as brilliant as thy skies,
Shall realise a poet's proudest dream,

And make thee Europe's nightingale of song;
    So that all present speech to thine shall seem   30
The note of meaner birds, and every tongue
    Confess its barbarism when compared with thine.
    This shalt thou owe to him thou didst so wrong,
Thy Tuscan bard, the banish'd Ghibelline.
    Woe! woe! the veil of coming centuries
    Is rent,—a thousand years which yet supine
Lie like the ocean waves ere winds arise,
    Heaving in dark and sullen undulation,
    Float from eternity into these eyes;
The storms yet sleep, the clouds still keep their station,
    The unborn earthquake yet is in the womb,   41
    The bloody chaos yet expects creation,
But all things are disposing for thy doom;
    The elements await but for the word,
    'Let there be darkness!' and thou grow'st a tomb!
Yes! thou, so beautiful, shalt feel the sword,
    Thou, Italy! so fair that Paradise,
    Revived in thee, blooms forth to man restored:
Ah! must the sons of Adam lose it twice?
    Thou, Italy! whose ever golden fields,   50
    Plough'd by the sunbeams solely, would suffice
For the world's granary; thou, whose sky heaven
    gilds
    With brighter stars, and robes with deeper blue;
    Thou, in whose pleasant places Summer builds
Her palace, in whose cradle Empire grew,
    And form'd the Eternal City's ornaments
    From spoils of kings whom freemen overthrew;
Birthplace of heroes, sanctuary of saints,
    Where earthly first, then heavenly glory made
    Her home; thou, all which fondest fancy paints,   60
And finds her prior vision but portray'd
    In feeble colours, when the eye—from the Alp
    Of horrid snow, and rock, and shaggy shade
Of desert-loving pine, whose emerald scalp
    Nods to the storm—dilates and dotes o'er thee,
    And wistfully implores, as 'twere for help
To see thy sunny fields, my Italy,

Nearer and nearer yet, and dearer still
    The more approach'd, and dearest were they free,
Thou—thou must wither to each tyrant's will: 70
    The Goth hath been,—the German, Frank, and Hun
    Are yet to come,—and on the imperial hill
Ruin, already proud of the deeds done
    By the old barbarians, there awaits the new,
    Throned on the Palatine, while lost and won
Rome at her feet lies bleeding ; and the hue
    Of human sacrifice and Roman slaughter
    Troubles the clotted air, of late so blue,
And deepens into red the saffron water
    Of Tiber, thick with dead ; the helpless priest,   80
    And still more helpless nor less holy daughter,
Vow'd to their God, have shrieking fled, and ceased
    Their ministry : the nations take their prey,
    Iberian, Almain, Lombard, and the beast
And bird, wolf, vulture, more humane than they
    Are ; these but gorge the flesh and lap the gore
    Of the departed, and then go their way ;
But those, the human savages, explore
    All paths of torture, and insatiate yet,
    With Ugolino hunger prowl for more.   90
Nine moons shall rise o'er scenes like this and set ;
    The chiefless army of the dead, which late
    Beneath the traitor Prince's banner met,
Hath left its leader's ashes at the gate ;
    Had but the royal Rebel lived, perchance
    Thou hadst been spared, but his involved thy fate.
Oh ! Rome, the spoiler or the spoil of France,
    From Brennus to the Bourbon, never, never
    Shall foreign standard to thy walls advance,
But Tiber shall become a mournful river.   100
    Oh ! when the strangers pass the Alps and Po,
    Crush them, ye rocks ! floods whelm them, and for
        ever !
Why sleep the idle avalanches so,
    To topple on the lonely pilgrim's head ?
    Why doth Eridanus but overflow
The peasant's harvest from his turbid bed ?

Were not each barbarous horde a nobler prey ?
  Over Cambyses' host the desert spread
Her sandy ocean, and the sea-waves' sway
  Roll'd over Pharaoh and his thousands,—why.   110
  Mountains and waters, do ye not as they ?
And you, ye men ! Romans who dare not die,
  Sons of the conquerors who overthrew
  Those who o'erthrew proud Xerxes, where yet lie
The dead whose tomb Oblivion never knew,
  Are the Alps weaker than Thermopylæ ?
  Their passes more alluring to the view
Of an invader ? is it they, or ye,
  That to each host the mountain-gate unbar,
  And leave the march in peace, the passage free ?
Why, Nature's self detains the victor's car,   121
  And makes your land impregnable, if earth
  Could be so ; but alone she will not war,
Yet aids the warrior worthy of his birth
  In a soil where the mothers bring forth men :
  Not so with those whose souls are little worth ;
For them no fortress can avail,—the den
  Of the poor reptile which preserves its sting
  Is more secure than walls of adamant, when
The hearts of those within are quivering.   130
  Are ye not brave ? Yes, yet the Ausonian soil
  Hath hearts, and hands, and arms, and hosts to bring
Against Oppression ; but how vain the toil,
  While still Division sows the seeds of woe
  And weakness, till the stranger reaps the spoil !
Oh ! my own beauteous land ! so long laid low,
  So long the grave of thy own children's hopes,
  When there is but required a single blow
To break the chain, yet—yet the Avenger stops,   139
  And Doubt and Discord step 'twixt thine and thee,
  And join their strength to that which with thee
    copes ;
What is there wanting then to set thee free,
  And show thy beauty in its fullest light ?
  To make the Alps impassable ; and we,
Her sons, may do this with *one* deed——Unite.

CANTO THE THIRD

FROM out the mass of never-dying ill,
   The Plague, the Prince, the Stranger, and the Sword,
   Vials of wrath but emptied to refill
And flow again, I cannot all record
   That crowds on my prophetic eye : the earth
   And ocean written o'er would not afford
Space for the annal, yet it shall go forth ;
   Yes, all, though not by human pen, is graven,
   There where the farthest suns and stars have birth,
Spread like a banner at the gate of heaven,   10
   The bloody scroll of our millennial wrongs
   Waves, and the echo of our groans is driven
Athwart the sound of archangelic songs,
   And Italy, the martyr'd nation's gore,
   Will not in vain arise to where belongs
Omnipotence and mercy evermore :
   Like to a harp-string stricken by the wind,
   The sound of her lament shall, rising o'er
The seraph voices, touch the Almighty Mind.
   Meantime I, humblest of thy sons, and of   20
   Earth's dust by immortality refined
To sense and suffering, though the vain may scoff,
   And tyrants threat, and meeker victims bow
   Before the storm because its breath is rough,
To thee, my country ! whom before, as now,
   I loved and love, devote the mournful lyre
   And melancholy gift high powers allow
To read the future ; and if now my fire
   Is not as once it shone o'er thee, forgive !
   I but foretell thy fortunes—then expire ;   30
Think not that I would look on them and live.
   A spirit forces me to see and speak,
   And for my guerdon grants *not* to survive ;
My heart shall be pour'd over thee and break :
   Yet for a moment, ere I must resume
   Thy sable web of sorrow, let me take
Over the gleams that flash athwart thy gloom

A softer glimpse; some stars shine through thy night,
   And many meteors, and above thy tomb
Leans sculptured Beauty, which Death cannot blight:
   And from thine ashes boundless spirits rise   41
To give thee honour, and the earth delight;
Thy soil shall still be pregnant with the wise,
   The gay, the learn'd, the generous, and the brave,
   Native to thee as summer to thy skies,
Conquerors on foreign shores, and the far wave,
   Discoverers of new worlds, which take their name;
   For *thee* alone they have no arm to save,
And all thy recompense is in their fame,
   A noble one to them, but not to thee—   50
   Shall they be glorious, and thou still the same?
Oh! more than these illustrious far shall be
   The being—and even yet he may be born—
   The mortal saviour who shall set thee free,
And see thy diadem, so changed and worn
   By fresh barbarians, on thy brow replaced;
   And the sweet sun replenishing thy morn,
Thy moral morn, too long with clouds defaced,
   And noxious vapours from Avernus risen,
   Such as all they must breathe who are debased   60
By servitude, and have the mind in prison.
   Yet through this centuried eclipse of woe
   Some voices shall be heard, and earth shall listen;
Poets shall follow in the path I show,
   And make it broader: the same brilliant sky
   Which cheers the birds to song shall bid them glow,
And raise their notes as natural and high;
   Tuneful shall be their numbers; they shall sing
   Many of love, and some of liberty,
But few shall soar upon that eagle's wing,   70
   And look in the sun's face with eagle's gaze,
   All free and fearless as the feather'd king,
But fly more near the earth; how many a phrase
   Sublime shall lavish'd be on some small prince
   In all the prodigality of praise!
And language, eloquently false, evince

The harlotry of genius, which, like beauty,
Too oft forgets its own self-reverence,
And looks on prostitution as a duty.
He who once enters in a tyrant's hall   80
As guest is slave, his thoughts become a booty,
And the first day which sees the chain enthral
A captive, sees his half of manhood gone—
The soul's emasculation saddens all
His spirit ; thus the Bard too near the throne
Quails from his inspiration, bound to *please*,—
How servile is the task to please alone !
To smooth the verse to suit his sovereign's ease
And royal leisure, nor too much prolong
Aught save his eulogy, and find, and seize,   90
Or force, or forge fit argument of song !
Thus trammell'd, thus condemn'd to Flattery's trebles,
He toils through all, still trembling to be wrong :
For fear some noble thoughts, like heavenly rebels,
Should rise up in high treason to his brain,
He sings, as the Athenian spoke, with pebbles
In 's mouth, lest truth should stammer through his
     strain.
But out of the long file of sonneteers
There shall be some who will not sing in vain,
And he, their prince, shall rank among my peers,   100
And love shall be his torment ; but his grief
Shall make an immortality of tears,
And Italy shall hail him as the Chief
Of Poet-lovers, and his higher song
Of Freedom wreathe him with as green a leaf.
But in a farther age shall rise along
The banks of Po two greater still than he ;
The world which smiled on him shall do them
     wrong
Till they are ashes, and repose with me.
The first will make an epoch with his lyre,   110
And fill the earth with feats of chivalry :
His fancy like a rainbow, and his fire,
Like that of Heaven, immortal, and his thought
Borne onward with a wing that cannot tire ;

Pleasure shall, like a butterfly new caught,
   Flutter her lovely pinions o'er his theme,
   And Art itself seem into Nature wrought
By the transparency of his bright dream.—
   The second, of a tenderer, sadder mood,
   Shall pour his soul out o'er Jerusalem ;   120
He, too, shall sing of arms, and Christian blood
   Shed where Christ bled for man ; and his high harp
   Shall, by the willow over Jordan's flood,
Revive a song of Sion, and the sharp
   Conflict, and final triumph of the brave
   And pious, and the strife of hell to warp
Their hearts from their great purpose, until wave
   The red-cross banners where the first red Cross
   Was crimson'd from his veins who died to save,
Shall be his sacred argument ; the loss   130
   Of years, of favour, freedom, even of fame
   Contested for a time, while the smooth gloss
Of courts would slide o'er his forgotten name
   And call captivity a kindness, meant
   To shield him from insanity or shame,
Such shall be his meet guerdon ! who was sent
   To be Christ's Laureate—they reward him well !
   Florence dooms me but death or banishment,
Ferrara him a pittance and a cell,
   Harder to bear and less deserved, for I   140
   Had stung the factions which I strove to quell ;
But this meek man, who with a lover's eye
   Will look on earth and heaven, and who will deign
   To embalm with his celestial flattery,
As poor a thing as e'er was spawn'd to reign,
   What will *he* do to merit such a doom ?
   Perhaps he'll *love*,—and is not love in vain
Torture enough without a living tomb ?
   Yet it will be so—he and his compeer,
   The Bard of Chivalry, will both consume   150
In penury and pain too many a year,
   And, dying in despondency, bequeath
   To the kind world, which scarce will yield a tear,
A heritage enriching all who breathe

With the wealth of a genuine poet's soul,
   And to their country a redoubled wreath,
Unmatch'd by time; not Hellas can unroll
   Through her olympiads two such names, though one
   Of hers be mighty;—and is this the whole
Of such men's destiny beneath the sun?   160
   Must all the finer thoughts, the thrilling sense,
   The electric blood with which their arteries run,
Their body's self turned soul with the intense
   Feeling of that which is, and fancy of
   That which should be, to such a recompense
Conduct? shall their bright plumage on the rough
   Storm be still scatter'd? Yes, and it must be;
   For, form'd of far too penetrable stuff,
These birds of Paradise but long to flee
   Back to their native mansion, soon they find   170
   Earth's mist with their pure pinions not agree,
And die or are degraded; for the mind
   Succumbs to long infection, and despair,
   And vulture passions flying close behind,
Await the moment to assail and tear;
   And when at length the winged wanderers stoop,
   Then is the prey-birds' triumph, then they share
The spoil, o'erpower'd at length by one fell swoop.
   Yet some have been untouch'd who learn'd to bear,
   Some whom no power could ever force to droop,
Who could resist themselves even, hardest care!   181
   And task most hopeless; but some such have been,
   And if my name amongst the number were,
That destiny austere, and yet serene,
   Were prouder than more dazzling fame unbless'd:
   The Alp's snow summit nearer heaven is seen
Than the volcano's fierce eruptive crest,
   Whose splendour from the black abyss is flung,
   While the scorch'd mountain, from whose burning breast
A temporary torturing flame is wrung,   190
   Shines for a night of terror, then repels
   Its fire back to the hell from whence it sprung,
The hell which in its entrails ever dwells.

CANTO THE FOURTH

MANY are poets who have never penn'd
   Their inspiration, and perchance the best:
   They felt, and loved, and died, but would not lend
Their thoughts to meaner beings; they compress'd
   The god within them, and rejoin'd the stars
   Unlaurell'd upon earth, but far more bless'd
Than those who are degraded by the jars
   Of passion, and their frailties link'd to fame,
   Conquerors of high renown, but full of scars.
Many are poets but without the name,   10
   For what is poesy but to create
   From overfeeling good or ill; and aim
At an external life beyond our fate,
   And be the new Prometheus of new men,
   Bestowing fire from heaven, and then, too late,
Finding the pleasure given repaid with pain,
   And vultures to the heart of the bestower,
   Who, having lavish'd his high gift in vain,
Lies chain'd to his lone rock by the sea-shore?
   So be it: we can bear.—But thus all they   20
   Whose intellect is an o'ermastering power
Which still recoils from its encumbering clay
   Or lightens it to spirit, whatsoe'er
   The form which their creations may essay,
Are bards; the kindled marble's bust may wear
   More poesy upon its speaking brow
   Than aught less than the Homeric page may bear;
One noble stroke with a whole life may glow,
   Or deify the canvas till it shine
   With beauty so surpassing all below,   30
That they who kneel to idols so divine
   Break no commandment, for high heaven is there
   Transfused, transfigurated: and the line
Of poesy, which peoples but the air
   With thought and beings of our thought reflected,
   Can do no more: then let the artist share
The palm, he shares the peril, and dejected

Faints o'er the labour unapproved—Alas!
   Despair and Genius are too oft connected.
Within the ages which before me pass   40
   Art shall resume and equal even the sway
   Which with Apelles and old Phidias
She held in Hellas' unforgotten day.
   Ye shall be taught by Ruin to revive
   The Grecian forms at least from their decay,
And Roman souls at last again shall live
   In Roman works wrought by Italian hands,
   And temples, loftier than the old temples, give
New wonders to the world; and while still stands
   The austere Pantheon, into heaven shall soar   50
   A dome, its image, while the base expands
Into a fane surpassing all before,
   Such as all flesh shall flock to kneel in: ne'er
   Such sight hath been unfolded by a door
As this, to which all nations shall repair
   And lay their sins at this huge gate of heaven.
   And the bold Architect unto whose care
The daring charge to raise it shall be given,
   Whom all hearts shall acknowledge as their lord,
   Whether into the marble chaos driven   60
His chisel bid the Hebrew, at whose word
   Israel left Egypt, stop the waves in stone,
   Or hues of Hell be by his pencil pour'd
Over the damn'd before the Judgement-throne,
   Such as I saw them, such as all shall see,
   Or fanes be built of grandeur yet unknown,
The stream of his great thoughts shall spring from me,
   The Ghibelline, who traversed the three realms
   Which form the empire of eternity.
Amidst the clash of swords, and clang of helms,   70
   The age which I anticipate, no less
   Shall be the Age of Beauty, and while whelms
Calamity the nations with distress,
   The genius of my country shall arise,
   A Cedar towering o'er the Wilderness,
Lovely in all its branches to all eyes,
   Fragrant as fair, and recognised afar,

Wafting its native incense through the skies.
Sovereigns shall pause amidst their sport of war,
   Wean'd for an hour from blood, to turn and gaze
   On canvas or on stone; and they who mar   81
All beauty upon earth, compell'd to praise,
   Shall feel the power of that which they destroy;
   And Art's mistaken gratitude shall raise
To tyrants who but take her for a toy,
   Emblems and monuments, and prostitute
   Her charms to pontiffs proud, who but employ
The man of genius as the meanest brute
   To bear a burthen, and to serve a need,
   To sell his labours, and his soul to boot.   90
Who toils for nations may be poor indeed,
   But free; who sweats for monarchs is no more
   Than the gilt chamberlain, who, clothed and fee'd,
Stands sleek and slavish, bowing at his door.
   Oh, Power that rulest and inspirest! how
   Is it that they on earth, whose earthly power
Is likest thine in heaven in outward show,
   Least like to thee in attributes divine,
   Tread on the universal necks that bow,
And then assure us that their rights are thine?   100
   And how is it that they, the sons of fame,
   Whose inspiration seems to them to shine
From high, they whom the nations oftest name,
   Must pass their days in penury or pain,
   Or step to grandeur through the paths of shame,
And wear a deeper brand and gaudier chain?
   Or if their destiny be born aloof
   From lowliness, or tempted thence in vain,
In their own souls sustain a harder proof,
   The inner war of passions deep and fierce?   110
   Florence! when thy harsh sentence razed my roof,
I loved thee; but the vengeance of my verse,
   The hate of injuries which every year
   Makes greater, and accumulates my curse,
Shall live, outliving all thou holdest dear,
   Thy pride, thy wealth, thy freedom, and even *that*,
   The most infernal of all evils here,

The sway of petty tyrants in a state ;
  For such sway is not limited to kings,
  And demagogues yield to them but in date,   120
As swept off sooner ; in all deadly things,
  Which make men hate themselves, and one another,
  In discord, cowardice, cruelty, all that springs,
From Death the Sin-born's incest with his mother,
  In rank oppression in its rudest shape,
  The faction Chief is but the Sultan's brother,
And the worst despot's far less human ape :
  Florence ! when this lone spirit, which so long
  Yearn'd, as the captive toiling at escape,
To fly back to thee in despite of wrong,   130
  An exile, saddest of all prisoners,
  Who has the whole world for a dungeon strong,
Seas, mountains, and the horizon's verge for bars,
  Which shut him from the sole small spot of earth,
  Where—whatsoe'er his fate—he still were hers,
His country's, and might die where he had birth—
  Florence ! when this lone spirit shall return
  To kindred spirits, thou wilt feel my worth,
And seek to honour with an empty urn
  The ashes thou shalt ne'er obtain—Alas !   140
  ' What have I done to thee, my people ? ' Stern
Are all thy dealings, but in this they pass
  The limits of man's common malice, for
  All that a citizen could be I was ;
Raised by thy will, all thine in peace or war,
  And for this thou hast warr'd with me—'Tis done :
  I may not overleap the eternal bar
Built up between us, and will die alone,
  Beholding with the dark eye of a seer
  The evil days to gifted souls foreshown,   150
Foretelling them to those who will not hear.
  As in the old time, till the hour be come
  When Truth shall strike their eyes through many
    a tear,
And make them own the Prophet in his tomb.

MANFRED

A DRAMATIC POEM

'There are more things in heaven and earth, Horatio,
Than are dreamt of in your philosophy.'

DRAMATIS PERSONÆ

MANFRED	WITCH OF THE ALPS
CHAMOIS HUNTER	ARIMANES
ABBOT OF ST. MAURICE	NEMESIS
MANUEL	THE DESTINIES
HERMAN	SPIRITS, &c.

The Scene of the Drama is amongst the Higher Alps—partly in the Castle of Manfred, and partly in the Mountains.

ACT I

SCENE I.—MANFRED *alone.—Scene, a Gothic Gallery.—Time, Midnight.*

Man. The lamp must be replenish'd, but even then
It will not burn so long as I must watch:
My slumbers—if I slumber—are not sleep,
But a continuance of enduring thought,
Which then I can resist not: in my heart
There is a vigil, and these eyes but close
To look within; and yet I live, and bear
The aspect and the form of breathing men.
But grief should be the instructor of the wise;
Sorrow is knowledge: they who know the most   10
Must mourn the deepest o'er the fatal truth,
The Tree of Knowledge is not that of Life.
Philosophy and science, and the springs
Of wonder, and the wisdom of the world,

I have essay'd, and in my mind there is
A power to make these subject to itself—
But they avail not : I have done men good,
And I have met with good even among men—
But this avail'd not : I have had my foes,
And none have baffled, many fallen before me—   20
But this avail'd not :—Good, or evil, life,
Powers, passions, all I see in other beings,
Have been to me as rain unto the sands,
Since that all-nameless hour. I have no dread,
And feel the curse to have no natural fear,
Nor fluttering throb, that beats with hopes or wishes,
Or lurking love of something on the earth.
Now to my task.—
                        Mysterious Agency !
Ye spirits of the unbounded Universe !
Whom I have sought in darkness and in light—   30
Ye, who do compass earth about, and dwell
In subtler essence—ye, to whom the tops
Of mountains inaccessible are haunts,
And earth's and ocean's caves familiar things—
I call upon ye by the written charm
Which gives me power upon you—Rise ! Appear !
                                        [*A pause.*

They come not yet.—Now by the voice of him
Who is the first among you—by this sign,
Which makes you tremble—by the claims of him
Who is undying,—Rise ! Appear !——Appear !   40
                                        [*A pause.*

If it be so—Spirits of earth and air,
Ye shall not thus elude me : by a power,
Deeper than all yet urged, a tyrant-spell,
Which had its birthplace in a star condemn'd,
The burning wreck of a demolish'd world,
A wandering hell in the eternal space ;
By the strong curse which is upon my soul,
The thought which is within me and around me,
I do compel ye to my will.—Appear !
            [*A star is seen at the darker end of the gallery :
            it is stationary ; and a voice is heard singing.*

FIRST SPIRIT.

Mortal! to thy bidding bow'd,   50
From my mansion in the cloud,
Which the breath of twilight builds,
And the summer's sunset gilds
With the azure and vermilion,
Which is mix'd for my pavilion;
Though thy quest may be forbidden,
On a star-beam I have ridden,
To thine adjuration bow'd,
Mortal—be thy wish avow'd!

Voice of the SECOND SPIRIT.

Mont Blanc is the monarch of mountains;   60
  They crown'd him long ago
On a throne of rocks, in a robe of clouds,
  With a diadem of snow.
Around his waist are forests braced,
  The Avalanche in his hand;
But ere it fall, that thundering ball
  Must pause for my command.
The Glacier's cold and restless mass
  Moves onward day by day;
But I am he who bids it pass,   70
  Or with its ice delay.
I am the spirit of the place,
  Could make the mountain bow
And quiver to his cavern'd base—
  And what with me wouldst *Thou*?

Voice of the THIRD SPIRIT.

In the blue depth of the waters,
  Where the wave hath no strife,
Where the wind is a stranger,
  And the sea-snake hath life,
Where the Mermaid is decking   80
  Her green hair with shells,
Like the storm on the surface
  Came the sound of thy spells;

O'er my calm Hall of Coral
    The deep echo roll'd—
To the Spirit of Ocean
    Thy wishes unfold !

FOURTH SPIRIT.

Where the slumbering earthquake
    Lies pillow'd on fire,
And the lakes of bitumen   90
    Rise boilingly higher ;
Where the roots of the Andes
    Strike deep in the earth,
As their summits to heaven
    Shoot soaringly forth ;
I have quitted my birthplace,
    Thy bidding to bide—
Thy spell hath subdued me,
    Thy will be my guide !

FIFTH SPIRIT.

I am the Rider of the wind,   100
    The Stirrer of the storm ;
The hurricane I left behind
    Is yet with lightning warm ;
To speed to thee, o'er shore and sea
    I swept upon the blast :
The fleet I met sail'd well, and yet
    'Twill sink ere night be past.

SIXTH SPIRIT.

My dwelling is the shadow of the night,
Why doth thy magic torture me with light ?

SEVENTH SPIRIT.

The star which rules thy destiny   110
Was ruled, ere earth began, by me :
It was a world as fresh and fair
As e'er revolved round sun in air
Its course was free and regular,
Space bosom'd not a lovelier star.

The hour arrived—and it became
A wandering mass of shapeless flame,
A pathless comet, and a curse,
The menace of the universe ;
Still rolling on with innate force,   120
Without a sphere, without a course,
A bright deformity on high,
The monster of the upper sky !
And thou ! beneath its influence born—
Thou worm ! whom I obey and scorn—
Forced by a power (which is not thine,
And lent thee but to make thee mine)
For this brief moment to descend,
Where these weak spirits round thee bend
And parley with a thing like thee—   130
What wouldst thou, Child of Clay ! with me ?

The SEVEN SPIRITS.

Earth, ocean, air, night, mountains, winds, thy star,
  Are at thy beck and bidding, Child of Clay !
Before thee at thy quest their spirits are—
  What wouldst thou with us, son of mortals—say ?

Man.   Forgetfulness——
First Spirit.   Of what—of whom—and why ?
Man.   Of that which is within me ; read it there—
Ye know it, and I cannot utter it.
Spirit. We can but give thee that which we possess :
Ask of us subjects, sovereignty, the power   140
O'er earth—the whole, or portion—or a sign
Which shall control the elements, whereof
We are the dominators,—each and all,
These shall be thine.
Man.   Oblivion, self-oblivion !
Can ye not wring from out the hidden realms
Ye offer so profusely what I ask ?
Spirit. It is not in our essence, in our skill ;
But—thou may'st die.
Man.   Will death bestow it on me ?
Spirit. We are immortal, and do not forget ;

We are eternal; and to us the past   150
Is, as the future, present.   Art thou answer'd ?
   Man.   Ye mock me—but the power which brought
ye here
Hath made you mine.   Slaves, scoff not at my will !
The mind, the spirit, the Promethean spark,
The lightning of my being, is as bright,
Pervading, and far darting as your own,
And shall not yield to yours, though coop'd in clay !
Answer, or I will teach you what I am.
   Spirit.   We answer as we answer'd ; our reply
Is even in thine own words.
   Man.   Why say ye so ?   160
   Spirit.   If, as thou say'st, thine essence be as ours,
We have replied in telling thee, the thing
Mortals call death hath nought to do with us.
   Man.   I then have call'd ye from your realms in vain ;
Ye cannot, or ye will not, aid me.
   Spirit.   Say—
What we possess we offer ; it is thine :
Bethink ere thou dismiss us ; ask again ;
Kingdom, and sway, and strength, and length of
    days——
   Man.   Accursed ! what have I to do with days ?
They are too long already.—Hence—begone !   170
   Spirit.   Yet pause : being here, our will would do
   thee service :
Bethink thee, is there then no other gift
Which we can make not worthless in thine eyes ?
   Man.   No, none : yet stay—one moment, ere we part,
I would behold ye face to face.   I hear
Your voices, sweet and melancholy sounds,
As music on the waters ; and I see
The steady aspect of a clear large star ;
But nothing more.   Approach me as ye are,
Or one, or all, in your accustom'd forms.   180
   Spirit.   We have no forms, beyond the elements
Of which we are the mind and principle :
But choose a form—in that we will appear.
   Man.   I have no choice ; there is no form on earth

Hideous or beautiful to me.   Let him,
Who is most powerful of ye, take such aspect
As unto him may seem most fitting—Come !
 Seventh Spirit (appearing in the shape of a beautiful
           female figure).   Behold !

 Man.   Oh God ! if it be thus, and *thou*
Art not a madness and a mockery,
I yet might be most happy.   I will clasp thee, 190
And we again will be——

        [*The figure vanishes.*
      My heart is crush'd !
       [MANFRED *falls senseless.*

(*A voice is heard in the Incantation which follows.*)

 When the moon is on the wave,
  And the glow-worm in the grass,
 And the meteor on the grave,
  And the wisp on the morass ;
 When the falling stars are shooting,
 And the answer'd owls are hooting,
 And the silent leaves are still
 In the shadow of the hill,
 Shall my soul be upon thine,   200
 With a power and with a sign.

 Though thy slumber may be deep,
 Yet thy spirit shall not sleep ;
 There are shades which will not vanish,
 There are thoughts thou canst not banish ;
 By a power to thee unknown,
 Thou canst never be alone ;
 Thou art wrapt as with a shroud,
 Thou art gather'd in a cloud ;
 And for ever shalt thou dwell   210
 In the spirit of this spell.

 Though thou seest me not pass by,
 Thou shalt feel me with thine eye
 As a thing that, though unseen,
 Must be near thee, and hath been ;

And when in that secret dread
Thou hast turn'd around thy head,
Thou shalt marvel I am not
As thy shadow on the spot,
And the power which thou dost feel   220
Shall be what thou must conceal.

And a magic voice and verse
Hath baptized thee with a curse;
And a spirit of the air
Hath begirt thee with a snare;
In the wind there is a voice
Shall forbid thee to rejoice;
And to thee shall Night deny
All the quiet of her sky;
And the day shall have a sun,   230
Which shall make thee wish it done.

From thy false tears I did distil
An essence which hath strength to kill;
From thy own heart I then did wring
The black blood in its blackest spring;
From thy own smile I snatch'd the snake,
For there it coil'd as in a brake;
From thy own lip I drew the charm
Which gave all these their chiefest harm;
In proving every poison known,   240
I found the strongest was thine own.

By thy cold breast and serpent smile,
By thy unfathom'd gulfs of guile,
By that most seeming virtuous eye,
By thy shut soul's hypocrisy;
By the perfection of thine art
Which pass'd for human thine own heart;
By thy delight in others' pain,
And by thy brotherhood of Cain,
I call upon thee! and compel   250
Thyself to be thy proper Hell!

And on thy head I pour the vial
Which doth devote thee to this trial;
Nor to slumber, nor to die,
Shall be in thy destiny;
Though thy death shall still seem near
To thy wish, but as a fear;
Lo! the spell now works around thee,
And the clankless chain hath bound thee:
O'er thy heart and brain together   260
Hath the word been pass'd—now wither!

SCENE II

The Mountain of the Jungfrau.—Time, Morning.—
MANFRED *alone upon the Cliffs.*

Man. The spirits I have raised abandon me,
The spells which I have studied baffle me,
The remedy I reck'd of tortured me;
I lean no more on superhuman aid;
It hath no power upon the past, and for
The future, till the past be gulf'd in darkness,
It is not of my search.—My mother Earth!
And thou fresh breaking Day, and you, ye Mountains,
Why are ye beautiful? I cannot love ye.
And thou, the bright eye of the universe,   10
That openest over all, and unto all
Art a delight—thou shin'st not on my heart.
And you, ye crags, upon whose extreme edge
I stand, and on the torrent's brink beneath
Behold the tall pines dwindled as to shrubs
In dizziness of distance; when a leap,
A stir, a motion, even a breath, would bring
My breast upon its rocky bosom's bed
To rest for ever—wherefore do I pause?
I feel the impulse—yet I do not plunge;   20
I see the peril—yet do not recede;
And my brain reels—and yet my foot is firm:
There is a power upon me which withholds,
And makes it my fatality to live,—

If it be life to wear within myself
This barrenness of spirit, and to be
My own soul's sepulchre, for I have ceased
To justify my deeds unto myself—
The last infirmity of evil. Ay,
Thou winged and cloud-cleaving minister,   30
                              [*An eagle passes.*
Whose happy flight is highest into heaven,
Well may'st thou swoop so near me—I should be
Thy prey, and gorge thine eaglets; thou art gone
Where the eye cannot follow thee; but thine
Yet pierces downward, onward, or above,
With a pervading vision.—Beautiful!
How beautiful is all this visible world!
How glorious in its action and itself!
But we, who name ourselves its sovereigns, we,
Half dust, half deity, alike unfit   40
To sink or soar, with our mix'd essence make
A conflict of its elements, and breathe
The breath of degradation and of pride,
Contending with low wants and lofty will,
Till our mortality predominates,
And men are—what they name not to themselves,
And trust not to each other. Hark! the note,
          [*The Shepherd's pipe in the distance is heard*
The natural music of the mountain reed——
For here the patriarchal days are not
A pastoral fable—pipes in the liberal air,   5c
Mix'd with the sweet bells of the sauntering herd;
My soul would drink those echoes. Oh, that I were
The viewless spirit of a lovely sound,
A living voice, a breathing harmony,
A bodiless enjoyment—born and dying
With the blest tone which made me!

Enter from below a CHAMOIS HUNTER.

Chamois Hunter.   Even so
This way the chamois leapt: her nimble feet
Have baffled me; my gains to-day will scarce
Repay my break-neck travail.—What is here?

Who seems not of my trade, and yet hath reach'd   60
A height which none even of our mountaineers,
Save our best hunters, may attain : his garb
Is goodly, his mien manly, and his air
Proud as a free-born peasant's, at this distance :
I will approach him nearer.

    Man. (*not perceiving the other*).   To be thus—
Grey-hair'd with anguish, like these blasted pines,
Wrecks of a single winter, barkless, branchless,
A blighted trunk upon a cursed root,
Which but supplies a feeling to decay—
And to be thus, eternally but thus,   70
Having been otherwise ! Now furrow'd o'er
With wrinkles, plough'd by moments,—not by years,—
And hours, all tortured into ages—hours
Which I outlive !—Ye toppling crags of ice !
Ye avalanches, whom a breath draws down
In mountainous o'erwhelming, come and crush me !
I hear ye momently above, beneath,
Crash with a frequent conflict ; but ye pass,
And only fall on things that still would live ;
On the young flourishing forest, or the hut   80
And hamlet of the harmless villager.

    C. Hun. The mists begin to rise from up the valley ;
I'll warn him to descend, or he may chance
To lose at once his way and life together.

    Man. The mists boil up around the glaciers ; clouds
Rise curling fast beneath me, white and sulphury,
Like foam from the roused ocean of deep Hell,
Whose every wave breaks on a living shore,
Heap'd with the damn'd like pebbles.—I am giddy.

    C. Hun. I must approach him cautiously ; if near,
A sudden step will startle him, and he   91
Seems tottering already.

    Man.   Mountains have fallen,
Leaving a gap in the clouds, and with the shock
Rocking their Alpine brethren ; filling up
The ripe green valleys with destruction's splinters ;
Damming the rivers with a sudden dash,
Which crush'd the waters into mist, and made

Their fountains find another channel—thus,
Thus, in its old age, did Mount Rosenberg—
Why stood I not beneath it ?
   C. Hun.   Friend ! have a care,   100
Your next step may be fatal !—for the love
Of Him who made you, stand not on that brink !
   Man. (*not hearing him*). Such would have been for
me a fitting tomb ;
My bones had then been quiet in their depth ;
They had not then been strewn upon the rocks
For the wind's pastime—as thus—thus they shall be—
In this one plunge.—Farewell, ye opening heavens !
Look not upon me thus reproachfully—
You were not meant for me—Earth ! take these atoms !
       [*As* MANFRED *is in act to spring from the cliff,*
         the CHAMOIS HUNTER *seizes and retains him*
         with a sudden grasp.
   C. Hun. Hold, madman !—though aweary of thy
life,   110
Stain not our pure vales with thy guilty blood :
Away with me——I will not quit my hold.
   Man. I am most sick at heart—nay, grasp me not—
I am all feebleness—the mountains whirl
Spinning around me——I grow blind——What art
thou ?
   C. Hun. I'll answer that anon.—Away with me—
The clouds grow thicker——there—now lean on me—
Place your foot here—here, take this staff, and cling
A moment to that shrub—now give me your hand,
And hold fast by my girdle—softly—well—   120
The Chalet will be gain'd within an hour :
Come on, we'll quickly find a surer footing,
And something like a pathway, which the torrent
Hath wash'd since winter.—Come, 'tis bravely done—
You should have been a hunter.—Follow me.
       [*As they descend the rocks with difficulty, the*
      scene closes.

ACT II

SCENE I.—*A Cottage amongst the Bernese Alps.*
MANFRED *and the* CHAMOIS HUNTER.

C. Hun. No, no—yet pause—thou must not yet go
            forth :
Thy mind and body are alike unfit
To trust each other, for some hours, at least ;
When thou art better, I will be thy guide—
But whither ?
    Man.   It imports not : I do know
My route full well, and need no further guidance.
    C. Hun. Thy garb and gait bespeak thee of high
            lineage—
One of the many chiefs, whose castled crags
Look o'er the lower valleys—which of these
May call thee lord ? I only know their portals ;   **10**
My way of life leads me but rarely down
To bask by the huge hearths of those old halls,
Carousing with the vassals ; but the paths,
Which step from out our mountains to their doors,
I know from childhood—which of these is thine ?
    Man. No matter.
    C. Hun.   Well, sir, pardon me the question,
And be of better cheer. Come, taste my wine ;
'Tis of an ancient vintage ; many a day
'T has thaw'd my veins among our glaciers, now
Let it do thus for thine—Come, pledge me fairly.   **20**
    Man. Away, away ! there 's blood upon the brim !
Will it then never—never sink in the earth ?
    C. Hun. What dost thou mean ? thy senses wander
            from thee.
    Man. I say 'tis blood—my blood ! the pure warm
            stream
Which ran in the veins of my fathers, and in ours
When we were in our youth, and had one heart,
And loved each other as we should not love,
And this was shed : but still it rises up,
Colouring the clouds, that shut me out from heaven,

Where thou art not—and I shall never be.   30
   C. Hun. Man of strange words, and some half-
      maddening sin,
Which makes thee people vacancy, whate'er
Thy dread and sufferance be, there's comfort yet—
The aid of holy men, and heavenly patience—
   Man. Patience and patience ! Hence—that word
      was made
For brutes of burthen, not for birds of prey !
Preach it to mortals of a dust like thine,—
I am not of thine order.
   C. Hun.   Thanks to Heaven !
I would not be of thine for the free fame
Of William Tell ; but whatsoe'er thine ill,   40
It must be borne, and these wild starts are useless.
   Man. Do I not bear it ?—Look on me—I live.
   C. Hun. This is convulsion, and no healthful life.
   Man. I tell thee, man ! I have lived many years,
Many long years, but they are nothing now
To those which I must number : ages—ages—
Space and eternity—and consciousness,
With the fierce thirst of death—and still unslaked !
   C. Hun. Why, on thy brow the seal of middle
      age
Hath scarce been set ; I am thine elder far.   50
   Man. Think'st thou existence doth depend on
      time ?
It doth ; but actions are our epochs : mine
Have made my days and nights imperishable,
Endless, and all alike, as sands on the shore,
Innumerable atoms ; and one desert,
Barren and cold, on which the wild waves break,
But nothing rests, save carcasses and wrecks,
Rocks, and the salt-surf weeds of bitterness.
   C. Hun. Alas ! he's mad—but yet I must not
      leave him.
   Man. I would I were—for then the things I see
Would be but a distemper'd dream.
   C. Hun.   What is it   61
That thou dost see, or think thou look'st upon ?

Man. Myself, and thee—a peasant of the Alps—
Thy humble virtues, hospitable home,
And spirit patient, pious, proud, and free;
Thy self-respect, grafted on innocent thoughts;
Thy days of health, and nights of sleep; thy toils,
By danger dignified, yet guiltless; hopes
Of cheerful old age and a quiet grave,
With cross and garland over its green turf,   70
And thy grandchildren's love for epitaph;
This do I see—and then I look within—
It matters not—my soul was scorch'd already!
    C. Hun. And wouldst thou then exchange thy lot
      for mine?
    Man. No, friend! I would not wrong thee, nor
      exchange
My lot with living being: I can bear—
However wretchedly, 'tis still to bear—
In life what others could not brook to dream,
But perish in their slumber.
    C. Hun. And with this—
This cautious feeling for another's pain,   80
Canst thou be black with evil?—say not so.
Can one of gentle thoughts have wreak'd revenge
Upon his enemies?
    Man. Oh! no, no, no!
My injuries came down on those who loved me—
On those whom I best loved: I never quell'd
An enemy, save in my just defence—
But my embrace was fatal.
    C. Hun. Heaven give thee rest!
And penitence restore thee to thyself;
My prayers shall be for thee.
    Man. I need them not—
But can endure thy pity. I depart—   90
'Tis time—farewell!—Here's gold, and thanks for
      thee—
No words—it is thy due.—Follow me not—
I know my path—the mountain peril's past:
And once again I charge thee, follow not!
                      [*Exit* MANFRED.

SCENE II

A lower Valley in the Alps.—A Cataract.

Enter MANFRED.

It is not noon—the sunbow's rays still arch
The torrent with the many hues of heaven,
And roll the sheeted silver's waving column
O'er the crag's headlong perpendicular,
And fling its lines of foaming light along,
And to and fro, like the pale courser's tail,
The Giant steed, to be bestrode by Death,
As told in the Apocalypse.   No eyes
But mine now drink this sight of loveliness;
I should be sole in this sweet solitude,   10
And with the Spirit of the place divide
The homage of these waters.—I will call her.

[MANFRED *takes some of the water into the palm
of his hand, and flings it into the air, muttering
the adjuration.   After a pause, the* WITCH OF
THE ALPS *rises beneath the arch of the sunbow
of the torrent.*

Beautiful Spirit! with thy hair of light,
And dazzling eyes of glory, in whose form
The charms of earth's least mortal daughters grow
To an unearthly stature, in an essence
Of purer elements; while the hues of youth,—
Carnation'd like a sleeping infant's cheek,
Rock'd by the beating of her mother's heart,
Or the rose tints, which summer's twilight leaves   20
Upon the lofty glacier's virgin snow,
The blush of earth embracing with her heaven,—
Tinge thy celestial aspect, and make tame
The beauties of the sunbow which bends o'er thee.
Beautiful Spirit! in thy calm clear brow,
Wherein is glass'd serenity of soul,
Which of itself shows immortality,
I read that thou wilt pardon to a Son
Of Earth, whom the abstruser powers permit
At times to commune with them—if that he   30

Avail him of his spells—to call thee thus,
And gaze on thee a moment.
  Witch.   Son of Earth !
I know thee, and the powers which give thee power ;
I know thee for a man of many thoughts,
And deeds of good and ill, extreme in both,
Fatal and fated in thy sufferings.
I have expected this—what wouldst thou with me ?
  Man. To look upon thy beauty—nothing further.
The face of the earth hath madden'd me, and I
Take refuge in her mysteries, and pierce   40
To the abodes of those who govern her—
But they can nothing aid me.   I have sought
From them what they could not bestow, and now
I search no further.
  Witch.   What could be the quest
Which is not in the power of the most powerful,
The rulers of the invisible ?
  Man.   A boon ;
But why should I repeat it ? 'twere in vain.
  Witch. I know not that ; let thy lips utter it.
  Man. Well, though it torture me, 'tis but the same ;
My pang shall find a voice.   From my youth upwards
My spirit walk'd not with the souls of men,   51
Nor look'd upon the earth with human eyes ;
The thirst of their ambition was not mine,
The aim of their existence was not mine ;
My joys, my griefs, my passions, and my powers,
Made me a stranger ; though I wore the form,
I had no sympathy with breathing flesh,
Nor midst the creatures of clay that girded me
Was there but one who—but of her anon.
I said with men, and with the thoughts of men, 60
I held but slight communion ; but instead,
My joy was in the wilderness,—to breathe
The difficult air of the iced mountain's top,
Where the birds dare not build, nor insect's wing
Flit o'er the herbless granite ; or to plunge
Into the torrent, and to roll along
On the swift whirl of the new breaking wave

Of river-stream, or ocean, in their flow.
In these my early strength exulted; or
To follow through the night the moving moon,   70
The stars and their development; or catch
The dazzling lightnings till my eyes grew dim;
Or to look, list'ning, on the scatter'd leaves,
While Autumn winds were at their evening song.
These were my pastimes, and to be alone;
For if the beings, of whom I was one,—
Hating to be so,—cross'd me in my path,
I felt myself degraded back to them,
And was all clay again. And then I dived,
In my lone wanderings, to the caves of death,   80
Searching its cause in its effect; and drew
From wither'd bones, and skulls, and heap'd up dust,
Conclusions most forbidden. Then I pass'd
The nights of years in sciences untaught,
Save in the old time; and with time and toil,
And terrible ordeal, and such penance
As in itself hath power upon the air,
And spirits that do compass air and earth,
Space, and the peopled infinite, I made
Mine eyes familiar with Eternity,   90
Such as, before me, did the Magi, and
He who from out their fountain dwellings raised
Eros and Anteros, at Gadara,
As I do thee;—and with my knowledge grew
The thirst of knowledge, and the power and joy
Of this most bright intelligence, until—
    Witch.   Proceed.
    Man.   Oh! I but thus prolong'd my words,
Boasting these idle attributes, because
As I approach the core of my heart's grief—
But to my task. I have not named to thee   100
Father or mother, mistress, friend, or being,
With whom I wore the chain of human ties;
If I had such, they seem'd not such to me—
Yet there was one—
    Witch.   Spare not thyself—proceed.
    Man. She was like me in lineaments; her eyes,

Her hair, her features, all, to the very tone
Even of her voice, they said were like to mine;
But soften'd all, and temper'd into beauty:
She had the same lone thoughts and wanderings,
The quest of hidden knowledge, and a mind   110
To comprehend the universe: nor these
Alone, but with them gentler powers than mine,
Pity, and smiles, and tears—which I had not;
And tenderness—but that I had for her;
Humility—and that I never had.
Her faults were mine—her virtues were her own—
I loved her, and destroy'd her!
    Witch.   With thy hand?
    Man. Not with my hand, but heart, which broke
      her heart;
It gazed on mine, and wither'd.   I have shed
Blood, but not hers—and yet her blood was shed;
I saw—and could not stanch it.
    Witch.   And for this—   121
A being of the race thou dost despise,
The order, which thine own would rise above,
Mingling with us and ours,—thou dost forgo
The gifts of our great knowledge, and shrink'st back
To recreant mortality——Away!
    Man. Daughter of Air! I tell thee, since that
      hour—
But words are breath—look on me in my sleep,
Or watch my watchings—Come and sit by me!
My solitude is solitude no more,   130
But peopled with the Furies;—I have gnash'd
My teeth in darkness till returning morn,
Then curs'd myself till sunset;—I have pray'd
For madness as a blessing—'tis denied me.
I have affronted death—but in the war
Of elements the waters shrunk from me,
And fatal things pass'd harmless; the cold hand
Of an all-pitiless demon held me back,
Back by a single hair, which would not break.
In fantasy, imagination, all   140
The affluence of my soul—which one day was

A Crœsus in creation—I plunged deep,
But, like an ebbing wave, it dash'd me back
Into the gulf of my unfathom'd thought.
I plunged amidst mankind—Forgetfulness
I sought in all, save where 'tis to be found,
And that I have to learn ;—my sciences,
My long-pursued and superhuman art,
Is mortal here : I dwell in my despair—
And live—and live for ever.

  Witch.   It may be   150
That I can aid thee.

  Man.   To do this thy power
Must wake the dead, or lay me low with them.
Do so—in any shape—in any hour—
With any torture—so it be the last.

  Witch. That is not in my province ; but if thou
Wilt swear obedience to my will, and do
My bidding, it may help thee to thy wishes.

  Man. I will not swear—Obey ! and whom ? the
      spirits
Whose presence I command, and be the slave
Of those who served me—Never !

  Witch.   Is this all ?   160
Hast thou no gentler answer ?—Yet bethink thee,
And pause ere thou rejectest.

  Man.   I have said it.

  Witch. Enough ! I may retire then—say !

  Man.   Retire !
           [*The* WITCH *disappears.*

  Man. (*alone*). We are the fools of time and terror :
     Days
Steal on us, and steal from us ; yet we live,
Loathing our life, and dreading still to die.
In all the days of this detested yoke—
This vital weight upon the struggling heart,
Which sinks with sorrow, or beats quick with pain,
Or joy that ends in agony or faintness—   170
In all the days of past and future, for
In life there is no present, we can number
How few—how less than few—wherein the soul

Forbears to pant for death, and yet draws back
As from a stream in winter, though the chill
Be but a moment's.   I have one resource
Still in my science—I can call the dead,
And ask them what it is we dread to be.
The sternest answer can but be the Grave,
And that is nothing: if they answer not——   180
The buried Prophet answered to the Hag
Of Endor; and the Spartan Monarch drew
From the Byzantine maid's unsleeping spirit
An answer and his destiny—he slew
That which he loved, unknowing what he slew,
And died unpardon'd—though he call'd in aid
The Phyxian Jove, and in Phigalia roused
The Arcadian Evocators to compel
The indignant shadow to depose her wrath,
Or fix her term of vengeance—she replied   190
In words of dubious import, but fulfill'd.
If I had never lived, that which I love
Had still been living; had I never loved,
That which I love would still be beautiful,
Happy and giving happiness.   What is she ?
What is she now ?—a sufferer for my sins—
A thing I dare not think upon—or nothing.
Within few hours I shall not call in vain—
Yet in this hour I dread the thing I dare:
Until this hour I never shrunk to gaze   200
On spirit, good or evil—now I tremble,
And feel a strange cold thaw upon my heart.
But I can act even what I most abhor,
And champion human fears.—The night approaches.
                                          [*Exit.*

SCENE III

The Summit of the Jungfrau Mountain.

Enter FIRST DESTINY.

The moon is rising broad, and round, and bright;
And here on snows, where never human foot
Of common mortal trod, we nightly tread,
And leave no traces: o'er the savage sea,

The glassy ocean of the mountain ice,
We skim its rugged breakers, which put on
The aspect of a tumbling tempest's foam,
Frozen in a moment—a dead whirlpool's image:
And this most steep fantastic pinnacle,
The fretwork of some earthquake—where the clouds
Pause to repose themselves in passing by—   11
Is sacred to our revels, or our vigils;
Here do I wait my sisters, on our way
To the Hall of Arimanes, for to-night
Is our great festival—'tis strange they come not.

A Voice without, singing

The Captive Usurper,
   Hurl'd down from the throne,
Lay buried in torpor,
   Forgotten and lone;
I broke through his slumbers,   20
   I shiver'd his chain,
I leagued him with numbers—
   He's Tyrant again!
With the blood of a million he'll answer my care,
With a nation's destruction—his flight and despair.

Second Voice, without

The ship sail'd on, the ship sail'd fast,
But I left not a sail, and I left not a mast;
There is not a plank of the hull or the deck,
And there is not a wretch to lament o'er his wreck;
Save one, whom I held, as he swam, by the hair,   30
And he was a subject well worthy my care;
A traitor on land, and a pirate at sea—
But I saved him to wreak further havoc for me!

FIRST DESTINY, *answering*

The city lies sleeping;
   The morn, to deplore it,
May dawn on it weeping:
   Sullenly, slowly,

The black plague flew o'er it—
  Thousands lie lowly;
Tens of thousands shall perish;   40
  The living shall fly from
The sick they should cherish;
  But nothing can vanquish
The touch that they die from.
  Sorrow and anguish,
And evil and dread,
  Envelope a nation;
The blest are the dead,
Who see not the sight
  Of their own desolation,   50
This work of a night—
This wreck of a realm—this deed of my doing—
For ages I've done, and shall still be renewing!

Enter the SECOND *and* THIRD DESTINIES.

The Three
Our hands contain the hearts of men,
  Our footsteps are their graves;
We only give to take again
  The spirits of our slaves!

First Des. Welcome!—Where 's Nemesis?
  Second Des.   At some great work;
But what I know not, for my hands were full.
  Third Des. Behold she cometh.

Enter NEMESIS.

  First Des.   Say, where hast thou been?
My sisters and thyself are slow to-night.   61
  Nem. I was detain'd repairing shatter'd thrones,
Marrying fools, restoring dynasties,
Avenging men upon their enemies,
And making them repent their own revenge;
Goading the wise to madness; from the dull
Shaping out oracles to rule the world

Afresh, for they were waxing out of date,
And mortals dared to ponder for themselves,
To weigh kings in the balance, and to speak   70
Of freedom, the forbidden fruit.—Away!
We have outstay'd the hour—mount we our clouds!

                    [*Exeunt.*

Scene IV

The Hall of Arimanes—Arimanes on his Throne,
a Globe of Fire, surrounded by the Spirits

Hymn of the Spirits.

Hail to our Master!—Prince of Earth and Air!
    Who walks the clouds and waters—in his hand
The sceptre of the elements, which tear
    Themselves to chaos at his high command!
He breatheth—and a tempest shakes the sea;
    He speaketh—and the clouds reply in thunder;
He gazeth—from his glance the sunbeams flee;
    He moveth—earthquakes rend the world asunder.
Beneath his footsteps the volcanoes rise;
    His shadow is the Pestilence; his path   10
The comets herald through the crackling skies;
    And planets turn to ashes at his wrath.
To him War offers daily sacrifice;
    To him Death pays his tribute; Life is his,
With all its infinite of agonies—
    And his the spirit of whatever is!

Enter the Destinies and Nemesis.

First Des. Glory to Arimanes! on the earth
His power increaseth—both my sisters did
His bidding, nor did I neglect my duty!
    Second Des. Glory to Arimanes! we who bow   20
The necks of men, bow down before his throne!
    Third Des. Glory to Arimanes! we await
His nod!
    Nem. Sovereign of Sovereigns! we are thine.

And all that liveth, more or less, is ours,
And most things wholly so ; still to increase
Our power, increasing thine, demands our care,
And we are vigilant. Thy late commands
Have been fulfill'd to the utmost.

Enter MANFRED.

  A Spirit.   What is here ?
A mortal !—Thou most rash and fatal wretch,
Bow down and worship !
  Second Spirit.   I do know the man—   **30**
A Magian of great power, and fearful skill !
  Third Spirit.   Bow down and worship, slave !—
    What, know'st thou not
Thine and our Sovereign ?—Tremble, and obey !
  All the Spirits.   Prostrate thyself, and thy con-
    demned clay,
Child of the Earth ! or dread the worst.
  Man.   I know it ;
And yet ye see I kneel not.
  Fourth Spirit.   'Twill be taught thee.
  Man. 'Tis taught already ;—many a night on the
    earth,
On the bare ground, have I bow'd down my face,
And strew'd my head with ashes ; I have known
The fulness of humiliation, for   **40**
I sunk before my vain despair, and knelt
To my own desolation.
  Fifth Spirit.   Dost thou dare
Refuse to Arimanes on his throne
What the whole earth accords, beholding not
The terror of his glory ?—Crouch ! I say.
  Man.   Bid *him* bow down to that which is above him,
The overruling Infinite—the Maker
Who made him not for worship—let him kneel,
And we will kneel together.
  The Spirits.   Crush the worm !
Tear him in pieces !—
  First Des.   Hence ! Avaunt !—he 's mine.   **50**

Prince of the Powers invisible ! This man
Is of no common order, as his port
And presence here denote ; his sufferings
Have been of an immortal nature, like
Our own ; his knowledge, and his powers and will,
As far as is compatible with clay,
Which clogs the ethereal essence, have been such
As clay hath seldom borne ; his aspirations
Have been beyond the dwellers of the earth,
And they have only taught him what we know—   60
That knowledge is not happiness, and science
But an exchange of ignorance for that
Which is another kind of ignorance.
This is not all—the passions, attributes
Of earth and heaven, from which no power, nor
        being,
Nor breath from the worm upwards is exempt,
Have pierced his heart, and in their consequence
Made him a thing which I, who pity not,
Yet pardon those who pity. He is mine,
And thine, it may be ; be it so, or not,   70
No other Spirit in this region hath
A soul like his—or power upon his soul.
    Nem. What doth he here then ?
    First Des.   Let him answer that.
    Man. Ye know what I have known ; and without
        power
I could not be amongst ye : but there are
Powers deeper still beyond—I come in quest
Of such, to answer unto what I seek.
    Nem. What wouldst thou ?
    Man.   Thou canst not reply to me.
Call up the dead—my question is for them.
    Nem. Great Arimanes, doth thy will avouch   80
The wishes of this mortal ?
    Ari.   Yea.
    Nem.   Whom wouldst thou
Uncharnel ?
    Man.   One without a tomb—call up
Astarte.

NEMESIS

Shadow ! or Spirit !
    Whatever thou art,
Which still doth inherit
    The whole or a part
Of the form of thy birth,
    Of the mould of thy clay,
Which return'd to the earth,   9c
    Re-appear to the day !
Bear what thou borest,
    The heart and the form,
And the aspect thou worest
    Redeem from the worm.
Appear !—Appear !—Appear !
Who sent thee there requires thee here !

                    [*The Phantom of* ASTARTE *rises and
                              stands in the midst.*

Man. Can this be death ? there 's bloom upon her
    cheek ;
But now I see it is no living hue,
But a strange hectic—like the unnatural red   10c
Which Autumn plants upon the perish'd leaf.
It is the same ! Oh, God ! that I should dread
To look upon the same—Astarte !—No,
I cannot speak to her—but bid her speak—
Forgive me or condemn me.

NEMESIS

By the power which hath broken
    The grave which enthrall'd thee,
Speak to him who hath spoken,
    Or those who have call'd thee !
Man.   She is silent,
And in that silence I am more than answer'd.   110
    Nem. My power extends no further. Prince of Air !
It rests with thee alone—command her voice.
    Ari. Spirit—obey this sceptre !
    Nem.   Silent still !
She is not of our order, but belongs
To the other powers. Mortal ! thy quest is vain,

And we are baffled also.

    Man.　　　　　　　　　Hear me, hear me—
Astarte! my beloved! speak to me:
I have so much endured—so much endure—
Look on me! the grave hath not changed thee more
Than I am changed for thee.　Thou lovedst me　　120
Too much, as I loved thee: we were not made
To torture thus each other, though it were
The deadliest sin to love as we have loved.
Say that thou loath'st me not—that I do bear
This punishment for both—that thou wilt be
One of the blessed—and that I shall die;
For hitherto all hateful things conspire
To bind me in existence—in a life
Which makes me shrink from immortality—
A future like the past.　I cannot rest.　　　130
I know not what I ask, nor what I seek:
I feel but what thou art, and what I am;
And I would hear yet once before I perish
The voice which was my music—Speak to me!
For I have call'd on thee in the still night,
Startled the slumbering birds from the hush'd boughs,
And woke the mountain wolves, and made the caves
Acquainted with thy vainly echoed name,
Which answer'd me—many things answer'd me—
Spirits and men—but thou wert silent all.　　140
Yet speak to me! I have outwatch'd the stars,
And gazed o'er heaven in vain in search of thee.
Speak to me! I have wander'd o'er the earth,
And never found thy likeness—Speak to me!
Look on the fiends around—they feel for me:
I fear them not, and feel for thee alone—
Speak to me! though it be in wrath;—but say—
I reck not what—but let me hear thee once—
This once—once more!

    Phantom of Astarte.　　Manfred!

    Man.　　　　　　　　　　　Say on, say on—
I live but in the sound—it is thy voice!　　　150

    Phan.　Manfred! To-morrow ends thine earthly ills.
Farewell!

Man.   Yet one word more—am I forgiven ?
Phan.   Farewell !
Man.   Say, shall we meet again ?
Phan.   Farewell !
Man.   One word for mercy ! Say, thou lovest me.
Phan.   Manfred !

          [*The Spirit of* ASTARTE *disappears.*
Nem.   She 's gone, and will not be recall'd ;
Her words will be fulfill'd.   Return to the earth.
A Spirit.   He is convulsed.—This is to be a mortal,
And seek the things beyond mortality.
Another Spirit.   Yet, see, he mastereth himself, and
makes
His torture tributary to his will.   160
Had he been one of us, he would have made
An awful spirit.
Nem.   Hast thou further question
Of our great sovereign, or his worshippers ?
Man.   None.
Nem.   Then for a time farewell.
Man.   We meet then ! Where ? On the earth ?—
Even as thou wilt : and for the grace accorded
I now depart a debtor.   Fare ye well !

                              [*Exit* MANFRED.

            (*Scene closes.*)

ACT III

SCENE I.—*A Hall in the Castle of Manfred.*

MANFRED *and* HERMAN.

Man.   What is the hour ?
Her.   It wants but one till sunset,
And promises a lovely twilight.
Man.   Say,
Are all things so disposed of in the tower
As I directed ?
Her.   All, my lord, are ready :
Here is the key and casket.
Man.   It is well :

Thou may'st retire.   [*Exit* HERMAN.
  Man. (*alone*).   There is a calm upon me—
Inexplicable stillness ! which till now
Did not belong to what I knew of life.
If that I did not know philosophy
To be of all our vanities the motliest,   10
The merest word that ever fool'd the ear
From out the schoolman's jargon, I should deem
The golden secret, the sought ' Kalon ', found,
And seated in my soul. It will not last,
But it is well to have known it, though but once :
It hath enlarged my thoughts with a new sense,
And I within my tablets would note down
That there is such a feeling. Who is there ?

Re-enter HERMAN.

  Her. My lord, the abbot of St. Maurice craves
To greet your presence.

Enter the ABBOT OF ST. MAURICE.

  Abbot.   Peace be with Count Manfred !   20
  Man. Thanks, holy father ! welcome to these walls ;
Thy presence honours them, and blesseth those
Who dwell within them.
  Abbot.   Would it were so, Count !—
But I would fain confer with thee alone.
  Man. Herman, retire.—What would my reverend
    guest ?
  Abbot. Thus, without prelude :—Age and zeal, my
    office,
And good intent must plead my privilege ;
Our near, though not acquainted neighbourhood,
May also be my herald. Rumours strange,
And of unholy nature, are abroad,   30
And busy with thy name ; a noble name
For centuries : may he who bears it now
Transmit it unimpair'd!
  Man.   Proceed,—I listen.
  Abbot. 'Tis said thou holdest converse with the
    things

Which are forbidden to the search of man ;
That with the dwellers of the dark abodes,
The many evil and unheavenly spirits
Which walk the valley of the shade of death,
Thou communest. I know that with mankind,
Thy fellows in creation, thou dost rarely   40
Exchange thy thoughts, and that thy solitude
Is as an anchorite's, were it but holy.

   Man. And what are they who do avouch these
     things ?

   Abbot. My pious brethren—the scared peasantry—
Even thy own vassals—who do look on thee
With most unquiet eyes. Thy life 's in peril.

   Man. Take it.

   Abbot.   I come to save, and not destroy :
I would not pry into thy secret soul ;
But if these things be sooth, there still is time
For penitence and pity : reconcile thee   50
With the true church, and through the church to
     Heaven.

   Man. I hear thee. This is my reply : whate'er
I may have been, or am, doth rest between
Heaven and myself. I shall not choose a mortal
To be my mediator. Have I sinn'd
Against your ordinances ? prove and punish !

   Abbot. My son ! I did not speak of punishment,
But penitence and pardon ;—with thyself
The choice of such remains—and for the last,
Our institutions and our strong belief   60
Have given me power to smooth the path from sin
To higher hope and better thoughts ; the first
I leave to Heaven,—' Vengeance is mine alone ! '
So saith the Lord, and with all humbleness
His servant echoes back the awful word.

   Man. Old man ! there is no power in holy men,
Nor charm in prayer, nor purifying form
Of penitence, nor outward look, nor fast,
Nor agony—nor, greater than all these,
The innate tortures of that deep despair,   70
Which is remorse without the fear of hell.

But all in all sufficient to itself
Would make a hell of heaven—can exorcise
From out the unbounded spirit the quick sense
Of its own sins, wrongs, sufferance, and revenge
Upon itself ; there is no future pang
Can deal that justice on the self-condemn'd
He deals on his own soul.

    Abbot.   All this is well ;
For this will pass away, and be succeeded
By an auspicious hope, which shall look up   80
With calm assurance to that blessed place,
Which all who seek may win, whatever be
Their earthly errors, so they be atoned :
And the commencement of atonement is
The sense of its necessity. Say on—
And all our church can teach thee shall be taught ;
And all we can absolve thee shall be pardon'd.

    Man. When Rome's sixth emperor was near his last,
The victim of a self-inflicted wound,
To shun the torments of a public death   90
From senates once his slaves, a certain soldier,
With show of loyal pity, would have stanch'd
The gushing throat with his officious robe ;
The dying Roman thrust him back, and said—
Some empire still in his expiring glance—
'It is too late—is this fidelity ?'

    Abbot. And what of this ?

    Man.   I answer with the Roman—
'It is too late !'

    Abbot.   It never can be so,
To reconcile thyself with thy own soul,
And thy own soul with Heaven. Hast thou no hope ?
'Tis strange—even those who do despair above,   101
Yet shape themselves some fantasy on earth,
To which frail twig they cling, like drowning men.

    Man. Aye—father ! I have had those earthly visions,
And noble aspirations in my youth,
To make my own the mind of other men,
The enlightener of nations ; and to rise
I knew not whither—it might be to fall ;

But fall, even as the mountain-cataract,
Which having leapt from its more dazzling height,
Even in the foaming strength of its abyss,   111
(Which casts up misty columns that become
Clouds raining from the re-ascended skies,)
Lies low but mighty still.—But this is past,
My thoughts mistook themselves.
   Abbot.   And wherefore so ?
   Man. I could not tame my nature down ; for he
Must serve who fain would sway ; and soothe, and sue,
And watch all time, and pry into all place,
And be a living lie, who would become
A mighty thing amongst the mean,—and such   120
The mass are ; I disdain'd to mingle with
A herd, though to be leader—and of wolves.
The lion is alone, and so am I.
   Abbot. And why not live and act with other men ?
   Man. Because my nature was averse from life :
And yet not cruel ; for I would not make,
But find a desolation. Like the wind,
The red-hot breath of the most lone simoom,
Which dwells but in the desert, and sweeps o'er
The barren sands which bear no shrubs to blast,   130
And revels o'er their wild and arid waves,
And seeketh not, so that it is not sought,
But being met is deadly,—such hath been
The course of my existence ; but there came
Things in my path which are no more.
   Abbot.   Alas !
I 'gin to fear that thou art past all aid
From me and from my calling ; yet so young,
I still would—
   Man.   Look on me ! there is an order
Of mortals on the earth, who do become
Old in their youth, and die ere middle age,   140
Without the violence of warlike death ;
Some perishing of pleasure, some of study,
Some worn with toil, some of mere weariness,
Some of disease, and some insanity,
And some of wither'd, or of broken hearts ;

For this last is a malady which slays
More than are number'd in the lists of Fate,
Taking all shapes, and bearing many names.
Look upon me ! for even of all these things
Have I partaken ; and of all these things,   150
One were enough ; then wonder not that I
Am what I am, but that I ever was,
Or having been, that I am still on earth.
 Abbot. Yet, hear me still——
 Man.   Old man ! I do respect
Thine order, and revere thine years ; I deem
Thy purpose pious, but it is in vain :
Think me not churlish ; I would spare thyself,
Far more than me, in shunning at this time
All further colloquy—and so—farewell.
         [*Exit* MANFRED.
 Abbot. This should have been a noble creature : he
Hath all the energy which would have made   161
A goodly frame of glorious elements,
Had they been wisely mingled ; as it is,
It is an awful chaos—light and darkness,—
And mind and dust,—and passions and pure thoughts
Mix'd, and contending without end or order,—
All dormant or destructive : he will perish,
And yet he must not ; I will try once more.
For such are worth redemption ; and my duty
Is to dare all things for a righteous end.   170
I'll follow him—but cautiously, though surely.
         [*Exit* ABBOT.

SCENE II

Another Chamber.

MANFRED *and* HERMAN.

 Her. My lord, you bade me wait on you at sunset :
He sinks behind the mountain.
 Man.   Doth he so ?
I will look on him. [MANFRED *advances to the Window*
         of the Hall.

  Glorious Orb ! the idol

Of early nature, and the vigorous race
Of undiseased mankind, the giant sons
Of the embrace of angels, with a sex
More beautiful than they, which did draw down
The erring spirits who can ne'er return.—
Most glorious orb! that wert a worship, ere
The mystery of thy making was reveal'd!   10
Thou earliest minister of the Almighty,
Which gladden'd, on their mountain tops, the hearts
Of the Chaldean shepherds, till they pour'd
Themselves in orisons! Thou material God!
And representative of the Unknown—
Who chose thee for his shadow! Thou chief star!
Centre of many stars! which mak'st our earth
Endurable, and temperest the hues
And hearts of all who walk within thy rays!
Sire of the seasons! Monarch of the climes,   20
And those who dwell in them! for near or far,
Our inborn spirits have a tint of thee
Even as our outward aspects;—thou dost rise,
And shine, and set in glory. Fare thee well!
I ne'er shall see thee more. As my first glance
Of love and wonder was for thee, then take
My latest look; thou wilt not beam on one
To whom the gifts of life and warmth have been
Of a more fatal nature. He is gone:
I follow.   [*Exit* MANFRED.

SCENE III

*The Mountains—The Castle of Manfred at some dis-
tance—A Terrace before a Tower.—Time, Twilight.*

HERMAN, MANUEL, *and other Dependants of*
MANFRED.

Her. 'Tis strange enough; night after night, for
      years,
He hath pursued long vigils in this tower,
Without a witness. I have been within it,—
So have we all been oft-times; but from it,

Or its contents, it were impossible
To draw conclusions absolute, of aught
His studies tend to. To be sure, there is
One chamber where none enter: I would give
The fee of what I have to come these three years,
To pore upon its mysteries.
    Manuel.   'Twere dangerous ;   10
Content thyself with what thou know'st already.
    Her. Ah ! Manuel ! thou art elderly and wise,
And couldst say much ; thou hast dwelt within the
      castle—
How many years is 't ?
    Manuel.   Ere Count Manfred's birth,
I served his father, whom he nought resembles.
    Her. There be more sons in like predicament.
But wherein do they differ ?
    Manuel.   I speak not
Of features or of form, but mind and habits ;
Count Sigismund was proud, but gay and free,—
A warrior and a reveller ; he dwelt not   20
With books and solitude, nor made the night
A gloomy vigil, but a festal time,
Merrier than day ; he did not walk the rocks
And forests like a wolf, nor turn aside
From men and their delights.
    Her.   Beshrew the hour,
But those were jocund times ! I would that such
Would visit the old walls again ; they look
As if they had forgotten them.
    Manuel.   These walls
Must change their chieftain first. Oh ! I have seen
Some strange things in them, Herman.
    Her.   Come, be friendly ;   30
Relate me some to while away our watch :
I've heard thee darkly speak of an event
Which happen'd hereabouts, by this same tower.
    Manuel. That was a night indeed ! I do remember
'Twas twilight, as it may be now, and such
Another evening ;—yon red cloud, which rests
On Eigher's pinnacle, so rested then,—

So like that it might be the same ; the wind
Was faint and gusty, and the mountain snows
Began to glitter with the climbing moon ;   40
Count Manfred was, as now, within his tower,—
How occupied, we knew not, but with him
The sole companion of his wanderings
And watchings—her, whom of all earthly things
That lived, the only thing he seem'd to love,—
As he, indeed, by blood was bound to do,
The Lady Astarte, his—

                Hush ! who comes here ?

Enter the ABBOT.

   Abbot. Where is your master ?
   Her.   Yonder in the tower.
   Abbot. I must speak with him.
   Manuel.   'Tis impossible ;
He is most private, and must not be thus   50
Intruded on.
   Abbot.   Upon myself I take
The forfeit of my fault, if fault there be—
But I must see him.
   Her.   Thou hast seen him once
This eve already.
   Abbot.   Herman ! I command thee,
Knock, and apprize the Count of my approach.
   Her. We dare not.
   Abbot.   Then it seems I must be herald
Of my own purpose.
   Manuel.   Reverend father, stop—
I pray you pause.
   Abbot.   Why so ?
   Manuel.   But step this way,
And I will tell you further.   [*Exeunt.*

Scene IV

Interior of the Tower.

Manfred *alone.*

The stars are forth, the moon above the tops
Of the snow-shining mountains.—Beautiful !
I linger yet with Nature, for the Night
Hath been to me a more familiar face
Than that of man ; and in her starry shade
Of dim and solitary loveliness,
I learn'd the language of another world.
I do remember me, that in my youth,
When I was wandering,—upon such a night
I stood within the Coliseum's wall, 10
'Midst the chief relics of almighty Rome ;
The trees which grew along the broken arches
Waved dark in the blue midnight, and the stars
Shone through the rents of ruin ; from afar
The watch-dog bay'd beyond the Tiber ; and
More near from out the Cæsars' palace came
The owl's long cry, and, interruptedly,
Of distant sentinels the fitful song
Begun and died upon the gentle wind.
Some cypresses beyond the time-worn breach 20
Appear'd to skirt the horizon, yet they stood
Within a bowshot. Where the Cæsars dwelt,
And dwell the tuneless birds of night, amidst
A grove which springs through levell'd battlements,
And twines its roots with the imperial hearths,
Ivy usurps the laurel's place of growth ;
But the gladiators' bloody Circus stands,
A noble wreck in ruinous perfection,
While Cæsar's chambers, and the Augustan halls,
Grovel on earth in indistinct decay. 30
And thou didst shine, thou rolling moon, upon
All this, and cast a wide and tender light,
Which soften'd down the hoar austerity
Of rugged desolation, and fill'd up,
As 'twere anew, the gaps of centuries ;

Leaving that beautiful which still was so,
And making that which was not, till the place
Became religion, and the heart ran o'er
With silent worship of the great of old,—
The dead but sceptred sovereigns, who still rule   40
Our spirits from their urns.
                'Twas such a night!
'Tis strange that I recall it at this time;
But I have found our thoughts take wildest flight
Even at the moment when they should array
Themselves in pensive order.

Enter the ABBOT

  Abbot.   My good lord!
I crave a second grace for this approach;
But yet let not my humble zeal offend
By its abruptness—all it hath of ill
Recoils on me; its good in the effect
May light upon your head—could I say *heart*—   50
Could I touch *that*, with words or prayers, I should
Recall a noble spirit which hath wander'd,
But is not yet all lost.
  Man.   Thou know'st me not;
My days are number'd, and my deeds recorded:
Retire, or 'twill be dangerous—Away!
  Abbot. Thou dost not mean to menace me?
  Man.   Not I;
I simply tell thee peril is at hand,
And would preserve thee.
  Abbot.   What dost thou mean?
  Man.   Look there!
What dost thou see?
  Abbot.   Nothing.
  Man.   Look there, I say,
And stedfastly;—now tell me what thou seest?   60
  Abbot. That which should shake me, but I fear it
     not:
I see a dusk and awful figure rise,
Like an infernal god, from out the earth;
His face wrapt in a mantle, and his form

Robed as with angry clouds : he stands between
Thyself and me—but I do fear him not.
 Man. Thou hast no cause—he shall not harm thee—
  but
His sight may shock thine old limbs into palsy.
I say to thee—Retire !
 Abbot.   And I reply—
Never—till I have battled with this fiend :—   70
What doth he here ?
 Man.   Why—aye—what doth he here ?
I did not send for him,—he is unbidden.
 Abbot. Alas ! lost mortal ! what with guests like
  these
Hast thou to do ? I tremble for thy sake :
Why doth he gaze on thee, and thou on him ?
Ah ! he unveils his aspect : on his brow
The thunder-scars are graven : from his eye
Glares forth the immortality of hell—
Avaunt !—
 Man. Pronounce—what is thy mission ?
 Spirit.   Come !
 Abbot. What art thou, unknown being ? answer !—
  speak !   80
 Spirit. The genius of this mortal.—Come ! 'tis time.
 Man. I am prepared for all things, but deny
The power which summons me. Who sent thee here ?
 Spirit. Thou'lt know anon—Come ! come !
 Man.   I have commanded
Things of an essence greater far than thine,
And striven with thy masters. Get thee hence !
 Spirit. Mortal ! thine hour is come—Away ! I say.
 Man. I knew, and know my hour is come, but not
To render up my soul to such as thee :
Away ! I'll die as I have lived—alone.   90
 Spirit. Then I must summon up my brethren.—
  Rise !

           [*Other Spirits rise up.*
 Abbot. Avaunt ! ye evil ones !—Avaunt ! I say ;
Ye have no power where piety hath power,
And I do charge ye in the name——

Spirit.   Old man !
We know ourselves, our mission, and thine order ;
Waste not thy holy words on idle uses,
It were in vain : this man is forfeited.
Once more I summon him—Away ! Away !
    Man. I do defy ye,—though I feel my soul
Is ebbing from me, yet I do defy ye ;   100
Nor will I hence, while I have earthly breath
To breathe my scorn upon ye—earthly strength
To wrestle, though with spirits ; what ye take
Shall be ta'en limb by limb.
    Spirit.   Reluctant mortal !
Is this the Magian who would so pervade
The world invisible, and make himself
Almost our equal ? Can it be that thou
Art thus in love with life ? the very life
Which made thee wretched ?
    Man.   Thou false fiend, thou liest !
My life is in its last hour,—*that* I know,   110
Nor would redeem a moment of that hour ;
I do not combat against death, but thee
And thy surrounding angels ; my past power
Was purchased by no compact with thy crew,
But by superior science—penance, daring,
And length of watching, strength of mind, and skill
In knowledge of our fathers—when the earth
Saw men and spirits walking side by side,
And gave ye no supremacy : I stand
Upon my strength—I do defy—deny—   120
Spurn back, and scorn ye !—
    Spirit.   But thy many crimes
Have made thee——
    Man.   What are they to such as thee ?
Must crimes be punish'd but by other crimes,
And greater criminals ?—Back to thy hell !
Thou hast no power upon me, *that* I feel ;
Thou never shalt possess me, *that* I know :
What I have done is done ; I bear within
A torture which could nothing gain from thine :
The mind which is immortal makes itself

Requital for its good or evil thoughts,— 130
Is its own origin of ill and end—
And its own place and time : its innate sense,
When stripp'd of this mortality, derives
No colour from the fleeting things without,
But is absorb'd in sufferance or in joy,
Born from the knowledge of its own desert.
Thou didst not tempt me, and thou couldst not tempt
    me ;
I have not been thy dupe, nor am thy prey—
But was my own destroyer, and will be
My own hereafter.—Back, ye baffled fiends !— 140
The hand of death is on me—but not yours !

                    [The Demons disappear.
  Abbot. Alas ! how pale thou art—thy lips are white—
And thy breast heaves—and in thy gasping throat
The accents rattle : Give thy prayers to Heaven—
Pray—albeit but in thought,—but die not thus.
  Man. 'Tis over—my dull eyes can fix thee not ;
But all things swim around me, and the earth
Heaves as it were beneath me. Fare thee well !
Give me thy hand.
  Abbot.   Cold—cold—even to the heart—
But yet one prayer—Alas ! how fares it with thee ?
  Man. Old man ! 'tis not so difficult to die. 151

                      [MANFRED *expires.*
  Abbot. He 's gone—his soul hath ta'en its earthless
    flight ;
Whither ? I dread to think—but he is gone.

MARINO FALIERO, DOGE OF VENICE

From *Marino Faliero, Doge of Venice.*

ACT V. SCENE III

*The Court of the Ducal Palace ; the outer gates are shut
against the people.—The* DOGE *enters in his ducal
robes, in procession with the Council of Ten and other
Patricians, attended by the Guards, till they arrive at
the top of the ' Giants' Staircase' (where the Doges
took the oaths) ; the Executioner is stationed there with
his sword.—On arriving, a Chief of the Ten takes off
the ducal cap from the Doge's head.*

Doge. So now the Doge is nothing, and at last
I am again Marino Faliero :
'Tis well to be so, though but for a moment.
Here was I crown'd, and here, bear witness, Heaven !
With how much more contentment I resign
That shining mockery, the ducal bauble,
Than I received the fatal ornament.
   One of the Ten. Thou tremblest, Faliero !
   Doge.   'Tis with age, then.
   Ben. Faliero ! hast thou aught further to commend,
Compatible with justice, to the senate ?   10
   Doge. I would commend my nephew to their mercy,
My consort to their justice ; for methinks
My death, and such a death, might settle all
Between the state and me.
   Ben.   They shall be cared for ;
Even notwithstanding thine unheard-of crime.
   Doge. Unheard of ! aye, there 's not a history
But shows a thousand crown'd conspirators
Against the people ; but to set them free,
One sovereign only died, and one is dying.   19
   Ben. And who were they who fell in such a cause ?
   Doge. The King of Sparta and the Doge of Venice—
Agis and Faliero !
   Ben.   Hast thou more
To utter or to do ?

Doge.   May I speak ?
Ben.   Thou may'st ;
But recollect the people are without,
Beyond the compass of the human voice.
  Doge.   I speak to Time and to Eternity,
Of which I grow a portion, not to man.
Ye elements ! in which to be resolved
I hasten, let my voice be as a spirit
Upon you ! Ye blue waves ! which bore my banner,
Ye winds ! which flutter'd o'er as if you loved it,   31
And fill'd my swelling sails as they were wafted
To many a triumph ! Thou, my native earth,
Which I have bled for ! and thou, foreign earth,
Which drank this willing blood from many a wound !
Ye stones, in which my gore will not sink, but
Reek up to heaven ! Ye skies, which will receive it !
Thou sun ! which shinest on these things, and Thou !
Who kindlest and who quenchest suns !—Attest !
I am not innocent—but are these guiltless ?   40
I perish, but not unavenged : far ages
Float up from the abyss of time to be,
And show these eyes, before they close, the doom
Of this proud city, and I leave my curse
On her and hers for ever !——Yes, the hours
Are silently engendering of the day,
When she, who built 'gainst Attila a bulwark,
Shall yield, and bloodlessly and basely yield,
Unto a bastard Attila, without
Shedding so much blood in her last defence,   50
As these old veins, oft drain'd in shielding her,
Shall pour in sacrifice.—She shall be bought
And sold, and be an appanage to those
Who shall despise her !—She shall stoop to be
A province for an empire, petty town
In lieu of capital, with slaves for senates,
Beggars for nobles, panders for a people !
Then when the Hebrew 's in thy palaces,
The Hun in thy high places, and the Greek
Walks o'er thy mart, and smiles on it for his :   60
When thy patricians beg their bitter bread

In narrow streets, and in their shameful need
Make their nobility a plea for pity;
Then, when the few who still retain a wreck
Of their great fathers' heritage shall fawn
Round a barbarian Vice of Kings' Vicegerent,
Even in the palace where they sway'd as sovereigns,
Even in the palace where they slew their sovereign,
Proud of some name they have disgraced, or sprung
From an adulteress boastful of her guilt   70
With some large gondolier or foreign soldier,
Shall bear about their bastardy in triumph
To the third spurious generation;—when
Thy sons are in the lowest scale of being,
Slaves turn'd o'er to the vanquish'd by the victors,
Despised by cowards for greater cowardice,
And scorn'd even by the vicious for such vices
As in the monstrous grasp of their conception
Defy all codes to image or to name them;
Then, when of Cyprus, now thy subject kingdom,   80
All thine inheritance shall be her shame
Entail'd on thy less virtuous daughters, grown
A wider proverb for worse prostitution;—
When all the ills of conquer'd states shall cling thee,
Vice without splendour, sin without relief
Even from the gloss of love to smooth it o'er,
But in its stead, coarse lusts of habitude,
Prurient yet passionless, cold studied lewdness,
Depraving nature's frailty to an art;—
When these and more are heavy on thee, when   90
Smiles without mirth, and pastimes without pleasure,
Youth without honour, age without respect,
Meanness and weakness, and a sense of woe
'Gainst which thou wilt not strive, and dar'st not
        murmur,
Have made thee last and worst of peopled deserts,
Then, in the last gasp of thine agony,
Amidst thy many murders, think of *mine !*
Thou den of drunkards with the blood of princes !
Gehenna of the waters ! thou sea Sodom !
Thus I devote thee to the infernal gods !   100

354 MARINO FALIERO, DOGE OF VENICE

Thee and thy serpent seed !

[*Here the* DOGE *turns and addresses the Executioner.*

Slave, do thine office !
Strike as I struck the foe ! Strike as I would
Have struck those tyrants ! Strike deep as my curse !
Strike—and but once !

[*The* DOGE *throws himself upon his knees, and as the Executioner raises his sword the scene closes.*

THE SWIMMER

(From *The Two Foscari*, I. i)

How many a time have I
Cloven with arm still lustier, breast more daring,
The wave all roughen'd ; with a swimmer's stroke
Flinging the billows back from my drench'd hair,
And laughing from my lip the audacious brine,
Which kiss'd it like a wine-cup, rising o'er
The waves as they arose, and prouder still
The loftier they uplifted me ; and oft,
In wantonness of spirit, plunging down
Into their green and glassy gulfs, and making   10
My way to shells and sea-weed, all unseen
By those above, till they wax'd fearful ; then
Returning with my grasp full of such tokens
As show'd that I had search'd the deep : exulting,
With a far-dashing stroke, and drawing deep
The long-suspended breath, again I spurn'd
The foam which broke around me, and pursued
My track like a sea-bird.—I was a boy then.

CAIN: A MYSTERY

ACT II

Scene I.—*The Abyss of Space*

Cain.   I tread on air, and sink not; yet I fear
To sink.

Lucifer.   Have faith in me, and thou shalt be
Borne on the air, of which I am the prince.

Cain.   Can I do so without impiety?

Lucifer.   Believe—and sink not! doubt—and
perish! thus
Would run the edict of the other God,
Who names me demon to his angels; they
Echo the sound to miserable things,
Which, knowing nought beyond their shallow senses,
Worship the word which strikes their ear, and deem
Evil or good what is proclaim'd to them   11
In their abasement.   I will have none such:
Worship or worship not, thou shalt behold
The worlds beyond thy little world, nor be
Amerced for doubts beyond thy little life,
With torture of *my* dooming.   There will come
An hour, when, toss'd upon some water-drops,
A man shall say to a man, 'Believe in me,
And walk the waters;' and the man shall walk
The billows and be safe.   *I* will not say,   20
Believe in *me*, as a conditional creed
To save thee; but fly with me o'er the gulf
Of space an equal flight, and I will show
What thou dar'st not deny,—the history
Of past, and present, and of future worlds.

Cain.   Oh, god, or demon, or whate'er thou art,
Is yon our earth?

Lucifer.   Dost thou not recognise

The dust which form'd your father ?
 Cain.   Can it be ?
Yon small blue circle, swinging in far ether,
With an inferior circlet near it still,   30
Which looks like that which lit our earthly night ?
Is this our Paradise ? Where are its walls,
And they who guard them ?
 Lucifer.   Point me out the site
Of Paradise.
 Cain.   How should I ? As we move
Like sunbeams onward, it grows small and smaller,
And as it waxes little, and then less,
Gathers a halo round it, like the light
Which shone the roundest of the stars, when I
Beheld them from the skirts of Paradise :
Methinks they both, as we recede from them,   40
Appear to join the innumerable stars
Which are around us ; and, as we move on,
Increase their myriads.
 Lucifer.   And if there should be
Worlds greater than thine own, inhabited
By greater things, and they themselves far more
In number than the dust of thy dull earth,
Though multiplied to animated atoms,
All living, and all doom'd to death, and wretched,
What wouldst thou think ?
 Cain.   I should be proud of thought
Which knew such things.
 Lucifer.   But if that high thought were
Link'd to a servile mass of matter, and,   51
Knowing such things, aspiring to such things,
And science still beyond them, were chain'd down
To the most gross and petty paltry wants,
All foul and fulsome, and the very best
Of thine enjoyments a sweet degradation,
A most enervating and filthy cheat
To lure thee on to the renewal of
Fresh souls and bodies, all foredoom'd to be
As frail, and few so happy——
 Cain.   Spirit ! I   ∞

Know nought of death, save as a dreadful thing
Of which I have heard my parents speak, as of
A hideous heritage I owe to them
No less than life; a heritage not happy,
If I may judge, till now. But, spirit! if
It be as thou hast said (and I within
Feel the prophetic torture of its truth),
Here let me die: for to give birth to those
Who can but suffer many years, and die,
Methinks is merely propagating death,   70
And multiplying murder.
  Lucifer.   Thou canst not
All die—there is what must survive.
  Cain.   The Other
Spake not of this unto my father, when
He shut him forth from Paradise, with death
Written upon his forehead. But at least
Let what is mortal of me perish, that
I may be in the rest as angels are.
  Lucifer. I am angelic: wouldst thou be as I am?
  Cain. I know not what thou art: I see thy
     power,
And see thou show'st me things beyond *my* power,
Beyond all power of my born faculties,   81
Although inferior still to my desires
And my conceptions.
  Lucifer.   What are they which dwell
So humbly in their pride, as to sojourn
With worms in clay?
  Cain.   And what art thou who dwellest
So haughtily in spirit, and canst range
Nature and immortality—and yet
Seem'st sorrowful?
  Lucifer.   I seem that which I am;
And therefore do I ask of thee, if thou
Wouldst be immortal?
  Cain.   Thou hast said I must be   90
Immortal in despite of me. I knew not
This until lately—but since it must be,
Let me, or happy or unhappy, learn

To anticipate my immortality.
    Lucifer.   Thou didst before I came upon thee.
    Cain.   How?
    Lucifer.   By suffering.
    Cain.   And must torture be immortal?
    Lucifer.   We and thy sons will try. But now, be-
        hold!
Is it not glorious?
    Cain.   Oh, thou beautiful
And unimaginable ether! and
Ye multiplying masses of increased   100
And still increasing lights! what are ye? what
Is this blue wilderness of interminable
Air, where ye roll along, as I have seen
The leaves along the limpid streams of Eden?
Is your course measured for ye? Or do ye
Sweep on in your unbounded revelry
Through an aërial universe of endless
Expansion—at which my soul aches to think—
Intoxicated with eternity?
O God! O Gods! or whatsoe'er ye are!   110
How beautiful ye are! how beautiful
Your works, or accidents, or whatsoe'er
They may be! Let me die, as atoms die
(If that they die), or know ye in your might
And knowledge! My thoughts are not in this **hour**
Unworthy what I see, though my dust is;
Spirit! let me expire, or see them nearer.
    Lucifer.   Art thou not nearer? look back to thine
        earth!
    Cain.   Where is it? I see nothing save a mass
Of most innumerable lights.
    Lucifer.   Look there!   120
    Cain.   I cannot see it.
    Lucifer.   Yet it sparkles still.
    Cain.   That!—yonder!
    Lucifer.   Yea.
    Cain.   And wilt thou tell me so?
Why, I have seen the fire-flies and fire-worms
Sprinkle the dusky groves and the green banks

In the dim twilight, brighter than yon world
Which bears them.
    Lucifer.   Thou hast seen both worms and worlds,
Each bright and sparkling—what dost think of them ?
    Cain.   That they are beautiful in their own sphere,
And that the night, which makes both beautiful,
The little shining fire-fly in its flight,   **130**
And the immortal star in its great course,
Must both be guided.
    Lucifer.   But by whom or what ?
    Cain. Show me.
    Lucifer.   Dar'st thou behold ?
    Cain.   How know I what
I *dare* behold ? As yet, thou hast shown nought
I dare not gaze on further.
    Lucifer.   On, then, with me.

ACT III

SCENE I.—*The Earth, near Eden, as in Act I.*

Enter CAIN *and* ADAH.

    Adah. Hush, tread softly, Cain.
    Cain.   I will ; but wherefore ?
    Adah. Our little Enoch sleeps upon yon bed
Of leaves, beneath the cypress.
    Cain.   Cypress ! 'tis
A gloomy tree, which looks as if it mourn'd
O'er what it shadows ; wherefore didst thou choose it
For our child's canopy ?
    Adah.   Because its branches
Shut out the sun like night, and therefore seem'd
Fitting to shadow slumber.
    Cain.   Ay, the last—
And longest ; but no matter—lead me to him.
                    [They go up to the child.
How lovely he appears ! his little cheeks,   **10**
In their pure incarnation, vying with

The rose leaves strewn beneath them.

   Adah.   And his lips, too,
How beautifully parted ! No ; you shall not
Kiss him, at least not now : he will awake soon.
His hour of mid-day rest is nearly over ;
But it were pity to disturb him till
'Tis closed.

   Cain.   You have said well ; I will contain
My heart till then. He smiles, and sleeps !—Sleep on,
And smile, thou little, young inheritor   19
Of a world scarce less young : sleep on, and smile !
Thine are the hours and days when both are cheering
And innocent ! *thou* hast not pluck'd the fruit—
Thou know'st not thou art naked ! Must the time
Come thou shalt be amerced for sins unknown,
Which were not thine nor mine ? But now sleep on !
His cheeks are reddening into deeper smiles,
And shining lids are trembling o'er his long
Lashes, dark as the cypress which waves o'er them ;
Half open, from beneath them the clear blue
Laughs out, although in slumber. He must dream—
Of what ? Of Paradise !—Ay ! dream of it,   31
My disinherited boy ! 'Tis but a dream ;
For never more thyself, thy sons, nor fathers,
Shall walk in that forbidden place of joy !

   Adah.   Dear Cain ! Nay, do not whisper o'er our son
Such melancholy yearnings o'er the past :
Why wilt thou always mourn for Paradise ?
Can we not make another ?

   Cain.   Where ?

   Adah.   Here, or
Where'er thou wilt : where'er thou art, I feel not
The want of this so much regretted Eden.   40
Have I not thee, our boy, our sire, and brother,
And Zillah—our sweet sister, and our Eve,
To whom we owe so much besides our birth ?

   Cain. Yes—death, too, is amongst the debts we
      owe her.

   Adah. Cain ! that proud spirit, who withdrew thee
      hence,

Hath sadden'd thine still deeper. I had hoped
The promised wonders which thou hast beheld,
Visions, thou say'st, of past and present worlds,
Would have composed thy mind into the calm
Of a contented knowledge; but I see   50
Thy guide hath done thee evil: still I thank him,
And can forgive him all, that he so soon
Hath given thee back to us.

   Cain.   So soon?

   Adah.   'Tis scarcely
Two hours since ye departed: two *long* hours
To *me*, but only *hours* upon the sun.

   Cain. And yet I have approach'd that sun, and seen
Worlds which he once shone on, and never more
Shall light; and worlds he never lit: methought
Years had roll'd o'er my absence.

   Adah.   Hardly hours.

   Cain. The mind then hath capacity of time,   60
And measures it by that which it beholds,
Pleasing or painful; little or almighty.
I had beheld the immemorial works
Of endless beings; skirr'd extinguish'd worlds;
And, gazing on eternity, methought
I had borrow'd more by a few drops of ages
From its immensity: but now I feel
My littleness again. Well said the spirit,
That I was nothing!

   Adah.   Wherefore said he so?
Jehovah said not that.

   Cain.   No: *he* contents him   70
With making us the *nothing* which we are;
And after flattering dust with glimpses of
Eden and Immortality, resolves
It back to dust again—for what?

   Adah.   Thou know'st—
Even for our parents' error.

   Cain.   What is that
To us? they sinn'd, then *let them* die!

   Adah. Thou hast not spoken well, nor is that
     thought

Thy own, but of the spirit who was with thee.
Would *I* could die for them, so *they* might live!
   Cain. Why, so say I—provided that one victim
Might satiate the insatiable of life,   81
And that our little rosy sleeper there
Might never taste of death nor human sorrow,
Nor hand it down to those who spring from him.
   Adah. How know we that some such atonement
          one day
May not redeem our race?
   Cain.   By sacrificing
The harmless for the guilty? what atonement
Were there? why, *we* are innocent: what have we
Done, that we must be victims for a deed
Before our birth, or need have victims to   90
Atone for this mysterious, nameless sin—
If it be such a sin to seek for knowledge?
   Adah. Alas! thou sinnest now, my Cain: thy words
Sound impious in mine ears.
   Cain.   Then leave me!
   Adah.   Never,
Though thy God left thee.
   Cain.   Say, what have we here?
   Adah. Two altars, which our brother Abel made
During thine absence, whereupon to offer
A sacrifice to God on thy return.
   Cain. And how knew *he*, that *I* would be so ready
With the burnt offerings, which he daily brings   100
With a meek brow, whose base humility
Shows more of fear than worship, as a bribe
To the Creator?
   Adah.   Surely, 'tis well done.
   Cain. One altar may suffice; *I* have no offering.
   Adah. The fruits of the earth, the early, beautiful
Blossom and bud, and bloom of flowers and fruits;
These are a goodly offering to the Lord,
Given with a gentle and a contrite spirit.
   Cain. I have toil'd, and till'd, and sweaten in the
         sun,
According to the curse:—must I do more?   110

For what should I be gentle ? for a war
With all the elements ere they will yield
The bread we eat ? For what must I be grateful ?
For being dust, and grovelling in the dust,
Till I return to dust ? If I am nothing—
For nothing shall I be an hypocrite,
And seem well-pleased with pain ? For what should I
Be contrite ? for my father's sin, already
Expiate with what we all have undergone,
And to be more than expiated by   120
The ages prophesied, upon our seed.
Little deems our young blooming sleeper, there,
The germs of an eternal misery
To myriads is within him ! better 'twere
I snatch'd him in his sleep, and dash'd him 'gainst
The rocks, than let him live to——
   Adah.   Oh, my God !
Touch not the child—my child ! *thy* child ! Oh, Cain !
   Cain. Fear not ! for all the stars, and all the power
Which sways them, I would not accost yon infant
With ruder greeting than a father's kiss.   130
   Adah. Then, why so awful in thy speech ?
   Cain.   I said,
'Twere better that he ceased to live, than give
Life to so much of sorrow as he must
Endure, and, harder still, bequeath ; but since
That saying jars you, let us only say—
'Twere better that he never had been born.
   Adah. Oh, do not say so ! Where were then the
      joys,
The mother's joys of watching, nourishing,
And loving him ? Soft ! he awakes. Sweet Enoch !
                        [*She goes to the child.*
Oh, Cain ! look on him ; see how full of life,   140
Of strength, of bloom, of beauty, and of joy,
How like to me—how like to thee, when gentle,
For *then* we are *all* alike ; is't not so, Cain ?
Mother, and sire, and son, our features are
Reflected in each other ; as they are
In the clear waters, when *they* are *gentle*, and

When *thou* art *gentle.*   Love us, then, my Cain!
And love thyself for our sakes, for we love thee.
Look! how he laughs and stretches out his arms,
And opens wide his blue eyes upon thine,   150
To hail his father; while his little form
Flutters as wing'd with joy.   Talk not of pain!
The childless cherubs well might envy thee
The pleasures of a parent!   Bless him, Cain!
As yet he hath no words to thank thee, but
His heart will, and thine own too.
      Cain.   Bless thee, boy!
If that a mortal blessing may avail thee,
To save thee from the serpent's curse!
      Adah.   It shall.
Surely a father's blessing may avert
A reptile's subtlety.
      Cain.   Of that I doubt;   160
But bless him ne'er the less.
      Adah.   Our brother comes.
      Cain.   Thy brother Abel.

                    Enter ABEL.

      Abel.   Welcome, Cain!   My brother,
The peace of God be on thee!
      Cain.   Abel, hail!
      Abel.   Our sister tells me that thou hast been
            wandering,
In high communion with a spirit, far
Beyond our wonted range.   Was he of those
We have seen and spoken with, like to our father?
      Cain.   No.
      Abel.   Why then commune with him?   he may be
A foe to the Most High.
      Cain.   And friend to man.
Has the Most High been so—if so you term him?   170
      Abel.   *Term him!*   your words are strange to-day,
            my brother.
My sister Adah, leave us for awhile—
We mean to sacrifice.
      Adah.   Farewell, my Cain;

But first embrace thy son. May his soft spirit,
And Abel's pious ministry, recall thee
To peace and holiness !

                   [*Exit* ADAH, *with her child.*

   Abel.   Where hast thou been ?
   Cain.   I know not.
   Abel.   Nor what thou hast seen ?
   Cain.   The dead,
The immortal, the unbounded, the omnipotent,
The overpowering mysteries of space—
The innumerable worlds that were and are—   180
A whirlwind of such overwhelming things,
Suns, moons, and earths, upon their loud-voiced spheres
Singing in thunder round me, as have made me
Unfit for mortal converse : leave me, Abel.
   Abel.   Thine eyes are flashing with unnatural light—
Thy cheek is flush'd with an unnatural hue—
Thy words are fraught with an unnatural sound—
What may this mean ?
   Cain.   It means——I pray thee, leave me.
   Abel.   Not till we have pray'd and sacrificed to-
         gether.
   Cain.   Abel, I pray thee, sacrifice alone—   190
Jehovah loves thee well.
   Abel.   *Both* well, I hope.
   Cain.   But thee the better : I care not for that ;
Thou art fitter for his worship than I am ;
Revere him, then—but let it be alone—
At least, without me.
   Abel.   Brother, I should ill
Deserve the name of our great father's son,
If, as my elder, I revered thee not,
And in the worship of our God, call'd not
On thee to join me, and precede me in
Our priesthood—'tis thy place.
   Cain.   But I have ne'er   200
Asserted it.
   Abel.   The more my grief ; I pray thee
To do so now : thy soul seems labouring in
Some strong delusion ; it will calm thee.

Cain.   No;
Nothing can calm me more.   *Calm!* say I?   Never
Knew I what calm was in the soul, although
I have seen the elements still'd.   My Abel, leave me!
Or let me leave thee to thy pious purpose.

Abel.   Neither; we must perform our task together.
Spurn me not.

Cain.   If it must be so——well, then,
What shall I do?

Abel.   Choose one of those two altars.   210

Cain.   Choose for me: they to me are so much turf
And stone.

Abel.   Choose thou!

Cain.   I have chosen.

Abel.   'Tis the highest,
And suits thee, as the elder.   Now prepare
Thine offerings.

Cain.   Where are thine?

Abel.   Behold them here—
The firstlings of the flock, and fat thereof—
A shepherd's humble offering.

Cain.   I have no flocks;
I am a tiller of the ground, and must
Yield what it yieldeth to my toil—its fruit:

                                [He gathers fruits.
Behold them in their various bloom and ripeness.

                *[They dress their altars, and kindle a flame
                                        upon them.*

Abel.   My brother, as the elder, offer first   220
Thy prayer and thanksgiving with sacrifice.

Cain.   No—I am new to this; lead thou the way,
And I will follow—as I may.

Abel (*kneeling*).   Oh, God!
Who made us, and who breathed the breath of life
Within our nostrils, who hath blessed us,
And spared, despite our father's sin, to make
His children all lost, as they might have been,
Had not thy justice been so temper'd with
The mercy which is thy delight, as to
Accord a pardon like a Paradise,   230

Compared with our great crimes :—Sole Lord of light,
Of good, and glory, and eternity !
Without whom all were evil, and with whom
Nothing can err, except to some good end
Of thine omnipotent benevolence—
Inscrutable, but still to be fulfill'd—
Accept from out thy humble first of shepherds'
First of the first-born flocks—an offering,
In itself nothing—as what offering can be
Aught unto thee ?—but yet accept it for   240
The thanksgiving of him who spreads it in
The face of thy high heaven, bowing his own
Even to the dust, of which he is, in honour
Of thee, and of thy name, for evermore !

   Cain (standing erect during this speech).
Spirit ! whate'er or whosoe'er thou art,
Omnipotent, it may be—and, if good,
Shown in the exemption of thy deeds from evil ;
Jehovah upon earth ! and God in heaven !
And it may be with other names, because
Thine attributes seem many, as thy works :—   250
If thou must be propitiated with prayers,
Take them ! If thou must be induced with altars,
And soften'd with a sacrifice, receive them !
Two beings here erect them unto thee.
If thou lov'st blood, the shepherd's shrine, which smokes
On my right hand, hath shed it for thy service
In the first of his flock, whose limbs now reek
In sanguinary incense to thy skies ;
Or if the sweet and blooming fruits of earth,
And milder seasons, which the unstain'd turf   260
I spread them on now offers in the face
Of the broad sun which ripen'd them, may seem
Good to thee, inasmuch as they have not
Suffer'd in limb or life, and rather form
A sample of thy works, than supplication
To look on ours ! If a shrine without victim,
And altar without gore, may win thy favour,
Look on it ! and for him who dresseth it,

He is—such as thou mad'st him; and seeks nothing
Which must be won by kneeling: if he 's evil,   270
Strike him! thou art omnipotent, and may'st—
For what can he oppose? If he be good,
Strike him, or spare him, as thou wilt! since all
Rests upon thee; and good and evil seem
To have no power themselves, save in thy will;
And whether that be good or ill I know not,
Not being omnipotent, nor fit to judge
Omnipotence, but merely to endure
Its mandate; which thus far I have endured.

[*The fire upon the altar of* ABEL *kindles into a column
of the brightest flame, and ascends to heaven; while
a whirlwind throws down the altar of* CAIN, *and
scatters the fruits abroad upon the earth.*

Abel (*kneeling*). Oh, brother, pray! Jehovah 's
wroth with thee.   280
Cain. Why so?
Abel.   Thy fruits are scatter'd on the earth.
Cain. From earth they came, to earth let them
return;
Their seed will bear fresh fruit there ere the summer:
Thy burnt flesh-off'ring prospers better; see
How heaven licks up the flames, when thick with blood!
Abel. Think not upon my offering's acceptance,
But make another of thine own before
It is too late.
Cain.   I will build no more altars,
Nor suffer any——
Abel (*rising*). Cain! what meanest thou?
Cain. To cast down yon vile flatt'rer of the clouds,
The smoky harbinger of thy dull prayers—   291
Thine altar, with its blood of lambs and kids,
Which fed on milk, to be destroy'd in blood.
Abel (*opposing him*). Thou shalt not:—add not
impious works to impious
Words! let that altar stand—'tis hallow'd now
By the immortal pleasure of Jehovah,
In his acceptance of the victims.
Cain.   His!

His pleasure! what was his high pleasure in
The fumes of scorching flesh and smoking blood,
To the pain of the bleating mothers, which   300
Still yearn for their dead offspring ? or the pang
Of the sad ignorant victims underneath
Thy pious knife ? Give way ! this bloody record
Shall not stand in the sun, to shame creation !

    Abel. Brother, give back ! thou shalt not touch my
        altar
With violence : if that thou wilt adopt it,
To try another sacrifice, 'tis thine.

    Cain. Another sacrifice ! Give way, or else
That sacrifice may be——

    Abel.   What mean'st thou ?

    Cain.   Give—
Give way !—thy God loves blood !—then look to it :—
Give way, ere he hath *more !*

    Abel.   In *his* great name,   311
I stand between thee and the shrine which hath
Had his acceptance.

    Cain.   If thou lov'st thyself,
Stand back till I have strew'd this turf along
Its native soil :—else——

    Abel (opposing him).   I love God far more
Than life.

    Cain (striking him with a brand, on the temples, which
                  he snatches from the altar).
           Then take thy life unto thy God,
Since he loves lives.

    Abel (falls). What hast thou done, my brother ?

    Cain. Brother !

    Abel.   Oh, God ! receive thy servant, and
Forgive his slayer, for he knew not what   319
He did—Cain, give me—give me thy hand ; and tell
Poor Zillah—

    Cain (after a moment's stupefaction). My hand ! 'tis
        all red, and with——
What ?
                [*A long pause.—Looking slowly round.*
        Where am I ? alone ! Where 's Abel ? where

Cain ? Can it be that I am he ? My brother,
Awake !—why liest thou so on the green earth ?
'Tis not the hour of slumber ;—why so pale ?
What hast thou !—thou wert full of life this morn !
Abel ! I pray thee, mock me not ! I smote
Too fiercely, but not fatally. Ah, why
Wouldst thou oppose me ? This is mockery ;
And only done to daunt me :—'twas a blow—   330
And but a blow. Stir—stir—nay, only stir !
Why, so—that's well !—thou breath'st ! breathe upon
     me !
Oh, God ! Oh, God !

     Abel (*very faintly*). What 's he who speaks of
     God ?
     Cain. Thy murderer.
     Abel.   Then may God forgive him ! Cain,
Comfort poor Zillah :—she has but one brother
Now.   [ABEL *dies.*
     Cain. And I none !—Who makes me brotherless ?
His eyes are open ! then he is not dead !
Death is like sleep ; and sleep shuts down our lids.
His lips, too, are apart ; why then he breathes ;
And yet I feel it not.—His heart !—his heart !   340
Let me see, doth it beat ? methinks——No !—no !
This is a vision, else I am become
The native of another and worse world.
The earth swims round me :—what is this ?—'tis
     wet ;
     [*Puts his hand to his brow, and then looks at it.*
And yet there are no dews ! 'Tis blood—my blood—
My brother's and my own ! and shed by me !
Then what have I further to do with life,
Since I have taken life from my own flesh ?
But he cannot be dead !—Is silence death ?   349
No ; he will wake ; then let me watch by him.
Life cannot be so slight, as to be quench'd
Thus quickly !—he hath spoken to me since—
What shall I say to him ?—My brother !—No :
He will not answer to that name ; for brethren
     te not each other. Yet—yet—speak to me.

Oh ! for a word more of that gentle voice,
That I may bear to hear my own again !

Enter ZILLAH.

   Zillah. I heard a heavy sound ; what can it be ?
'Tis Cain ; and watching by my husband. What   359
Dost thou there, brother ? Doth he sleep ? Oh, heaven !
What means this paleness, and yon stream ?—No, no !
It is not blood ; for who would shed his blood ?
Abel ! what 's this ?—who hath done this ? He moves
   not ;
He breathes not : and his hands drop down from mine
With stony lifelessness ! Ah ! cruel Cain !
Why cam'st thou not in time to save him from
This violence ? Whatever hath assail'd him,
Thou wert the stronger, and shouldst have stepp'd in
Between him and aggression ! Father !—Eve !—
Adah !—come hither ! Death is in the world !   370
        [*Exit* ZILLAH, *calling on her Parents, &c.*
   Cain (solus). And who hath brought him there ?—
      I—who abhor
The name of Death so deeply, that the thought
Empoison'd all my life, before I knew
His aspect—I have led him here, and given
My brother to his cold and still embrace,
As if he would not have asserted his
Inexorable claim without my aid.
I am awake at last—a dreary dream
Had madden'd me ;—but *he* shall ne'er awake !

FROM 'THE DEFORMED TRANSFORMED'

The Transformation into the Shape of Achilles

Beautiful shadow
  Of Thetis's boy!
Who sleeps in the meadow
  Whose grass grows o'er Troy:
From the red earth, like Adam,
  Thy likeness I shape,
As the being who made him,
  Whose actions I ape.
Thou clay, be all glowing,
  Till the rose in his cheek   10
Be as fair as, when blowing
  It wears its first streak!
Ye violets, I scatter,
  Now turn into eyes!
And thou, sunshiny water,
  Of blood take the guise!
Let these hyacinth boughs
  Be his long flowing hair,
And wave o'er his brows
  As thou wavest in air!   20
Let his heart be this marble
  I tear from the rock!
But his voice as the warble
  Of birds on yon oak!
Let his flesh be the purest
  Of mould, in which grew
The lily-root surest,
  And drank the best dew!
Let his limbs be the lightest
  Which clay can compound,   30
And his aspect the brightest
  On earth to be found!

Elements, near me,
  Be mingled and stirr'd,
Know me, and hear me,
  And leap to my word!
Sunbeams, awaken
  This earth's animation!
'Tis done! He hath taken
  His stand in creation!   **40**

Song of the Soldiers

The black bands came over
  The Alps and their snow;
With Bourbon, the rover,
  They pass'd the broad Po.
We have beaten all foemen,
  We have captured a king,
We have turn'd back on no men,
  And so let us sing!
Here's the Bourbon for ever!
  Though penniless all,   **10**
We'll have one more endeavour
  At yonder old wall.
With the Bourbon we'll gather
  At day-dawn before
The gates, and together
  Or break or climb o'er
The wall: on the ladder
  As mounts each firm foot,
Our shout shall grow gladder,
  And death only be mute.   **20**
With the Bourbon we'll mount o'er
  The walls of old Rome,
And who then shall count o'er
  The spoils of each dome?
Up! up with the lily!
  And down with the keys!
In old Rome, the seven-hilly,
  We'll revel at ease.

Her streets shall be gory,
  Her Tiber all red,   30
And her temples so hoary
  Shall clang with our tread.
Oh, the Bourbon! the Bourbon!
  The Bourbon for aye!
Of our song bear the burden!
  And fire, fire away!
With Spain for the vanguard,
  Our varied host comes;
And next to the Spaniard
  Beat Germany's drums;   40
And Italy's lances
  Are couch'd at their mother;
But our leader from France is,
  Who warr'd with his brother.
Oh, the Bourbon! the Bourbon!
  Sans country or home,
We'll follow the Bourbon,
  To plunder old Rome.

CHORUS OF SPIRITS IN THE AIR

I

'Tis the morn, but dim and dark.
Whither flies the silent lark?
Whither shrinks the clouded sun?
Is the day indeed begun?
Nature's eye is melancholy
O'er the city high and holy:
But without there is a din
Should arouse the saints within,
And revive the heroic ashes
Round which yellow Tiber dashes.   10
Oh, ye seven hills! awaken,
Ere your very base be shaken!

II

Hearken to the steady stamp!
Mars is in their every tramp!
Not a step is out of tune,
As the tides obey the moon!
On they march, though to self-slaughter,
Regular as rolling water,
Whose high waves o'ersweep the border
Of huge moles, but keep their order,   20
Breaking only rank by rank.
Hearken to the armour's clank!
Look down o'er each frowning warrior,
How he glares upon the barrier:
Look on each step of each ladder,
As the stripes that streak an adder.

III

Look upon the bristling wall,
Mann'd without an interval!
Round and round, and tier on tier,
Cannon's black mouth, shining spear,   30
Lit match, bell-mouth'd musquetoon,
Gaping to be murderous soon;
All the warlike gear of old,
Mix'd with what we now behold,
In this strife 'twixt old and new,
Gather like a locusts' crew.
Shade of Remus! 'tis a time
Awful as thy brother's crime!
Christians war against Christ's shrine:—
Must its lot be like to thine?   40

IV

Near—and near—and nearer still,
As the earthquake saps the hill,
First with trembling, hollow motion,
Like a scarce awaken'd ocean,

Then with stronger shock and louder,
Till the rocks are crush'd to powder,—
Onward sweeps the rolling host!
Heroes of the immortal boast!
Mighty chiefs! eternal shadows!
First flowers of the bloody meadows   50
Which encompass Rome, the mother
Of a people without brother!
Will you sleep when nations' quarrels
Plough the root up of your laurels?
Ye who weep o'er Carthage burning,
Weep not—*strike!* for Rome is mourning!

V

Onward sweep the varied nations!
Famine long hath dealt their rations.
To the wall, with hate and hunger,
Numerous as wolves, and stronger,   60
On they sweep. Oh, glorious city!
Must thou be a theme for pity?
Fight, like your first sire, each Roman!
Alaric was a gentle foeman,
Match'd with Bourbon's black banditti!
Rouse thee, thou eternal city;
Rouse thee! Rather give the torch
With thine own hand to thy porch,
Than behold such hosts pollute
Your worst dwelling with their foot.   70

VI

Ah! behold yon bleeding spectre!
Ilion's children find no Hector;
Priam's offspring loved their brother;
Rome's great sire forgot his mother,
When he slew his gallant twin,
With inexpiable sin.
See the giant shadow stride
O'er the ramparts high and wide!

When the first o'erleapt thy wall,
Its foundation mourn'd thy fall.   80
Now, though towering like a Babel,
Who to stop his steps are able ?
Stalking o'er thy highest dome,
Remus claims his vengeance, Rome !

VII

Now they reach thee in their anger:
Fire and smoke and hellish clangour
Are around thee, thou world's wonder !
Death is in thy walls and under.
Now the meeting steel first clashes,
Downward then the ladder crashes,   90
With its iron load all gleaming,
Lying at its foot blaspheming !
Up again ! for every warrior
Slain, another climbs the barrier.
Thicker grows the strife : thy ditches
Europe's mingling gore enriches.
Rome ! although thy wall may perish,
Such manure thy fields will cherish,
Making gay the harvest-home ;
But thy hearths, alas ! oh, Rome !—   100
Yet be Rome amidst thine anguish,
Fight as thou wast wont to vanquish !

VIII

Yet once more, ye old Penates !
Let not your quench'd hearths be Até's !
Yet again, ye shadowy heroes,
Yield not to these stranger Neros !
Though the son who slew his mother
Shed Rome's blood, he was your brother;
'Twas the Roman curb'd the Roman ;—
Brennus was a baffled foeman.   110
Yet again, ye saints and martyrs,
Rise ! for yours are holier charters !
Mighty gods of temples falling,
Yet in ruin still appalling !

Mightier founders of those altars,
True and Christian,—strike the assaulters !
Tiber ! Tiber ! let thy torrent
Show even nature's self abhorrent.
Let each breathing heart dilated
Turn, as doth the lion baited !   120
Rome be crush'd to one wide tomb,
But be still the Roman's Rome !

Chorus of Peasants.

I

The wars are over,
    The spring is come ;
The bride and her lover
    Have sought their home :
They are happy, we rejoice ;
Let their hearts have an echo in every voice !

II

The spring is come ; the violet's gone,
The first-born child of the early sun :
With us she is but a winter's flower,
The snow on the hills cannot blast her bower,
And she lifts up her dewy eye of blue   11
To the youngest sky of the self-same hue.

III

And when the spring comes with her host
Of flowers, that flower beloved the most
Shrinks from the crowd that may confuse
Her heavenly odour and virgin hues.

IV

Pluck the others, but still remember
Their herald out of dim December—
The morning star of all the flowers,
The pledge of daylight's lengthen'd hours ;   20
Nor, midst the roses, e'er forget
The virgin, virgin violet.

Enter CÆSAR.

Cæs. (*singing*).   The wars are all over,
        Our swords are all idle,
        The steed bites the bridle.
The casque's on the wall.
There's rest for the rover ;
        But his armour is rusty,
        And the veteran grows crusty,
As he yawns in the hall.   30
        He drinks—but what's drinking ?
        A mere pause from thinking !
No bugle awakes him with life-and-death call

Chorus.

But the hound bayeth loudly,
    The boar's in the wood,
And the falcon longs proudly
    To spring from her hood :
On the wrist of the noble
    She sits like a crest,
And the air is in trouble   40
    With birds from their nest.

Cæs.   Oh ! shadow of glory !
        Dim image of war !
But the chase hath no story,
    Her hero no star,
Since Nimrod, the founder
    Of empire and chase,
Who made the woods wonder
    And quake for their race.

When the lion was young,   50
  In the pride of his might,
Then 'twas sport for the strong
  To embrace him in fight;
To go forth, with a pine
  For a spear, 'gainst the mammoth,
Or strike through the ravine
  At the foaming behemoth;
While man was in stature
  As towers in our time,
The first-born of Nature,   60
  And, like her, sublime!

Chorus.

But the wars are over,
  The spring is come;
The bride and her lover
  Have sought their home;
They are happy, and we rejoice;
Let their hearts have an echo from every voice!

       [Exeunt the Peasantry, singing.

ITALY AND ENGLAND

(From *Beppo*, xli–xlix)

WITH all its sinful doings, I must say,
  That Italy's a pleasant place to me,
Who love to see the Sun shine every day,
  And vines (not nail'd to walls) from tree to tree
Festoon'd, much like the back scene of a play,
  Or melodrame, which people flock to see,
When the first act is ended by a dance
In vineyards copied from the south of France.

I like on Autumn evenings to ride out,
  Without being forced to bid my groom be sure 10
My cloak is round his middle strapp'd about,
  Because the skies are not the most secure;

I know too that, if stopp'd upon my route,
 Where the green alleys windingly allure,
Reeling with grapes red waggons choke the way,—
In England 'twould be dung, dust, or a dray.

I also like to dine on becaficas,
 To see the Sun set, sure he'll rise to-morrow,
Not through a misty morning twinkling weak as
 A drunken man's dead eye in maudlin sorrow,   20
But with all Heaven t'himself; the day will break as
 Beauteous as cloudless, nor be forced to borrow
That sort of farthing candlelight which glimmers
Where reeking London's smoky caldron simmers.

I love the language, that soft bastard Latin,
 Which melts like kisses from a female mouth,
And sounds as if it should be writ on satin,
 With syllables which breathe of the sweet South,
And gentle liquids gliding all so pat in,
 That not a single accent seems uncouth,   30
Like our harsh northern whistling, grunting guttural,
Which we're obliged to hiss, and spit, and sputter all.

I like the women too (forgive my folly),
 From the rich peasant cheek of ruddy bronze,
And large black eyes that flash on you a volley
 Of rays that say a thousand things at once,
To the high dama's brow, more melancholy,
 But clear, and with a wild and liquid glance,
Heart on her lips, and soul within her eyes,
Soft as her clime, and sunny as her skies.   40

Eve of the land which still is Paradise!
 Italian beauty! didst thou not inspire
Raphael, who died in thy embrace, and vies
 With all we know of Heaven, or can desire,
In what he hath bequeath'd us?—in what guise,
 Though flashing from the fervour of the lyre,
Would *words* describe thy past and present glow,
While yet Canova can create below?

'England! with all thy faults I love thee still,'
 I said at Calais, and have not forgot it; 50
I like to speak and lucubrate my fill;
 I like the government (but that is not it);
I like the freedom of the press and quill;
 I like the Habeas Corpus (when we've got it);
I like a parliamentary debate,
Particularly when 'tis not too late;

I like the taxes, when they're not too many;
 I like a seacoal fire, when not too dear;
I like a beef-steak, too, as well as any;
 Have no objection to a pot of beer; 60
I like the weather, when it is not rainy,
 That is, I like two months of every year.
And so God save the Regent, Church, and King!
Which means that I like all and everything.

Our standing army, and disbanded seamen,
 Poor's rate, Reform, my own, the nation's debt,
Our little riots just to show we are free men,
 Our trifling bankruptcies in the Gazette,
Our cloudy climate, and our chilly women,
 All these I can forgive, and those forget, 70
And greatly venerate our recent glories,
And wish they were not owing to the Tories.

FROM 'DON JUAN'

WANTED—A HERO

(Canto I, i–v)

I want a hero: an uncommon want,
    When every year and month sends forth a new one,
Till, after cloying the gazettes with cant,
    The age discovers he is not the true one:
Of such as these I should not care to vaunt,
    I'll therefore take our ancient friend Don Juan—
We all have seen him, in the pantomime,
Sent to the devil somewhat ere his time.

Vernon, the butcher Cumberland, Wolfe, Hawke,
    Prince Ferdinand, Granby, Burgoyne, Keppel, Howe,
Evil and good, have had their tithe of talk,   11
    And fill'd their sign-posts then, like Wellesley now;
Each in their turn like Banquo's monarchs stalk,
    Followers of fame, 'nine farrow' of that sow:
France, too, had Buonaparté and Dumourier
Recorded in the Moniteur and Courier.

Barnave, Brissot, Condorcet, Mirabeau,
    Pétion, Clootz, Danton, Marat, La Fayette,
Were French, and famous people, as we know;
    And there were others, scarce forgotten yet,   20
Joubert, Hoche, Marceau, Lannes, Desaix, Moreau,
    With many of the military set,
Exceedingly remarkable at times,
But not at all adapted to my rhymes.

Nelson was once Britannia's god of war,
    And still should be so, but the tide is turn'd;
There's no more to be said of Trafalgar,
    'Tis with our hero quietly inurn'd;
Because the army's grown more popular,
    At which the naval people are concern'd,   30
Besides, the prince is all for the land-service,
Forgetting Duncan, Nelson, Howe, and Jervis.

Brave men were living before Agamemnon
　　And since, exceeding valorous and sage,
A good deal like him too, though quite the same none;
　　But then they shone not on the poet's page,
And so have been forgotten:—I condemn none.
　　But can't find any in the present age
Fit for my poem (that is, for my new one);
So, as I said, I'll take my friend Don Juan.　　40

THE SWEETS OF LIFE

(Canto I, cxxii–cxxvii)

　　　　　　　　　　'Tis sweet to hear
　　At midnight on the blue and moonlit deep
The song and oar of Adria's gondolier,
　　By distance mellow'd, o'er the waters sweep;
'Tis sweet to see the evening star appear;
　　'Tis sweet to listen as the night-winds creep
From leaf to leaf; 'tis sweet to view on high
The rainbow, based on ocean, span the sky.

'Tis sweet to hear the watch-dog's honest bark
　　Bay deep-mouth'd welcome as we draw near home;
'Tis sweet to know there is an eye will mark　　11
　　Our coming, and look brighter when we come;
'Tis sweet to be awaken'd by the lark,
　　Or lull'd by falling waters; sweet the hum
Of bees, the voice of girls, the song of birds,
The lisp of children, and their earliest words.

Sweet is the vintage, when the showering grapes
　　In Bacchanal profusion reel to earth,
Purple and gushing; sweet are our escapes
　　From civic revelry to rural mirth;
Sweet to the miser are his glittering heaps,　　20
　　Sweet to the father is his first-born's birth,
Sweet is revenge—especially to women,
Pillage to soldiers, prize-money to seamen.

Sweet is a legacy, and passing sweet
  The unexpected death of some old lady
Or gentleman of seventy years complete,
  Who've made ' us youth ' wait too—too long already
For an estate, or cash, or country seat,
  Still breaking, but with stamina so steady   30
That all the Israelites are fit to mob its
Next owner for their double-damn'd post-obits.

'Tis sweet to win, no matter how, one's laurels,
  By blood or ink ; 'tis sweet to put an end
To strife ; 'tis sometimes sweet to have our quarrels,
  Particularly with a tiresome friend :
Sweet is old wine in bottles, ale in barrels ;
  Dear is the helpless creature we defend
Against the world ; and dear the schoolboy spot
We ne'er forget, though there we are forgot.   40

But sweeter still than this, than these, than all,
  Is first and passionate love—it stands alone,
Like Adam's recollection of his fall ;
  The tree of knowledge has been pluck'd—all's known—
And life yields nothing further to recall
  Worthy of this ambrosial sin, so shown,
No doubt in fable, as the unforgiven
Fire which Prometheus filch'd for us from heaven.

JULIA'S LETTER

(CANTO I. cxcii—cxcviii).

" THEY tell me 'tis decided you depart :
  'Tis wise—'tis well, but not the less a pain ;
I have no further claim on your young heart,
  Mine is the victim, and would be again :
To love too much has been the only art
  I used ;—I write in haste, and if a stain
Be on this sheet, 'tis not what it appears ;
My eyeballs burn and throb, but have no tears.

" I loved, I love you, for this love have lost
　　State, station, heaven, mankind's, my own esteem,
And yet cannot regret what it hath cost,　　　　　11
　　So dear is still the memory of that dream ;
Yet, if I name my guilt, 'tis not to boast,
　　None can deem harshlier of me than I deem :
I trace this scrawl because I cannot rest—
I've nothing to reproach or to request.

" Man's love is of man's life a thing apart,
　　'Tis woman's whole existence ; man may range
The court, camp, church, the vessel, and the mart ;
　　Sword, gown, gain, glory, offer in exchange　　20
Pride, fame, ambition, to fill up his heart,
　　And few there are whom these cannot estrange ;
Men have all these resources, we but one,
To love again, and be again undone.

" You will proceed in pleasure, and in pride,
　　Beloved and loving many ; all is o'er
For me on earth, except some years to hide
　　My shame and sorrow deep in my heart's core :
These I could bear, but cannot cast aside
　　The passion which still rages as before, —　　30
And so farewell—forgive me, love me—No,
That word is idle now—but let it go.

" My breast has been all weakness, is so yet ;
　　But still I think I can collect my mind ;
My blood still rushes where my spirit 's set,
　　As roll the waves before the settled wind ;
My heart is feminine, nor can forget—
　　To all, except one image, madly blind ;
So shakes the needle, and so stands the pole,
As vibrates my fond heart to my fix'd soul.　　40

" I have no more to say, but linger still,
　　And dare not set my seal upon this sheet,
And yet I may as well the task fulfil,
　　My misery can scarce be more complete :

I had not lived till now, could sorrow kill ;
   Death shuns the wretch who fain the blow would
      meet,
And I must even survive this last adieu,
And bear with life to love and pray for you ! "

This note was written upon gilt-edged paper
   With a neat little crow-quill, slight and new ;   50
Her small white hand could hardly reach the taper,
   It trembled as magnetic needles do,
And yet she did not let one tear escape her ;
   The seal a sun-flower ; " *Elle vous suit partout,*"
The motto, cut upon a white cornelian ;
The wax was superfine, its hue vermilion.

POETICAL COMMANDMENTS

(Canto I. cc—ccvi)

My poem 's epic, and is meant to be
   Divided in twelve books ; each book containing,
With love, and war, a heavy gale at sea,
   A list of ships, and captains, and kings reigning,
New characters ; the episodes are three :
   A panoramic view of hell 's in training,
After the style of Virgil and of Homer,
So that my name of Epic 's no misnomer.

All these things will be specified in time,
   With strict regard to Aristotle's rules,   10
The *Vade Mecum* of the true sublime,
   Which makes so many poets, and some fools :
Prose poets like blank-verse, I'm fond of rhyme,
   Good workmen never quarrel with their tools ;
I've got new mythological machinery,
And very handsome supernatural scenery.

There 's only one slight difference between
   Me and my epic brethren gone before,
And here the advantage is my own, I ween
   (Not that I have not several merits more,   20

But this will more peculiarly be seen);
  They so embellish, that 'tis quite a bore
Their labyrinth of fables to thread through,
  Whereas this story 's actually true.

If any person doubt it, I appeal
  To history, tradition, and to facts,
To newspapers, whose truth all know and feel,
  To plays in five, and operas in three acts ;
All these confirm my statement a good deal,
  But that which more completely faith exacts   30
Is, that myself, and several now in Seville,
  Saw Juan's last elopement with the devil.

If ever I should condescend to prose,
  I'll write poetical commandments, which
Shall supersede beyond all doubt all those
  That went before ; in these I shall enrich
My text with many things that no one knows,
  And carry precept to the highest pitch :
I'll call the work " Longinus o'er a Bottle,
Or, Every Poet his *own* Aristotle.'   40

Thou shalt believe in Milton, Dryden, Pope ;
  Thou shalt not set up Wordsworth, Coleridge, Southey;
Because the first is crazed beyond all hope,
  The second drunk, the third so quaint and mouthy :
With Crabbe it may be difficult to cope,
  And Campbell's Hippocrene is somewhat drouthy :
Thou shalt not steal from Samuel Rogers, nor
Commit—flirtation with the muse of Moore.

Thou shalt not covet Mr. Sotheby's Muse,
  His Pegasus, nor anything that 's his ;   50
Thou shalt not bear false witness like " the Blues "—
  (There 's one, at least, is very fond of this) ;
Thou shalt not write, in short, but what I choose ;
  This is true criticism, and you may kiss—
Exactly as you please, or not,—the rod ;
But if you don't, I'll lay it on, by G—d !

THE SHIPWRECK

(Canto II. xxiv—liii)

The ship, call'd the most holy 'Trinidada,'
   Was steering duly for the port Leghorn ;
For there the Spanish family Moncada
   Were settled long ere Juan's sire was born :
They were relations, and for them he had a
   Letter of introduction, which the morn
Of his departure had been sent him by
His Spanish friends for those in Italy.

His suite consisted of three servants and
   A tutor, the licentiate Pedrillo,   10
Who several languages did understand,
   But now lay sick and speechless on his pillow,
And, rocking in his hammock, long'd for land,
   His headache being increased by every billow ;
And the waves oozing through the port-hole made
His berth a little damp, and him afraid.

'Twas not without some reason, for the wind
   Increased at night, until it blew a gale ;
And though 'twas not much to a naval mind,
   Some landsmen would have look'd a little pale,   20
For sailors are, in fact, a different kind :
   At sunset they began to take in sail,
For the sky show'd it would come on to blow,
And carry away, perhaps, a mast or so.

At one o'clock the wind with sudden shift
   Threw the ship right into the trough of the sea,
Which struck her aft, and made an awkward rift,
   Started the stern-post, also shatter'd the
Whole of her stern-frame, and, ere she could lift
   Herself from out her present jeopardy,   30
The rudder tore away : 'twas time to sound
The pumps, and there were four feet water found.

One gang of people instantly was put
  Upon the pumps, and the remainder set
To get up part of the cargo, and what not ;
  But they could not come at the leak as yet ;
At last they did get at it really, but
  Still their salvation was an even bet :
The water rush'd through in a way quite puzzling,
While they thrust sheets, shirts, jackets, bales of muslin,

Into the opening ; but all such ingredients   41
  Would have been vain, and they must have gone
    down,
Despite of all their efforts and expedients,
  But for the pumps : I'm glad to make them known
To all the brother tars who may have need hence,
  For fifty tons of water were upthrown
By them per hour, and they all had been undone,
But for the maker, Mr. Mann, of London.

As day advanced the weather seem'd to abate,
  And then the leak they reckon'd to reduce,   50
And keep the ship afloat, though three feet yet
  Kept two hand and one chain-pump still in use.
The wind blew fresh again : as it grew late
  A squall came on, and while some guns broke loose,
A gust—which all descriptive power transcends—
Laid with one blast the ship on her beam ends.

There she lay, motionless, and seem'd upset ;
  The water left the hold, and wash'd the decks,
And made a scene men do not soon forget ;
  For they remember battles, fires, and wrecks,   60
Or any other thing that brings regret,
  Or breaks their hopes, or hearts, or heads, or necks ;
Thus drownings are much talk'd of by the divers,
And swimmers, who may chance to be survivors.

Immediately the masts were cut away,
  Both main and mizen : first the mizen went,
The main-mast follow'd ; but the ship still lay
  Like a mere log, and baffled our intent.

Foremast and bowsprit were cut down, and they
    Eased her at last (although we never meant   70
To part with all till every hope was blighted),
And then with violence the old ship righted.

It may be easily supposed, while this
    Was going on, some people were unquiet,
That passengers would find it much amiss
    To lose their lives, as well as spoil their diet;
That even the able seaman, deeming his
    Days nearly o'er, might be disposed to riot,
As upon such occasions tars will ask
For grog, and sometimes drink rum from the cask.   80

There 's nought, no doubt, so much the spirit calms
    As rum and true religion: thus it was,
Some plunder'd, some drank spirits, some sung psalms,
    The high wind made the treble, and as bass
The hoarse harsh waves kept time; fright cured the
        qualms
    Of all the luckless landsmen's sea-sick maws:
Strange sounds of wailing, blasphemy, devotion,
Clamour'd in chorus to the roaring ocean.

Perhaps more mischief had been done, but for
    Our Juan, who, with sense beyond his years,   90
Got to the spirit-room, and stood before
    It with a pair of pistols; and their fears,
As if Death were more dreadful by his door
    Of fire than water, spite of oaths and tears,
Kept still aloof the crew, who, ere they sunk,
Thought it would be becoming to die drunk.

'Give us more grog,' they cried, 'for it will be
    All one an hour hence.' Juan answer'd, 'No!
'Tis true that death awaits both you and me,
    But let us die like men, not sink below   100
Like brutes:'—and thus his dangerous post kept he,
    And none liked to anticipate the blow;
And even Pedrillo, his most reverend tutor,
Was for some rum a disappointed suitor.

The **good old** gentleman was quite aghast,
    And made a loud and pious lamentation;
Repented all his sins, and made a last
    Irrevocable vow of reformation;
Nothing should tempt him more (this peril past)
    To quit his academic occupation,   110
In cloisters of the classic Salamanca,
To follow Juan's wake, like Sancho Panca.

But now there came a flash of hope once more;
    Day broke, and the wind lull'd: the masts were gone;
The leak increased; shoals round her, but no shore,
    The vessel swam, yet still she held her own.
They tried the pumps again, and though before
    Their desperate efforts seem'd all useless grown,
A glimpse of sunshine set some hands to bale—
The stronger pump'd, the weaker thrumm'd a sail.

Under the vessel's keel the sail was pass'd,   121
    And for the moment it had some effect;
But with a leak, and not a stick of mast,
    Nor rag of canvas, what could they expect?
But still 'tis best to struggle to the last,
    'Tis never too late to be wholly wreck'd:
And though 'tis true that man can only die once,
'Tis not so pleasant in the Gulf of Lyons.

There winds and waves had hurl'd them, and from
    thence,
    Without their will, they carried them away;   130
For they were forced with steering to dispense,
    And never had as yet a quiet day
On which they might repose, or even commence
    A jurymast or rudder, or could say
The ship would swim an hour, which, by good luck,
Still swam—though not exactly like a duck.

The wind, in fact, perhaps, was rather less,
    But the ship labour'd so, they scarce could hope
To weather out much longer; the distress
    Was also great with which they had to cope   140

For want of water, and their solid mess
    Was scant enough : in vain the telescope
Was used—nor sail nor shore appear'd in sight,
Nought but the heavy sea, and coming night.

Again the weather threaten'd,—again blew
    A gale, and in the fore and after hold
Water appear'd ; yet, though the people knew
    All this, the most were patient, and some bold,
Until the chains and leathers were worn through
    Of all our pumps :—a wreck complete she roll'd,
At mercy of the waves, whose mercies are   151
Like human beings during civil war.

Then came the carpenter, at last, with tears
    In his rough eyes, and told the captain, he
Could do no more : he was a man in years,
    And long had voyaged through many a stormy sea,
And if he wept at length, they were not fears
    That made his eyelids as a woman's be,
But he, poor fellow, had a wife and children,
Two things for dying people quite bewildering.   160

The ship was evidently settling now
    Fast by the head ; and, all distinction gone,
Some went to prayers again, and made a vow
    Of candles to their saints—but there were none
To pay them with ; and some look'd o'er the bow ;
    Some hoisted out the boats ; and there was one
That begg'd Pedrillo for an absolution,
Who told him to be damn'd—in his confusion.

Some lash'd them in their hammocks ; some put on
    Their best clothes, as if going to a fair ;   170
Some cursed the day on which they saw the sun,
    And gnash'd their teeth, and, howling, tore their hair ;
And others went on as they had begun,
    Getting the boats out, being well aware
That a tight boat will live in a rough sea,
Unless with breakers close beneath her lee.

The worst of all was, that in their condition,
　　Having been several days in great distress,
'Twas difficult to get out such provision
　　As now might render their long suffering less : 180
Men, even when dying, dislike inanition ;
　　Their stock was damaged by the weather's stress :
Two casks of biscuit, and a keg of butter,
Were all that could be thrown into the cutter.

But in the long-boat they contrived to stow
　　Some pounds of bread, though injured by the wet ;
Water, a twenty-gallon cask or so ;
　　Six flasks of wine : and they contrived to get
A portion of their beef up from below,
　　And with a piece of pork, moreover, met, 190
But scarce enough to serve them for a luncheon—
Then there was rum, eight gallons in a puncheon.

The other boats, the yawl and pinnace, had
　　Been stove in the beginning of the gale ;
And the long-boat's condition was but bad,
　　As there were but two blankets for a sail,
And one oar for a mast, which a young lad
　　Threw in by good luck over the ship's rail ;
And two boats could not hold, far less be stored,
To save one half the people then on board. 200

'Twas twilight, and the sunless day went down
　　Over the waste of waters ; like a veil,
Which, if withdrawn, would but disclose the frown
　　Of one whose hate is mask'd but to assail.
Thus to their hopeless eyes the night was shown,
　　And grimly darkled o'er the faces pale,
And the dim desolate deep : twelve days had Fear
Been their familiar, and now Death was here.

Some trial had been making at a raft,
　　With little hope in such a rolling sea, 210
A sort of thing at which one would have laugh'd,
　　If any laughter at such times could be,

Unless with people who too much have quaff'd,
    And have a kind of wild and horrid glee,
Half epileptical, and half hysterical:—
Their preservation would have been a miracle.

At half-past eight o'clock, booms, hencoops, spars,
    And all things, for a chance, had been cast loose,
That still could keep afloat the struggling tars,
    For yet they strove, although of no great use: 220
There was no light in heaven but a few stars,
    The boats put off o'ercrowded with their crews;
She gave a heel, and then a lurch to port,
And, going down head foremost—sunk, in short.

Then rose from sea to sky the wild farewell—
    Then shriek'd the timid, and stood still the brave—
Then some leap'd overboard with dreadful yell,
    As eager to anticipate their grave;
And the sea yawn'd around her like a hell,
    And down she suck'd with her the whirling wave,
Like one who grapples with his enemy,   231
And strives to strangle him before he die.

And first one universal shriek there rush'd,
    Louder than the loud ocean, like a crash
Of echoing thunder; and then all was hush'd,
    Save the wild wind and the remorseless dash
Of billows; but at intervals there gush'd,
    Accompanied with a convulsive splash,
A solitary shriek, the bubbling cry
Of some strong swimmer in his agony.   240

HAIDÉE

(Canto II, cxi—cxviii)

How long in his damp trance young Juan lay
  He knew not, for the earth was gone for him,
And Time had nothing more of night nor day
  For his congealing blood, and senses dim ;
And how this heavy faintness pass'd away
  He knew not, till each painful pulse and limb,
And tingling vein, seem'd throbbing back to life,
For Death, though vanquish'd, still retir'd with strife.

His eyes he open'd, shut, again unclosed,
  For all was doubt and dizziness ; he thought   10
He still was in the boat, and had but dozed,
  And felt again with his despair o'erwrought,
And wish'd it death in which he had reposed,
  And then once more his feelings back were brought,
And slowly by his swimming eyes was seen
A lovely female face of seventeen.

'Twas bending close o'er his, and the small mouth
  Seem'd almost prying into his for breath ;
And chafing him, the soft warm hand of youth
  Recall'd his answering spirits back from death ;   20
And, bathing his chill temples, tried to soothe
  Each pulse to animation, till beneath
Its gentle touch and trembling care, a sigh
To these kind efforts made a low reply.

Then was the cordial pour'd, and mantle flung
  Around his scarce-clad limbs ; and the fair arm
Raised higher the faint head which o'er it hung ;
  And her transparent cheek, all pure and warm,
Pillow'd his death-like forehead ; then she wrung
  His dewy curls, long drench'd by every storm ;
And watch'd with eagerness each throb that drew
A sigh from his heaved bosom—and hers, too.   32

And lifting him with care into the cave,
   The gentle girl, and her attendant,—one
Young, yet her elder, and of brow less grave,
   And more robust of figure—then begun
To kindle fire, and as the new flames gave
   Light to the rocks that roof'd them, which the sun
Had never seen, the maid, or whatsoe'er
She was, appear'd distinct, and tall, and fair.   40

Her brow was overhung with coins of gold,
   That sparkled o'er the auburn of her hair,
Her clustering hair, whose longer locks were roll'd
   In braids behind ; and though her stature were
Even of the highest for a female mould,
   They nearly reach'd her heel ; and in her air
There was a something which bespoke command,
As one who was a lady in the land.

Her hair, I said, was auburn ; but her eyes
   Were black as death, their lashes the same hue,   50
Of downcast length, in whose silk shadow lies
   Deepest attraction ; for when to the view
Forth from its raven fringe the full glance flies,
   Ne'er with such force the swiftest arrow flew ;
'Tis as the snake late coil'd, who pours his length,
And hurls at once his venom and his strength.

Her brow was white and low, her cheek's pure dye
   Like twilight rosy still with the set sun ;
Short upper lip—sweet lips ! that make us sigh
   Ever to have seen such ; for she was one   60
Fit for the model of a statuary
   (A race of mere impostors, when all's done—
I've seen much finer women, ripe and real,
Than all the nonsense of their stone ideal).

JUAN AND HAIDÉE

(Canto II, clxxxiii—clxxxix)

It was the cooling hour, just when the rounded
  Red sun sinks down behind the azure hill,
Which then seems as if the whole earth it bounded,
  Circling all nature, hush'd, and dim, and still,
With the far mountain-crescent half surrounded
  On one side, and the deep sea calm and chill,
Upon the other, and the rosy sky,
With one star sparkling through it like an eye.

And thus they wander'd forth, and hand in hand,
  Over the shining pebbles and the shells,   10
Glided along the smooth and harden'd sand,
  And in the worn and wild receptacles
Work'd by the storms, yet work'd as it were plann'd,
  In hollow halls, with sparry roofs and cells,
They turn'd to rest; and, each clasp'd by an arm,
Yielded to the deep twilight's purple charm.

They look'd up to the sky, whose floating glow
  Spread like a rosy ocean, vast and bright;
They gazed upon the glittering sea below,
  Whence the broad moon rose circling into sight;   20
They heard the waves splash, and the wind so low,
  And saw each other's dark eyes darting light
Into each other—and, beholding this,
Their lips drew near, and clung into a kiss;

A long, long kiss, a kiss of youth, and love,
  And beauty, all concentrating like rays
Into one focus, kindled from above;
  Such kisses as belong to early days,
Where heart, and soul, and sense, in concert move,
  And the blood's lava, and the pulse a blaze,   30
Each kiss a heart-quake,—for a kiss's strength,
I think, it must be reckon'd by its length.

By length I mean duration; theirs endured
   Heaven knows how long—no doubt they never
   reckon'd;
And if they had, they could not have secured
   The sum of their sensations to a second:
They had not spoken; but they felt allured,
   As if their souls and lips each other beckon'd,
Which, being join'd, like swarming bees they clung—
Their hearts the flowers from whence the honey sprung.

They were alone, but not alone as they   41
   Who shut in chambers think it loneliness;
The silent ocean, and the starlight bay,
   The twilight glow, which momently grew less,
The voiceless sands, and dropping caves, that lay
   Around them, made them to each other press,
As if there were no life beneath the sky
Save theirs, and that their life could never die.

They fear'd no eyes nor ears on that lone beach,
   They felt no terrors from the night; they were   50
All in all to each other; though their speech
   Was broken words, they *thought* a language there,—
And all the burning tongues the passions teach
   Found in one sigh the best interpreter
Of nature's oracle—first love,—that all
Which Eve has left her daughters since her fall.

ALAS! THE LOVE OF WOMEN!

(CANTO II, cxcix—cciv)

ALAS! the love of women! it is known
   To be a lovely and a fearful thing;
For all of theirs upon that die is thrown,
   And if 'tis lost, life hath no more to bring
To them but mockeries of the past alone,
   And their revenge is as the tiger's spring,
Deadly, and quick, and crushing; yet, as real
Torture is theirs,—what they inflict they feel.

They are right; for man, to man so oft unjust,
  Is always so to women; one sole bond   10
Awaits them, treachery is all their trust;
  Taught to conceal, their bursting hearts despond
Over their idol, till some wealthier lust
  Buys them in marriage—and what rests beyond?
A thankless husband, next a faithless lover,
Then dressing, nursing, praying, and all's over.

Some take a lover, some take drams or prayers,
  Some mind their household, others dissipation,
Some run away, and but exchange their cares,
  Losing the advantage of a virtuous station;   20
Few changes e'er can better their affairs,
  Theirs being an unnatural situation,
From the dull palace to the dirty hovel:
Some play the devil, and then write a novel.

Haidée was Nature's bride, and knew not this:
  Haidée was Passion's child, born where the sun
Showers triple light, and scorches even the kiss
  Of his gazelle-eyed daughters; she was one
Made but to love, to feel that she was his
  Who was her chosen: what was said or done   30
Elsewhere was nothing. She had nought to fear,
Hope, care, nor love beyond,—her heart beat *here*.

And oh! that quickening of the heart, that beat!
  How much it costs us! yet each rising throb
Is in its cause as its effect so sweet,
  That Wisdom, ever on the watch to rob
Joy of its alchemy, and to repeat
  Fine truths; even Conscience, too, has a tough job
To make us understand each good old maxim,
So good—I wonder Castlereagh don't tax 'em.   40

And now 'twas done—on the lone shore were plighted
  Their hearts; the stars, their nuptial torches, shed
Beauty upon the beautiful they lighted:
  Ocean their witness, and the cave their bed,

By their own feelings hallow'd and united,
  Their priest was Solitude, and they were wed:
And they were happy, for to their young eyes
Each was an angel, and earth paradise.

MARRIAGE AND THE MUSE

(Canto III, viii—xi)

There's doubtless something in domestic doings
  Which forms, in fact, true love's antithesis;
Romances paint at full length people's wooings,
  But only give a bust of marriages;
For no one cares for matrimonial cooings,
  There's nothing wrong in a connubial kiss:
Think you, if Laura had been Petrarch's wife,
He would have written sonnets all his life?

All tragedies are finish'd by a death,
  All comedies are ended by a marriage;   10
The future states of both are left to faith,
  For authors fear description might disparage
The worlds to come of both, or fall beneath,
  And then both worlds would punish their miscarriage;
So leaving each their priest and prayer-book ready,
They say no more of Death or of the Lady.

The only two that in my recollection
  Have sung of heaven and hell, or marriage, are
Dante and Milton, and of both the affection
  Was hapless in their nuptials, for some bar   20
Of fault or temper ruin'd the connexion
  (Such things, in fact, it don't ask much to mar);
But Dante's Beatrice and Milton's Eve
Were not drawn from their spouses, you conceive.

Some persons say that Dante meant theology
  By Beatrice, and not a mistress—I,
Although my opinion may require apology,
  Deem this a commentator's phantasy,

Unless indeed it was from his own knowledge he
   Decided thus, and show'd good reason why ;   30
I think that Dante's more abstruse ecstatics
Meant to personify the mathematics.

LAMBRO'S RETURN

(Canto III, xxvii—xli)

He saw his white walls shining in the sun,
   His garden trees all shadowy and green ;
He heard his rivulet's light bubbling run,
   The distant dog-bark ; and perceived between
The umbrage of the wood so cool and dun,
   The moving figures, and the sparkling sheen
Of arms (in the East all arm)—and various dyes
Of colour'd garbs, as bright as butterflies.

And as the spot where they appear he nears,
   Surprised at these unwonted signs of idling,   10
He hears—alas ! no music of the spheres,
   But an unhallow'd, earthly sound of fiddling !
A melody which made him doubt his ears,
   The cause being past his guessing or unriddling ;
A pipe, too, and a drum, and shortly after,
A most unoriental roar of laughter.

And still more nearly to the place advancing,
   Descending rather quickly the declivity,
Through the waved branches, o'er the greensward
     glancing,
   'Midst other indications of festivity,   20
Seeing a troop of his domestics dancing
   Like dervises, who turn as on a pivot, he
Perceived it was the Pyrrhic dance so martial,
To which the Levantines are very partial.

And further on a group of Grecian girls,
   The first and tallest her white kerchief waving,
Were strung together like a row of pearls,
   Link'd hand in hand, and dancing : each too having

Down her white neck long floating auburn curls—
    (The least of which would set ten poets raving);   30
Their leader sang—and bounded to her song,
With choral step and voice, the virgin throng.

And here, assembled cross-legg'd round their trays,
    Small social parties just begun to dine;
Pilaus and meats of all sorts met the gaze,
    And flasks of Samian and of Chian wine,
And sherbet cooling in the porous vase;
    Above them their dessert grew on its vine;—
The orange and pomegranate nodding o'er,
Dropp'd in their laps, scarce pluck'd, their mellow store.

A band of children, round a snow-white ram,   41
    There wreathe his venerable horns with flowers;
While peaceful as if still an unwean'd lamb,
    The patriarch of the flock all gently cowers
His sober head, majestically tame,
    Or eats from out the palm, or playful lowers
His brow, as if in act to butt, and then
Yielding to their small hands, draws back again.

Their classical profiles, and glittering dresses,
    Their large black eyes, and soft seraphic cheeks,   50
Crimson as cleft pomegranates, their long tresses.
    The gesture which enchants, the eye that speaks,
The innocence which happy childhood blesses,
    Made quite a picture of these little Greeks;
So that the philosophical beholder
Sigh'd for their sakes—that they should e'er grow older.

Afar, a dwarf buffoon stood telling tales
    To a sedate grey circle of old smokers,
Of secret treasures found in hidden vales,
    Of wonderful replies from Arab jokers,   60
Of charms to make good gold and cure bad ails,
    Of rocks bewitch'd that open to the knockers,
Of magic ladies who, by one sole act,
Transform'd their lords to beasts (but that's a fact).

Here was no lack of innocent diversion
    For the imagination or the senses,
Song, dance, wine, music, stories from the Persian,
    All pretty pastimes in which no offence is ;
But Lambro saw all these things with aversion,
    Perceiving in his absence such expenses,   70
Dreading that climax of all human ills,
The inflammation of his weekly bills.

Ah ! what is man ? what perils still environ
    The happiest mortals even after dinner !
A day of gold from out an age of iron
    Is all that life allows the luckiest sinner ;
Pleasure (whene'er she sings, at least)'s a siren,
    That lures, to flay alive, the young beginner ;
Lambro's reception at his people's banquet
Was such as fire accords to a wet blanket.   80

He—being a man who seldom used a word
    Too much, and wishing gladly to surprise
(In general he surprised men with the sword)
    His daughter—had not sent before to advise
Of his arrival, so that no one stirr'd ;
    And long he paused to reassure his eyes,
In fact much more astonish'd than delighted,
To find so much good company invited.

He did not know (alas ! how men will lie !)
    That a report (especially the Greeks)   90
Avouch'd his death (such people never die),
    And put his house in mourning several weeks,—
But now their eyes and also lips were dry ;
    The bloom, too, had return'd to Haidée's cheeks.
Her tears, too, being return'd into their fount,
She now kept house upon her own account.

Hence all this rice, meat, dancing, wine, and fiddling,
    Which turn'd the isle into a place of pleasure ;
The servants all were getting drunk or idling,
    A life which made them happy beyond measure. 100

Her father's hospitality seem'd middling,
　　Compared with what Haidée did with his treasure;
'Twas wonderful how things went on improving,
While she had not one hour to spare from loving.

Perhaps you think, in stumbling on this feast,
　　He flew into a passion, and in fact
There was no mighty reason to be pleased;
　　Perhaps you prophesy some sudden act,
The whip, the rack, or dungeon at the least,
　　To teach his people to be more exact,　　　　　110
And that, proceeding at a very high rate,
He show'd the royal *penchants* of a pirate.

You're wrong.—He was the mildest manner'd man
　　That ever scuttled ship or cut a throat,
With such true breeding of a gentleman,
　　You never could divine his real thought,
No courtier could, and scarcely woman can
　　Gird more deceit within a petticoat;
Pity he loved adventurous life's variety,
He was so great a loss to good society.　　　　　120

HAIDÉE AGAIN

(CANTO III, lxx—lxxvii).

OF all the dresses I select Haidée's:
　　She wore two jelicks—one was of pale yellow;
Of azure, pink, and white was her chemise—
　　'Neath which her breast heaved like a little billow:
With buttons form'd of pearls as large as peas,
　　All gold and crimson shone her jelick's fellow,
And the striped white gauze baracan that bound her,
Like fleecy clouds about the moon, flow'd round her.

One large gold bracelet clasp'd each lovely arm,
　　Lockless—so pliable from the pure gold,　　　　　10
That the hand stretch'd and shut it without harm,
　　The limb which it adorn'd its only mould;

So beautiful—its very shape would charm,
　　And clinging as if loath to lose its hold,
The purest ore enclosed the whitest skin
That e'er by precious metal was held in.

Around, as princess of her father's land,
　　A like gold bar above her instep roll'd
Announced her rank ; twelve rings were on her hand ;
　　Her hair was starr'd with gems ; her veil's fine fold
Below her breast was fasten'd with a band　　　　21
　　Of lavish pearls, whose worth could scarce be told ;
Her orange silk full Turkish trousers furl'd
About the prettiest ankle in the world.

Her hair's long auburn waves down to her heel
　　Flow'd like an Alpine torrent which the sun
Dyes with his morning light,—and would conceal
　　Her person if allow'd at large to run,
And still they seem'd resentfully to feel
　　The silken fillet's curb, and sought to shun　　30
Their bonds whene'er some Zephyr caught began
To offer his young pinion as her fan.

Round her she made an atmosphere of life,
　　The very air seem'd lighter from her eyes,
They were so soft and beautiful, and rife
　　With all we can imagine of the skies,
And pure as Psyche ere she grew a wife—
　　Too pure even for the purest human ties ;
Her overpowering presence made you feel
It would not be idolatry to kneel.　　　　　　40

Her eyelashes, though dark as night, were tinged
　　(It is the country's custom), but in vain ;
For those large black eyes were so blackly fringed,
　　The glossy rebels mock'd the jetty stain,
And in their native beauty stood avenged :
　　Her nails were touch'd with henna ; but again
The power of art was turn'd to nothing, for
They could not look more rosy than before.

The henna should be deeply dyed to make
   The skin relieved appear more fairly fair ;   50
She had no need of this, day ne'er will break
   On mountain-tops more heavenly white than her :
The eye might doubt if it were well awake,
   She was so like a vision ; I might err,
But Shakespeare also says, 'tis very silly
' To gild refined gold, or paint the lily.'

Juan had on a shawl of black and gold,
   But a white baracan, and so transparent
The sparkling gems beneath you might behold,
   Like small stars through the milky way apparent ;
His turban, furl'd in many a graceful fold,   61
   An emerald aigrette, with Haidée's hair in 't,
Surmounted, as its clasp, a glowing crescent,
Whose rays shone ever trembling, but incessant.

THE ISLES OF GREECE

1.

The isles of Greece, the isles of Greece !
   Where burning Sappho loved and sung,
Where grew the arts of war and peace,
   Where Delos rose, and Phœbus sprung !
Eternal summer gilds them yet,
But all, except their sun, is set.

2.

The Scian and the Teian muse,
   The hero's harp, the lover's lute,
Have found the fame your shores refuse :
   Their place of birth alone is mute   10
To sounds which echo further west
Than your sires' ' Islands of the Blest.'

3.

The mountains look on Marathon—
   And Marathon looks on the sea ;
And musing there an hour alone,

I dream'd that Greece might still be free;
For standing on the Persians' grave,
I could not deem myself a slave.

4.

A king sate on the rocky brow
　　Which looks o'er sea-born Salamis;　　　20
And ships, by thousands, lay below,
　　And men in nations;—all were his!
He counted them at break of day—
And when the sun set where were they?

5.

And where are they? and where art thou,
　　My country? On thy voiceless shore
The heroic lay is tuneless now—
　　The heroic bosom beats no more!
And must thy lyre, so long divine,
Degenerate into hands like mine?　　　30

6.

'Tis something, in the dearth of fame,
　　Though link'd among a fetter'd race,
To feel at least a patriot's shame,
　　Even as I sing, suffuse my face;
For what is left the poet here?
For Greeks a blush—for Greece a tear.

7.

Must we but weep o'er days more blest?
　　Must we but blush?—Our fathers bled.
Earth! render back from out thy breast
　　A remnant of our Spartan dead!　　　40
Of the three hundred grant but three,
To make a new Thermopylæ!

8.

What, silent still? and silent all?
　　Ah! no;—the voices of the dead
Sound like a distant torrent's fall,
　　And answer, 'Let one living head,
But one arise,—we come, we come!'
'Tis but the living who are dumb.

9.

In vain—in vain : strike other chords ;
   Fill high the cup with Samian wine !   50
Leave battles to the Turkish hordes,
   And shed the blood of Scio's vine !
Hark ! rising to the ignoble call—
How answers each bold Bacchanal !

10.

You have the Pyrrhic dance as yet ;
   Where is the Pyrrhic phalanx gone ?
Of two such lessons, why forget
   The nobler and the manlier one ?
You have the letters Cadmus gave—
Think ye he meant them for a slave ?   60

11.

Fill high the bowl with Samian wine !
   We will not think of themes like these !
It made Anacreon's song divine :
   He served—but served Polycrates—
A tyrant ; but our masters then
Were still, at least, our countrymen.

12.

The tyrant of the Chersonese
   Was freedom's best and bravest friend ;
That tyrant was Miltiades !
   Oh ! that the present hour would lend   70
Another despot of the kind !
Such chains as his were sure to bind.

13.

Fill high the bowl with Samian wine !
   On Suli's rock, and Parga's shore,
Exists the remnant of a line
   Such as the Doric mothers bore ;
And there, perhaps, some seed is sown,
The Heracleidan blood might own.

14.

Trust not for freedom to the Franks—
    They have a king who buys and sells ;   80
In native swords, and native ranks,
    The only hope of courage dwells :
But Turkish force, and Latin fraud,
Would break your shield, however broad.

15.

Fill high the bowl with Samian wine !
    Our virgins dance beneath the shade—
I see their glorious black eyes shine ;
    But gazing on each glowing maid,
My own the burning tear-drop laves,
To think such breasts must suckle slaves.   90

16.

Place me on Sunium's marbled steep,
    Where nothing, save the waves and I,
May hear our mutual murmurs sweep ;
    There, swan-like, let me sing and die :
A land of slaves shall ne'er be mine—
Dash down yon cup of Samian wine !

GREAT NAMES

(Canto III, lxxxviii—xciv)

But words are things, and a small drop of ink,
    Falling like dew, upon a thought, produces
That which makes thousands, perhaps millions, think ;
    'Tis strange, the shortest letter which man uses
Instead of speech, may form a lasting link
    Of ages ; to what straits old Time reduces
Frail man, when paper—even a rag like this,
Survives himself, his tomb, and all that's his !

And when his bones are dust, his grave a blank,
  His station, generation, even his nation,   10
Become a thing, or nothing, save to rank
  In chronological commemoration,
Some dull MS. oblivion long has sank,
  Or graven stone found in a barrack's station
In digging the foundation of a closet,
May turn his name up, as a rare deposit.

And glory long has made the sages smile;
  'Tis something, nothing, words, illusion, wind—
Depending more upon the historian's style
  Than on the name a person leaves behind: 20
Troy owes to Homer what whist owes to Hoyle:
  The present century was growing blind
To the great Marlborough's skill in giving knocks,
Until his late Life by Archdeacon Coxe.

Milton's the prince of poets—so we say;
  A little heavy, but no less divine:
An independent being in his day—
  Learn'd, pious, temperate in love and wine;
But his life falling into Johnson's way,
  We're told this great high priest of all the Nine   30
Was whipt at college—a harsh sire—odd spouse,
For the first Mrs. Milton left his house.

All these are, *certes*, entertaining facts,
  Like Shakespeare's stealing deer, Lord Bacon's bribes;
Like Titus' youth, and Cæsar's earliest acts;
  Like Burns (whom Doctor Currie well describes);
Like Cromwell's pranks;—but although truth exacts
  These amiable descriptions from the scribes,
As most essential to their hero's story,
They do not much contribute to his glory.   40

All are not moralists, like Southey, when
  He prated to the world of ' Pantisocrasy ; '
Or Wordsworth unexcised, unhired, who then
  Season'd his pedlar poems with democracy ;
Or Coleridge, long before his flighty pen
  Let to the Morning Post its aristocracy ;
When he and Southey, following the same path,
Espoused two partners (milliners of Bath).

Such names at present cut a convict figure,
  The very Botany Bay in moral geography ;   50
Their loyal treason, renegado rigour,
  Are good manure for their more bare biography,
Wordsworth's last quarto, by the way, is bigger
  Than any since the birthday of typography ;
A drowsy frowzy poem, call'd the ' Excursion ',
Writ in a manner which is my aversion.

WORDSWORTH

(Canto III. xcviii—c)

We learn from Horace, ' Homer sometimes sleeps ; '
  We feel without him, Wordsworth sometimes
    wakes,—
To show with what complacency he creeps,
  With his dear ' Waggoners,' around his lakes.
He wishes for " a boat " to sail the deeps—
  Of ocean ?—No, of air ; and then he makes
Another outcry for ' a little boat,'
And drivels seas to set it well afloat.

If he must fain sweep o'er the ethereal plain,
  And Pegasus runs restive in his ' Waggon,'   10
Could he not beg the loan of Charles's Wain ?
  Or pray Medea for a single dragon ?
Or if, too classic for his vulgar brain,
  He fear'd his neck to venture such a nag on,
And he must needs mount nearer to the moon,
Could not the blockhead ask for a balloon ?

" Pedlars," and " Boats," and " Waggons ! " Oh ! ye
    shades
Of Pope and Dryden, are we come to this ?
That trash of such sort not alone evades
    Contempt, but from the bathos' vast abyss   20
Floats scumlike uppermost, and these Jack Cades
    Of sense and song above your graves may hiss—
The ' little boatman ' and his ' Peter Bell '
Can sneer at him who drew ' Achitophel ' !

AVE MARIA

(CANTO III, ci—cix)

T' OUR tale.—The feast was over, the slaves gone,
    The dwarfs and dancing girls had all retired ;
The Arab lore and poet's song were done,
    And every sound of revelry expired ;
The lady and her lover, left alone,
    The rosy flood of twilight's sky admired ;—
Ave Maria ! o'er the earth and sea,
That heavenliest hour of Heaven is worthiest thee !

Ave Maria ! blessed be the hour !
    The time, the clime, the spot, where I so oft   10
Have felt that moment in its fullest power
    Sink o'er the earth so beautiful and soft,
While swung the deep bell in the distant tower,
    Or the faint dying day-hymn stole aloft,
And not a breath crept through the rosy air,
And yet the forest leaves seem'd stirr'd with prayer.

Ave Maria ! 'tis the hour of prayer !
    Ave Maria ! 'tis the hour of love !
Ave Maria ! may our spirits dare
    Look up to thine and to thy Son's above !   20
Ave Maria ! oh that face so fair !
    Those downcast eyes beneath the Almighty dove—
What though 'tis but a pictured image strike,—
That painting is no idol,—'tis too like.

Some kinder casuists are pleased to say,
    In nameless print—that I have no devotion;
But set those persons down with me to pray,
    And you shall see who has the properest notion
Of getting into heaven the shortest way;
    My altars are the mountains and the ocean,   30
Earth, air, stars,—all that springs from the great Whole,
Who hath produced, and will receive the soul.

Sweet hour of twilight!—in the solitude
    Of the pine forest, and the silent shore
Which bounds Ravenna's immemorial wood,
    Rooted where once the Adrian wave flow'd o'er,
To where the last Cæsarean fortress stood,
    Evergreen forest! which Boccaccio's lore
And Dryden's lay made haunted ground to me,
How have I loved the twilight hour and thee!   40

The shrill cicalas, people of the pine,
    Making their summer lives one ceaseless song,
Were the sole echoes, save my steed's and mine,
    And vesper bell's that rose the boughs along;
The spectre huntsman of Onesti's line,
    His hell-dogs, and their chase, and the fair throng
Which learn'd from this example not to fly
From a true lover,—shadow'd my mind's eye.

Oh, Hesperus! thou bringest all good things—
    Home to the weary, to the hungry cheer,   50
To the young bird the parent's brooding wings,
    The welcome stall to the o'erlabour'd steer;
Whate'er of peace about our hearthstone clings,
    Whate'er our household gods protect of dear,
Are gather'd round us by thy look of rest;
Thou bring'st the child, too, to the mother's breast.

Soft hour! which wakes the wish and melts the heart
    Of those who sail the seas, on the first day
When they from their sweet friends are torn apart;
    Or fills with love the pilgrim on his way   60

As the far bell of vesper makes him start,
  Seeming to weep the dying day's decay;
Is this a fancy which our reason scorns?
Ah! surely nothing dies but something mourns!

When Nero perish'd by the justest doom
  Which ever the destroyer yet destroy'd,
Amidst the roar of liberated Rome.
  Of nations freed, and the world overjoy'd,
Some hands unseen strew'd flowers upon his tomb:
  Perhaps the weakness of a heart not void   70
Of feeling for some kindness done, when power
Had left the wretch an uncorrupted hour.

TROY

(CANTO IV, lxxvi—lxxviii)

THERE, on the green and village-cotted hill, is
  (Flank'd by the Hellespont, and by the sea)
Entomb'd the bravest of the brave, Achilles;
  They say so—(Bryant says the contrary):
And further downward, tall and towering still, is
  The tumulus—of whom? Heaven knows; 't may be
Patroclus, Ajax, or Protesilaus;
All heroes, who if living still would slay us.

High barrows, without marble, or a name,
  A vast, untill'd, and mountain-skirted plain,   10
And Ida in the distance, still the same,
  And old Scamander (if 'tis he), remain;
The situation seems still form'd for fame—
  A hundred thousand men might fight again,
With ease; but where I sought for Ilion's walls,
The quiet sheep feeds, and the tortoise crawls;

Troops of untended horses; here and there
  Some little hamlets, with new names uncouth;
Some shepherds (unlike Paris), led to stare
  A moment at the European youth   20

Whom to the spot their school-boy feelings bear ;
    A Turk, with beads in hand, and pipe in mouth,
Extremely taken with his own religion,
Are what I found there—but the devil a Phrygian.

LIFE

(CANTO VII, i—vi and CANTO XV, xcix)

O LOVE ! O Glory ! what are you who fly
    Around us ever, rarely to alight ?
There 's not a meteor in the Polar sky
    Of such transcendent and more fleeting flight.
Chill, and chain'd to cold earth, we lift on high
    Our eyes in search of either lovely light ;
A thousand and a thousand colours they
Assume, then leave us on our freezing way.

And such as they are, such my present tale is,
    A nondescript and ever-varying rhyme,   10
A versified Aurora Borealis,
    Which flashes o'er a waste and icy clime.
When we know what all are, we must bewail us,
    But ne'ertheless I hope it is no crime
To laugh at *all* things—for I wish to know
What, after *all*, are *all* things—but a *show ?*

They accuse me—*Me*—the present writer of
    The present poem—of—I know not what—
A tendency to under-rate and scoff
    At human power and virtue, and all that ;   20
And this they say in language rather rough.
    Good God ! I wonder what they would be at !
I say no more than hath been said in Dante's
Verse, and by Solomon and by Cervantes ;

By Swift, by Machiavel, by Rochefoucault,
    By Fénélon, by Luther, and by Plato ;
By Tillotson, and Wesley, and Rousseau,
    Who knew this life was not worth a potato.

'Tis not their fault, nor mine, if this be so,—
    For my part, I pretend not to be Cato,   30
Nor even Diogenes.—We live and die,
    But which is best, you know no more than I.

Socrates said, our only knowledge was
    ' To know that nothing could be known ; ' a pleasant
Science enough, which levels to an ass
    Each man of wisdom, future, past, or present.
Newton (that proverb of the mind), alas !
    Declared, with all his grand discoveries recent,
That he himself felt only ' like a youth
Picking up shells by the great ocean—Truth.'   40

Ecclesiastes said, ' that all is vanity '—
    Most modern preachers say the same, or show it
By their examples of true Christianity :
    In short, all know, or very soon may know it ;
And in this scene of all-confess'd inanity,
    By saint, by sage, by preacher, and by poet,
Must I restrain me, through the fear of strife,
From holding up the nothingness of life ?

.   .   .   .

Between two worlds life hovers like a star,
    'Twixt night and morn, upon the horizon's verge.
How little do we know that which we are !   51
    How less what we may be ! The eternal surge
Of time and tide rolls on, and bears afar
    Our bubbles ; as the old burst, new emerge,
Lash'd from the foam of ages ; while the graves
Of empires heave but like some passing waves.

WELLINGTON

(CANTO IX, i—x).

OH, Wellington! (or 'Villainton'—for Fame
  Sounds the heroic syllables both ways;
France could not even conquer your great name,
  But punn'd it down to this facetious phrase—
Beating or beaten she will laugh the same,)
  You have obtain'd great pensions and much praise:
Glory like yours should any dare gainsay,
Humanity would rise, and thunder 'Nay!'

I don't think that you used Kinnaird quite well
  In Marinèt's affair—in fact, 'twas shabby,   10
And like some other things won't do to tell
  Upon your tomb in Westminster's old Abbey.
Upon the rest 'tis not worth while to dwell,
  Such tales being for the tea-hours of some tabby;
But though your years as *man* tend fast to zero,
In fact your Grace is still but a *young hero*.

Though Britain owes (and pays you too) so much,
  Yet Europe doubtless owes you greatly more:
You have repair'd Legitimacy's crutch,
  A prop not quite so certain as before: 20
The Spanish, and the French, as well as Dutch,
  Have seen, and felt, how strongly you *restore;*
And Waterloo has made the world your debtor
(I wish your bards would sing it rather better).

You are 'the best of cut-throats:'—do not start;
  The phrase is Shakespeare's, and not misapplied:—
War's a brain-spattering, windpipe-slitting art,
  Unless her cause by right be sanctified.
If you have acted *once* a generous part,
  The world, not the world's masters, will decide,   30
And I shall be delighted to learn who,
Save you and yours, have gain'd by Waterloo?

I am no flatterer—you've supp'd full of flattery:
   They say you like it too—'tis no great wonder.
He whose whole life has been assault and battery,
   At last may get a little tired of thunder;
And swallowing eulogy much more than satire, he
   May like being praised for every lucky blunder,
Call'd 'Saviour of the Nations'—not yet saved,
And 'Europe's Liberator'—still enslaved.   40

I've done.   Now go and dine from off the plate
   Presented by the Prince of the Brazils,
And send the sentinel before your gate
   A slice or two from your luxurious meals:
He fought, but has not fed so well of late.
   Some hunger, too, they say the people feels:—
There is no doubt that you deserve your ration,
But pray give back a little to the nation.

I don't mean to reflect—a man so great as
   You, my lord Duke ! is far above reflection: 50
The high Roman fashion, too, of Cincinnatus,
   With modern history has but small connexion:
Though as an Irishman you love potatoes,
   You need not take them under your direction;
And half a million for your Sabine farm
Is rather dear !—I'm sure I mean no harm.

Great men have always scorn'd great recompenses:
   Epaminondas saved his Thebes, and died,
Not leaving even his funeral expenses:
   George Washington had thanks, and nought beside,
Except the all-cloudless glory (which few men's is)   61
   To free his country: Pitt too had his pride,
And as a high-soul'd minister of state is
Renown'd for ruining Great Britain gratis.

Never had mortal man such opportunity,
   Except Napoleon, or abused it more:
You might have freed fallen Europe from the unity
   Of tyrants and been blest from shore to shore:

And *now*—what *is* your fame ? Shall the Muse tune
   it ye ?
   Now—that the rabble's first vain shouts are o'er ?
Go ! hear it in your famish'd country's cries !   71
Behold the world ! and curse your victories !

As these new cantos touch on warlike feats,
   To *you* the unflattering Muse deigns to inscribe
Truths, that you will not read in the Gazettes,
   But which 'tis time to teach the hireling tribe
Who fatten on their country's gore, and debts,
   Must be recited—and without a bribe.
You *did great* things: but not being *great* in mind,
Have left *undone* the *greatest*—and mankind.   80

LONDON

(CANTO X, lxxxi—lxxxvii).

THE sun went down, the smoke rose up, as from
   A half-unquench'd volcano, o'er a space
Which well beseem'd the ' Devil's drawing-room,'
   As some have qualified that wondrous place :
But Juan felt, though not approaching *home*,
   As one who, though he were not of the race,
Revered the soil, of those true sons the mother,
Who butcher'd half the earth, and bullied t'other.

A mighty mass of brick, and smoke, and shipping,
   Dirty and dusky, but as wide as eye   10
Could reach, with here and there a sail just skipping
   In sight, then lost amidst the forestry
Of masts ; a wilderness of steeples peeping
   On tiptoe through their sea-coal canopy ;
A huge, dun cupola, like a foolscap crown
On a fool's head—and there is London Town !

But Juan saw not this : each wreath of smoke
   Appear'd to him but as the magic vapour
Of some alchymic furnace, from whence broke
   The wealth of worlds (a wealth of tax and paper) :

The gloomy clouds, which o'er it as a yoke   21
   Are bow'd, and put the sun out like a taper,
Were nothing but the natural atmosphere,
Extremely wholesome, though but rarely clear.

He paused—and so will I; as doth a crew
   Before they give their broadside. By and by,
My gentle countrymen, we will renew
   Our old acquaintance; and at least I'll try
To tell you truths *you* will not take as true,
   Because they are so;—a male Mrs. Fry,   30
With a soft besom will I sweep your halls,
And brush a web or two from off the walls.

Oh Mrs. Fry! Why go to Newgate? Why
   Preach to poor rogues? And wherefore not begin
With Carlton, or with other houses? Try
   Your hand at harden'd and imperial sin.
To mend the people's an absurdity,
   A jargon, a mere philanthropic din,
Unless you make their betters better:—Fie!
I thought you had more religion, Mrs. Fry.   40

Teach them the decencies of good threescore;
   Cure them of tours, hussar and highland dresses;
Tell them that youth once gone returns no more,
   That hired huzzas redeem no land's distresses;
Tell them Sir William Curtis is a bore,
   Too dull even for the dullest of excesses,
The witless Falstaff of a hoary Hal,
A fool whose bells have ceased to ring at all.

Tell them, though it may be perhaps too late
   On life's worn confine, jaded, bloated, sated,   50
To set up vain pretence of being great,
   'Tis not so to be good; and be it stated,
The worthiest kings have ever loved least state;
   And tell them——But you won't, and I have prated
Just now enough; but by and by I'll prattle
Like Roland's horn in Roncesvalles' battle.

BYRON AND HIS CONTEMPORARIES

(CANTO XI, liii—lxiii).

JUAN knew several languages—as well
    He might—and brought them up with skill, in time
To save his fame with each accomplish'd belle,
    Who still regretted that he did not rhyme.
There wanted but this requisite to swell
    His qualities (with them) into sublime :
Lady Fitz-Frisky, and Miss Mævia Mannish,
Both long'd extremely to be sung in Spanish.

However, he did pretty well, and was
    Admitted as an aspirant to all   10
The coteries, and, as in Banquo's glass,
    At great assemblies or in parties small,
He saw ten thousand living authors pass,
    That being about their average numeral ;
Also the eighty ' greatest living poets,'
As every paltry magazine can show *it 's.*

In twice five years the ' greatest living poet,'
    Like to the champion in the fisty ring,
Is call'd on to support his claim, or show it,
    Although 'tis an imaginary thing.   20
Even I—albeit I'm sure I did not know it,
    Nor sought of foolscap subjects to be king,—
Was reckon'd, a considerable time,
The grand Napoleon of the realms of rhyme.

But Juan was my Moscow, and Faliero
    My Leipsic, and my Mont Saint Jean seems Cain :
La Belle Alliance of dunces down at zero,
    Now that the Lion 's fall'n, may rise again :
But I will fall at least as fell my hero ;
    Nor reign at all, or as a *monarch* reign ;   30
Or to some lonely isle of gaolers go,
With turncoat Southey for my turnkey Lowe.

Sir Walter reign'd before me ; Moore and Campbell
   Before and after : but now grown more holy,
The Muses upon Sion's hill must ramble
   With poets almost clergymen, or wholly :
And Pegasus has a psalmodic amble
   Beneath the very Reverend Rowley Powley,
Who shoes the glorious animal with stilts,
A modern Ancient Pistol—by the hilts !   40

Still he excels that artificial hard
   Labourer in the same vineyard, though the vine
Yields him but vinegar for his reward.—
   That neutralised dull Dorus of the Nine ;
That swarthy Sporus, neither man nor bard ;
   That ox of verse, who *ploughs* for every line :—
Cambyses' roaring Romans beat at least
The howling Hebrews of Cybele's priest.—

Then there 's my gentle Euphues,—who, they say,
   Sets up for being a sort of *moral me ;*   50
He'll find it rather difficult some day
   To turn out both, or either, it may be.
Some persons think that Coleridge hath the sway ;
   And Wordsworth has supporters, two or three ;
And that deep-mouth'd Bœotian ' Savage Landor '
Has taken for a swan rogue Southey's gander.

John Keats—who was kill'd off by one critique,
   Just as he really promised something great,
If not intelligible, without Greek
   Contrived to talk about the gods of late,   60
Much as they might have been supposed to speak.
   Poor fellow ! His was an untoward fate ;
'Tis strange the mind, that fiery particle,
Should let itself be snuff'd out by an article.

The list grows long of live and dead pretenders
   To that which none will gain—or none will know
The conqueror at least ; who, ere Time renders
   His last award, will have the long grass grow

Above his burnt-out brain, and sapless cinders.
    If I might augur, I should rate but low   70
Their chances ;—they're too numerous, like the thirty
Mock tyrants, when Rome's annals wax'd but dirty.

This is the literary *lower* empire,
    Where the prætorian bands take up the matter ;—
A 'dreadful trade,' like his who 'gathers samphire,'
    The insolent soldiery to soothe and flatter,
With the same feelings as you'd coax a vampire.
    Now, were I once at home, and in good satire,
I'd try conclusions with those Janizaries,
And show them *what* an intellectual war is.   80

I think I know a trick or two, would turn
    Their flanks ;—but it is hardly worth my while
With such small gear to give myself concern :
    Indeed I've not the necessary bile ;
My natural temper 's really aught but stern,
    And even my Muse's worst reproof 's a smile ;
And then she drops a brief and modern curtsy,
And glides away, assured she never hurts ye.

CARPE DIEM *enjoy the Day*

(Canto XI, lxxxii—lxxxvi).

Talk not of seventy years as age ; in seven
    I have seen more changes, down from monarchs to
The humblest individual under heaven,
    Than might suffice a moderate century through.
I knew that nought was lasting, but now even
    Change grows too changeable, without being new :
Nought 's permanent among the human race,
Except the Whigs *not* getting into place.

I have seen Napoleon, who seem'd quite a Jupiter,
    Shrink to a Saturn. I have seen a Duke   10
(No matter which) turn politician stupider,
    If that can well be, than his wooden look.

But it is time that I should hoist my 'blue Peter,'
  And sail for a new theme :—I have seen—and shook
To see it—the king hiss'd, and then caress'd ;
But don't pretend to settle which was best.

I have seen the Landholders without a rap—
  I have seen Joanna Southcote—I have seen
The House of Commons turn'd to a tax-trap—
  I have seen that sad affair of the late Queen— 20
I have seen crowns worn instead of a fool's cap—
  I have seen a Congress doing all that 's mean—
I have seen some nations, like o'erloaded asses,
Kick off their burthens—meaning the high classes.

I have seen small poets, and great prosers, and
  Interminable—*not eternal*—speakers—
I have seen the funds at war with house and land—
  I have seen the country gentlemen turn squeakers—
I have seen the people ridden o'er, like sand,
  By slaves on horseback—I have seen malt liquors
Exchanged for 'thin potations' by John Bull— 31
I have seen John half detect himself a fool—

But '*carpe diem*,' Juan, '*carpe, carpe !*'
  To-morrow sees another race as gay
And transient, and devour'd by the same harpy.
  'Life 's a poor player,'—then 'play out the play,
Ye villains !' and above all keep a sharp eye
  Much less on what you do than what you say :
Be hypocritical, be cautious, be
Not what you *seem*, but always what you *see*. 40

A RUINED ABBEY

(Canto XIII, lvi—lxiv).

It stood embosom'd in a happy valley,
  Crown'd by high woodlands, where the Druid oak
Stood, like Caractacus, in act to rally
  His host, with broad arms 'gainst the thunderstroke;
And from beneath his boughs were seen to sally
  The dappled foresters; as day awoke,
The branching stag swept down with all his herd,
To quaff a brook which murmur'd like a bird.

Before the mansion lay a lucid lake,
  Broad as transparent, deep, and freshly fed   10
By a river, which its soften'd way did take
  In currents through the calmer water spread
Around: the wildfowl nestled in the brake
  And sedges, brooding in their liquid bed:
The woods sloped downwards to its brink, and stood
With their green faces fix'd upon the flood.

Its outlet dash'd into a deep cascade,
  Sparkling with foam, until again subsiding,
Its shriller echoes—like an infant made
  Quiet—sank into softer ripples, gliding   20
Into a rivulet: and thus allay'd,
  Pursued its course, now gleaming, and now hiding
Its windings through the woods; now clear, now blue,
According as the skies their shadows threw.

A glorious remnant of the Gothic pile
  (While yet the church was Rome's) stood half apart
In a grand arch, which once screen'd many an aisle.
  These last had disappear'd—a loss to art:
The first yet frown'd superbly o'er the soil,
  And kindled feelings in the roughest heart,   30
Which mourn'd the power of time's or tempest's march,
In gazing on that venerable arch.

Within a niche, nigh to its pinnacle,
  Twelve saints had once stood sanctified in stone ;
But these had fallen, not when the friars fell,
  But in the war which struck Charles from his
      throne,
When each house was a fortalice—as tell
  The annals of full many a line undone,—
The gallant cavaliers, who fought in vain
For those who knew not to resign or reign.   40

But in a higher niche, alone, but crown'd,
  The Virgin-Mother of the God-born Child,
With her Son in her blessed arms, look'd round,
  Spared by some chance when all beside was spoil'd ;
She made the earth below seem holy ground.
  This may be superstition, weak or wild ;
But even the faintest relics of a shrine
Of any worship wake some thoughts divine.

A mighty window, hollow in the centre,
  Shorn of its glass of thousand colourings,   50
Through which the deepen'd glories once could enter,
  Streaming from off the sun like seraph's wings,
Now yawns all desolate : now loud, now fainter,
  The gale sweeps through its fretwork, and oft
      sings
The owl his anthem, where the silenced quire
Lie with their hallelujahs quench'd like fire.

But in the noontide of the moon, and when
  The wind is winged from one point of heaven,
There moans a strange unearthly sound, which then
  Is musical—a dying accent driven   60
Through the huge arch, which soars and sinks again.
  Some deem it but the distant echo given
Back to the night wind by the waterfall,
And harmonised by the old choral wall :

Others, that some original shape, or form
  Shaped by decay perchance, hath given the power
(Though less than that of Memnon's statue, warm
  In Egypt's rays, to harp at a fix'd hour)
To this grey ruin, with a voice to charm,
  Sad, but serene, it sweeps o'er tree or tower;   70
The cause I know not, nor can solve; but such
The fact:—I've heard it,—once perhaps too much.

INDEX OF TITLES

INDEX OF FIRST LINES

Printed in Great Britain by Neill & Co. Ltd., Edinburgh